Secrets of the Press

JOURNALISTS ON JOURNALISM

Edited by Stephen Glover

ALLEN LANE
THE PENGUIN PRESS

ALLEN LANE
THE PENGUIN PRESS
Published by the Penguin Group
Penguin Books Ltd, 27 Wrights Lane, London w8 5tz, England
Penguin Putnam Inc., 375 Hudson Street, New York, New York 10014, USA
Penguin Books Australia Ltd, Ringwood, Victoria, Australia
Penguin Books Canada Ltd, 10 Alcorn Avenue, Toronto, Ontario, Canada m4v 3b2
Penguin Books (NZ) Ltd, 182–190 Wairau Road, Auckland 10, New Zealand

Penguin Books Ltd, Registered Offices: Harmondsworth, Middlesex, England

First published 1999
1 3 5 7 9 10 8 6 4 2

The publishers would like to thank the Estate of Hilaire Belloc and
Peters Fraser and Dunlop for permission to quote from *The Happy Journalist*.
The publishers have made every effort to trace or contact all copyright holders.
They will be pleased to rectify any omissions brought to their notice.

Set in 11/14 pt PostScript Adobe Sabon
Typeset by Rowland Phototypesetting Ltd, Bury St Edmunds, Suffolk
Printed in England by The Bath Press, Bath

A CIP catalogue record for this book is available from the British Library

ISBN 0-713-99265-4

Contents

CONTENTS

Introduction

Most of us are newspaper readers but not all of us know very much about how journalists operate. I remember once meeting a perfectly intelligent woman who thought that the editor of a national newspaper was responsible for writing almost everything in it, with the possible exception of the sports pages. Admittedly newspapers were much thinner in those days, but all the same it was a funny thing to believe. She was incredulous when I informed her that most editors have several hundred people to help them do what she had thought was done virtually single-handedly, and when I told her that most editorials were not written by the editor, but by specially employed leader writers, she asked me to stop pulling her leg.

An extreme case, of course, but a telling one. We may think we understand newspapers because they come into our kitchens and sitting-rooms, and are a familiar part of most of our lives. And in one sense newspapers have no secrets. They lay out their wares for all to see. They usually, though not always, publish everything they know about a story, and in a manner that can be easily analysed. (This, incidentally, is why journalistic innovations do not remain innovations for long. They can be easily copied by rivals.) But for all our surface familiarity with newspapers, most of us have rather little idea how they are put together, or what goes on behind the scenes.

We may hate journalists – indeed, we rank them, according to some polls, below estate agents and politicians. But hating is not knowing them. How do they work? How is it done? What are the skills involved? How does one become a journalist? How does one remain one? These strike me as pretty interesting questions, since whatever we think of journalists it can hardly be denied that journalism is important. But they are questions which journalists do not normally go out of their way to answer. I don't think they are necessarily any more secretive than any other group of people, but that they should be secretive at all, given that they are dedicated to finding out and writing about other people's secrets, is definitely odd.

There haven't been many collections of living journalism. There have been innumerable anthologies of dead journalists; and from time to time quite well-known ones are encouraged by over-hopeful publishers to produce books of dead columns or forgotten articles. But I can barely think of another enterprise like this. Twenty-six leading journalists writing pieces for one book! They have laboured long and hard, and spent more time writing these essays than they do the articles in the press that have won them fame. They really have written with unusual candour about their trade. The point is not that there are dozens of scandalous revelations, though there are certainly some, but that these contributors are attempting to explain the inner workings of the parts of the press they best understand.

I've tried to spread the net wide, but of course you can't have everything. There is nothing on cartoons: I wondered for a long time whether I should ask my old friend Nicholas Garland, perhaps the outstanding political cartoonist of his generation, to contribute, but for some reason I decided against. There is nothing on the regional press or magazines or page three girls or crossword puzzles or gardening columns. There is also nothing about photography, though as someone who helped set up the *Independent*, famous for its moody black-and-white pictures, this is a subject I certainly care about. All I can say is that unless you want to read 200 pieces you can't have everything. On the other hand, there are some subjects so important that it would seem wrong to leave them in the hands of one contributor, however brilliant. There are three essays in this collection about foreign and war reporting, from Christopher Munnion, Emma Daly and Ann Leslie.

Why have I chosen these twenty-six contributors? It would be putting it a bit strong to say that they are the best twenty-six journalists in Britain. To make such a claim would be to invite other journalists to feel insecure, and possibly envious. What is undoubtedly true is that these are all writers I respect and mostly admire. It is also true that many journalists whom I also admire are not to be found within this book. In one or two cases an unwonted shyness overcame them, and nothing – not money, not glory – could persuade them to contribute. In other cases, for a variety of reasons, I could not bring myself to ask them. I am a huge fan of William Rees-Mogg, the *Times* columnist, though I appreciate it is one of those infatuations not necessarily understood by the rest of humanity. I mentally stood in front of his reputation and marvelled at the achievement as a climber may contemplate a particularly magnificent mountain, but for reasons I cannot wholly explain decided against tackling his slopes.

Some of the contributors are my friends, but the majority are not. A few I have never even met. My only dealings with Emma Daly, an intrepid war correspondent, have been via satellite telephone. Carol Sarler, who argues the superiority of tabloids over broadsheets, I have merely admired from afar. The same is true of Lynne Truss, the famous sports columnist. Other contributors have at some time attacked me in print: Paul Foot once devoted an entire article in the *New Statesman* to disembowelling me, while Lynn Barber crafted possibly the rudest book review I have ever read, about a book I had written. Unless I am much mistaken, in his brilliant essay on editors my friend Henry Porter has a little sideswipe at me for having criticized in the past his country neighbour and chum, Alan Rusbridger, editor of the *Guardian*. None of this worries me. If journalists have a fault, it is to bear grudges and nurse hatreds as a result of having had rude or harsh things written about them. They are much worse than politicians in this respect. I know this very well, having written a column about the press for some years. The wife of one of our leading editors, a man about whom I have occasionally written some innocuous things, chases and harangues me whenever she sees me.

What counts is only how good these journalists are, how effectively they can lift the veil on whichever aspect of journalism they best understand. These contributors represent as heterogeneous a group of people as you could hope to encounter, so that we have a member of the Socialist Workers Party and a High Tory MP nestling between the same pages. I fancy that if we were to lock our contributors in a room for forty-eight hours there would be a number of fights, and possibly one or two deaths. I may be mistaken but I seem to remember that Peter McKay, as author of the Ephraim Hardcastle column in the *Daily Mail*, has lampooned his fellow-contributors Petronella Wyatt and Alan Clark on several occasions. It is probable that Richard Ingrams has offended nearly everyone at some time or another. And it is almost certain that Lynn Barber, who has a passionate hatred of practically any article that brushes against politics, will be bored by Michael White's marvellous piece about spin doctors, or Anthony Howard's authoritative essay about the influence of the press on politicians.

I certainly don't agree with everything that is written here, although in almost every case the subject matter has been suggested by me. I rather think Peter McKay may have been too indulgent towards gossip columnists as a breed, and I do not quite share Niall Ferguson's high view of 'media dons', amongst whom he is admittedly an outstanding practitioner. I have bridled on several occasions during Alan Clark's tirade against the press. Are journalists really as revolting and dysfunctional as he suggests, and are our newspapers so uniformly driven by low commercial motives and vulgar preoccupations? I am sure some people will think so, but I'm not convinced. I don't agree with Paul Foot, in his brilliant polemic, that Rupert Murdoch's removal of his printing operations to Wapping was in every way regrettable, though I can see it may have had one or two bad consequences. For example, the demise of the Fleet Street printing unions brought about by Murdoch enabled publishers to produce much fatter newspapers, and no one could deny that much of what goes into them is hardly up to snuff. Also, the Fleet Street diaspora set off by Murdoch has meant a very much less congenial life for most journalists. The old, vanished Fleet Street of pubs and eccentrics and long afternoons is evocatively and movingly brought back to life by Alan Watkins and Francis Wheen.

A collection of pieces from the same standpoint, each reflecting

the *Weltanschauung* of the editor, would be a very dull one. I have
been struck, in reading and thinking about these pieces, by the
amazing variety of journalism. A. N. Wilson describes the young
writer Peter Ackroyd visiting the offices of the *Spectator* magazine
in the hope of getting a book to review. After having been rebuffed
he is offered the job of literary editor of the magazine by its editor,
George Gale, whose 'head appeared over the banisters' and
addressed the departing Ackroyd. In her vivid essay on war
reporting, Emma Daly describes the terrible aftermath of a bombing
in Bosnia. 'Dogs and cats, even fluffy, cuddly ones, will happily
feed off the dead.' This passage certainly made me look at my Irish
setter in a new light. It also, set alongside A. N. Wilson's evocation
of the clubby, gentlemanly world of the *Spectator*, induces a sense
of wonder at the extraordinary scope of journalism. Journalism *is*
life. It really does extend from the killing-fields of Bosnia to the
calm of the *Spectator* offices, from broadsheets to tabloids, from
the sports pages to the City pages, from interviews of 'celebrities'
to serious political articles. This is the dazzling range I have tried
to capture. It is because journalism has such variety that I can't
agree with Alan Clark. What he says may be true, but it is not the
whole truth, or not the truth about everything.

In one important respect our contributors do have something in
common. None of them is very young. There are some in their
thirties, including the brilliant Zoë Heller and the no less brilliant
Fiammetta Rocco; more in their forties, and some in their fifties
and sixties. I even asked a lady of eighty-seven to contribute, but
that didn't quite work out. I suppose that the average age of
contributors is about forty-five, and in an ageist, youth-obsessed
world that may seem almost geriatric. I don't apologize. If you were
writing a book about modern painters you would not, if you were
sensible, include all the recent graduates from art school who had
just learnt how to throw a pot of paint at a blank canvas. It usually
takes time to be a great interviewer or an outstanding foreign
correspondent or a first-rate book reviewer or an experienced gossip
columnist. For me much of the joy of this book lies in learning
how things are done. I suppose I am a reasonably seasoned foreign
traveller, having been abroad many times for newspapers, but I

learnt many new things from reading Ann Leslie's sparkling essay – including how to deal with recalcitrant officials. Anybody who has ever done an interview or hopes to do one should read Lynn Barber's marvellously informative piece. Of course, you might decide to do it in a different way, even the opposite way. But to read her piece is to be present at the wittiest of master-classes.

That partly explains why few of our contributors are in the first flush of youth, and some of them not far from the consolations of old age. They are expert craftsmen and women. There is another reason. They have a sense of history, of how things have changed in journalism, whether for the better or worse. There are too many young journalists who don't know about the histories of their newspapers, too many aspiring feature editors who are shamefully unaware of what happened on their watch the day before yesterday. The here-and-now is naturally what concerns journalists most. The future is pretty interesting too, as Andrew Brown shows in his fascinating essay about the Internet, and James Fergusson reminds us in his elegant contemplation of death, which I suppose looks back as well as forward. But journalism must have a sense of its past. That is where many of its secrets lie.

One must of course guard against nostalgia, against the idea that things used to be much better. I'm sure they weren't. I personally think that newspapers have got better *and* worse. They have become more like supermarkets and less like your corner shop, so that they now offer many more services, many of which you don't need. I think someone once worked out that it would take twenty-four hours to read the multi-section *Sunday Times* from cover to cover. Who would ever want to do that? Papers have become less intimate, less treasured, perhaps, but much more comprehensive. We take what we want and leave the rest. I suppose that most of them have 'dumbed down', but just as we accept that idea along comes Peregrine Worsthorne, in his characteristically brilliant and para-doxical way, pointing out that there is more 'fine writing' in news-papers than there was forty or fifty years ago.

No, I don't think one can say that papers in their entirety are worse, though some titles have undoubtedly declined. But I think it is certain that journalism for many journalists is less enjoyable than it was. Francis Wheen, Alan Watkins and Paul Foot lament a vanished world. They and others deprecate the new cost-conscious, accountant-dominated Fleet Street – a misnomer, since there are no longer any newspapers there – and they decry the modern, far-flung office blocks where teetotal journalists peer forlornly into their computer screens. What they are partly saying is that journalism is less fun in this strange new land, and I am sure that they are right. There is little room in the reformed Fleet Street for the eccentric, no time for swashbuckling correspondents like René McColl or Peter Younghusband (the latter, Christopher Munnion tells us, once swam to the island of Zanzibar to cover a revolution, leaving his *Daily Express* rival behind). In his essay on expenses, 'Anonymous' brings to life a baroque world that few will credit, where one foreign correspondent passed off a racehorse as a family pet, and another hired at vast expense a 'racing camel' which 'rendered magnificent, heart-rending service' to his paper. 'Anonymous', by the way, is a person of quite impeccable rectitude, prevented only by his – or her – natural reticence (not to mention a publisher who appreciates a come-on) from disclosing a full identity.

Much of that extravagant and charming world has passed away. But no doubt other things have improved. It is much easier for women journalists to advance, though Petronella Wyatt and Amanda Platell show that the path can still be strewn with briars. Speaking for myself, I feel blessed to be a journalist even in this new and rather pinched world. It is still fun. I am privileged that I can speak to people who might otherwise not want to speak to me, go places I might otherwise never visit, see things I might never see and, above all, attempt to understand things I could never otherwise understand. Journalism is a raft which speeds one through many of the complexities of our age. The journey is faster than is ideal, but at least one has been there. More than ever, journalists are here to explain, to make some sense of a world that is growing more mind-boggling by the minute.

Should the modern Mrs Worthington wish to put her son or daughter into journalism? Stephen Fay warns that every journalist is sacked in the end, and some sooner rather than later. It is a rum profession – more of a trade, really – offering about as much career security as a job as an air hostess on the *Hindenburg*. It's becoming increasingly like showbiz, and the higher you rise the faster you may fall. Yet more and more of our most brilliant graduates are attracted to it, oblivious to its dangers, and hugely exaggerating its glamour. I won't say they're wrong. You may be sacked. You *will* be sacked. You probably won't get rich. But whether you end up reviewing books or writing obituaries or reporting wars or subbing copy, you could still have a lot of fun and might even do some good. Here, anyway, are the secrets of the press.

STEPHEN GLOVER

The Deserted Village

FRANCIS WHEEN

All that I loved and hated,
All that I shunned and knew,
Clears in broad battle lightning,
Where they, and I, and you,
Run high the barricade that breaks
The barriers of the street,
And shout to them that shrink within,
The Prisoners of the Fleet.
(G. K. Chesterton,
'When I Came Back to Fleet Street')

I love to walk about at night
By nasty lanes and corners foul,
All shielded from the unfriendly light
And independent as the owl.
By dirty gates I love to lurk;
I often stoop to take a squint
At printers working at their work.
I muse upon the rot they print.
(Hilaire Belloc,
'The Happy Journalist')

The continuing debate was an essential feature of Fleet Street, the awful
pubs were the forum where people talked and a lot of the talk was rubbish
but we learned a lot from it too. This just doesn't happen any more.
(Keith Waterhouse, in *Fleet Street Remembered*, Heinemann, 1990)

When I first came to work in Fleet Street, as a seventeen-year-old office-boy, there were at least a dozen pubs between Ludgate Circus and the Wig and Pen club. The most Hogarthian was the King and Keys, a ghastly bearpit where wild-eyed savages swore and fought and extinguished their cigarettes in other people's glasses of whisky: an outsider would have been astonished to learn that these Bohemian bruisers were all employed by the *Daily Telegraph*, that champion of middle-class respectability. An equal but opposite surprise could be had in the Clachan, where journalists from the permissive, progressive *Guardian* sat quietly nursing half-pints of bitter while discussing the latest cricket scores – looking, to the untrained eye, remarkably like *Daily Telegraph* readers.

Fleet Street was a village of many tribes, but a village none the less. I loved to walk about at night by nasty lanes and corners foul – starting at the *Daily Mirror*'s in-house boozer on Fetter Lane, the gloriously named Stab in the Back, then sinking a few swift ones with the *Express* crowd at the Popinjay before adjourning to the neutral territory of El Vino, where champagne bottles were lined up like skittles. Notwithstanding the looming dome of St Paul's and the monastic flavour of the place-names – Blackfriars, Carmelite Street, the Temple – there was little evidence of righteousness, godliness or sobriety. Our *lares* and *penates* were Samuel Johnson and John Thaddeus Delane, W. T. Stead and G. K. Chesterton. Some of the newer landmarks, such as Lord Beaverbrook's Black Lubyanka, might have seemed strange to these ancient deities, but I think they would have recognized that the essential character of the place – its inky numen – had scarcely changed since the days of Addison and Steele.

The offices, like the pubs, were chaotic and rather smelly, furnished with peeling lino and a speckled carpet of cigarette ends. Noise rose in a crescendo through the day – the clatter of typewriters, the shouted instructions to errand-boys, and finally the tumultuous roar as presses started to roll. For me, at least, the thrill of it all never diminished with familiarity. There was something sexual about the daily rhythm, the accelerating urgency and excitement followed by that climactic moment when the first edition emerged; no wonder we felt the need for a few post-coital drinks and cigarettes.

And then, quite suddenly, the tumult and the shouting died; the denizens of the Clachan and the King and Keys departed. Rupert Murdoch claimed that he was setting journalists free by moving them out of the Street of Shame, but the glum faces of the hacks who were bussed into Wapping told a different story. A few days later, word emerged that Murdoch had banned all alcohol from the premises. At a stroke, he had broken two of the most important rules of the Fourth Estate: that journalists should be at the heart of the city, and that a hack without a drink is like a wingless eagle – or, if you prefer, a hairless dog.

The Prisoners of the Fleet exchanged the old Victorian penal colony of Chesterton's imagination for offices that look like privatized jails, even down to the Group 4 security men. In the joyless offices of today, journalists arrive at their workstations bright and early, without a hint of a hangover, log on to the computer and spend the next nine hours or so gazing at their screens in a kind of trance before heading home. The biggest thrill in their day is nibbling on a corned-beef sandwich at lunchtime, washed down with a little something from the water-cooler. And they never, ever leave the office during working hours if they can possibly help it: if you'd ever tried getting anywhere from Wapping or Canary Wharf, nor would you. For all the difference it makes, they might as well be on an ice-floe in Antarctica.

Readers often complain that newspapers these days seem obsessively self-regarding; but journalists have little else to write about. Stuck on the twenty-fifth floor of a hermetically sealed office block, with uniformed guards at every exit, they seldom meet anyone. For all the manifold sins and wickednesses of old Fleet Street at least its inhabitants did get out occasionally, if only to escape the discomfort of their desks. And yes, perhaps they drank too much – but the fact is that you're more likely to find a story while chatting to people in a pub than staring at a computer in Canary Wharf.

When I was a boy, the journalistic household names were reporters such as James Cameron, Sefton Delmer and Martha Gellhorn, or more recently John Pilger of the *Daily Mirror* and the Woodward–Bernstein team at the *Washington Post*. Now the stars of British journalism are all columnists, who – with a few honourable exceptions – fill their pages with self-regarding blather about what they saw on telly last night, or the state of their love life, or extempore opinions without any sort of anchorage in fact. In the words of Ian Jack, a former editor of the *Independent on Sunday*, 'Britain has developed a singular sort of media culture which places a high premium on excitement, controversy and sentimentality, in which information takes second place to the opinions it arouses.' There was an excellent example of this recently when a new editor at one of the broadsheets was advised by his proprietor to poach Matthew Parris from *The Times*. 'I don't care if we have to pay him £300,000 a year,' the editor was told. 'We must get Parris.' With a dowry of that size you could hire half a dozen energetic reporters; but any editor who suggested spending the money on news would undoubtedly be rebuked for needless extravagance.

Though top columnists may seem expensive because of their huge salaries, their running costs are agreeably low; they never go anywhere, and they can produce reams of daily copy with no difficulty since it all comes out of the top of their heads. Proper reporting takes time and money; it's much cheaper and easier to fill the pages with inflated gossip about footballers, or glorified public relations puffs for minor pop stars, or – most deadly of all – lifestyle features. Do blondes really have more fun? Are big breasts to be this season's fashion accessory? Is pink the new grey? Whither polenta? Not so long ago the *Sunday Times* started a new weekly feature in which famous men talk about their underpants. I've heard of navel-gazing, but this is ridiculous.

Harmless fun? Maybe, as long as it's quarantined within the Style supplement. But the virus has spread. When the *Sunday Times* published Adolf Hitler's secret diaries without bothering to check whether they were genuine – which, of course, they weren't – the most telling reaction was that of Rupert Murdoch, who appeared sublimely untroubled by this scandalous dereliction of journalistic duty. All he seemed to care about was that the *Sunday Times* had put on sales. 'After all,' he murmured, 'we are in the entertainment business.'

As the man who brought us *Home Alone*, Murdoch is indeed in the entertainment business. Why, however, have so many journalists sold the pass? Partly because they have little choice, since otherwise they'd be out of a job; and partly because they are well paid for doing it. But at the back of their minds there may also be a suspicion that, deep down, Murdoch is right: the public doesn't want to be informed. How else do you explain the fact that the biggest-selling daily newspaper in this country is the *Sun*, which has never pretended to inform its readers about the world – except for that small corner of celebrity-land occupied by Gazza, Ginger Spice and the cast of *Coronation Street*?

Like Belloc, I often muse upon the rot they print. Murdoch's executives insist that their newspapers are merely satisfying a public appetite for trivia and tosh, but I suspect that they also whet that appetite. One of the most interesting local papers in this country is the *Barnsley Chronicle*, where a couple of years ago the editor became so exasperated by the proliferation of vacuous lifestyle features that he chucked them all out and ordered his reporters to discover what was actually happening in the town. The result? Circulation has rocketed. Newspaper readers, it transpires, are rather more intelligent and curious than Rupert Murdoch would have us believe.

This is confirmed by my own experience. Many years ago I worked briefly for a small Scottish weekly, the *Lochaber Free Press*, which was essentially run by one person, a Yorkshireman called John Hatton. He was the editor, the chief reporter and the advertising manager: I think he even set the crossword. John directed his operations from a table in the local Railway Tavern, and readers who took offence at something he printed – a series of pungent editorials lambasting the Scots for their indifference to cricket, for instance – wouldn't bother writing to the Press Complaints Commission: they simply barged into the Railway Tavern and bawled him out, whereupon he pacified them with a pint of McEwan's or a large Scotch. Anyone who had a story – whether it was a farmer, a gamekeeper or even the local vicar – would also wander in for a drink or three and give him the gen.

Everyone read the *Lochaber Free Press* because it was a newspaper that was genuinely and constantly in touch with the community it served. In fact it was too successful for its own good:

after John had exposed several district councillors for corruption, the local political bigwigs decided to run him out of town by persuading the bank manager to withdraw the overdraft facility which covered the one day a week when John had paid the printing bill but hadn't yet collected the advertising revenue. Understandably furious at this censorship, he hurled a brick at the bank's window – which, alas, was made of reinforced glass. The brick bounced back, hitting him on the foot. Even so, the local police issued a warrant for his arrest and John had to make a quick getaway back to Yorkshire, or at least as quick as his bandaged foot allowed.

Thus ended John Hatton's *Lochaber Free Press*. But its spirit and attitude – so conspicuously absent from our distant, disembodied national press – linger on in a few outbuildings of the Fourth Estate. *Private Eye* magazine, where I work a couple of days a week, is based in a ramshackle old house in Soho, only a few yards from the nearest pub. Anyone can wander in off the street without having to fight their way past teams of security guards; and anyone does. I remember an occasion after Robert Maxwell died when a distraught woman, who appeared to hold us responsible for his demise, burst into the office and started throwing the furniture around before trying to strangle the editor, Ian Hislop. (Bizarrely, she turned out to be the daughter of Lord Hartwell, the former owner of the *Daily Telegraph*.) More recently a man travelled down from Walsall to inform me that the Lord Chancellor, the Pope and Boris Yeltsin were all tapping his phone. When I asked why all these important chaps had it in for him, he replied: 'You're the journalist. That's what I want you to find out.' From time to time, however, some apparent nutter will come to the office with an equally unlikely tale which is absolutely true – but which no other newspaper will touch.

Private Eye has always believed that there is no point in having freedom of the press if you don't use it. When Robert Maxwell was alive, I tried writing about him for any number of newspapers but always found myself having the same old conversation with editors and lawyers. 'You know he'll sue us if we print this,' they'd say. 'Yes,' I'd agree, 'but it's true, and I can prove it.' 'Well, that's as may be, but we'll have to spend the next two years fighting the case, which will be very expensive and very time-consuming. Is it really that important?' They usually decided that it wasn't, because most newspaper editors are, at heart, rather timid souls who want a quiet life.

At the *Eye*, on the other hand, we used to regard every libel writ from Maxwell as a campaign medal. I still have somewhere the last statement of claim he ever issued, in October 1991, a masterpiece of boiling indignation at our 'malicious' and 'mendacious' allegation that he was taking money from the Mirror Group pension fund. He fell off his yacht before we had the chance to see him in court, and a few weeks later it was revealed that he had indeed stolen about half a billion pounds from his wretched pensioners. Immediately, and belatedly, every newspaper in the land started thundering. Paul Johnson in the *Daily Mail* was particularly angry: 'Since Maxwell had been judged unfit to run a public company as long ago as 1971, what were the various regulators doing while he built up his crazy pyramid of debt? How did a man like Maxwell, who had This Man Is Dangerous written all over him in letters two feet high, manage to persuade senior bank executives to hand over to him hundreds of millions of their depositors' money? Who exactly were these generous, gullible fellows? What is their explanation?'

One explanation might be that they had taken the advice of Paul Johnson. This is what he wrote in July 1984, shortly after Robert Maxwell took over the Mirror Group: 'Maxwell is a hard man with a sharp nose for extravagance, waste and freeloading of any kind ... I don't care a damn about his early business record or what the Board of Trade said about him umpteen years ago. That is all ancient history.' Ancient history, as Johnson should know better than most, has a habit of coming back to haunt us. If a few more newspapers had been willing to challenge Maxwell during his lifetime, he might not have left such a trail of devastation after his death. But then again, why should they bother? John Thaddeus Delane's maxim that 'the business of the press is disclosure' seems quaintly old-fashioned, if not absurdly pompous, to his modern counterparts. We are, after all, in the entertainment business.

Of course there are still some free-spirited, buccaneering characters in the Fleet Street diaspora. But they struggle to survive in the boozeless, smokeless, air-conditioned, bean-counting newspaper offices of the 1990s. Whenever I am invited to address sixth-formers, I ask which of them hopes to go into journalism and why. The answers are depressingly predictable: 'I've heard it's really well paid,' or 'I'd like to be the next Bridget Jones.' A quarter of a century ago ambitious young trainees aspired to become Woodward and Bernstein, speaking truth to power; today, they want to be William Leith, tapping out a thousand words on the state of their toenails.

In a speech some years ago, John Major warned that 'we cannot afford to subject ourselves to the despotism of nostalgia'; he then proceeded to do just that by babbling about long shadows on county grounds, warm beer, invincible green suburbs and old maids bicycling to Holy Communion through the morning mist. It is a familiar problem. When nostalgic types say that things aren't what they used to be I am usually sceptical, but as soon as I walk down the old Street of Adventure I turn into a maudlin sentimentalist. The only nocturnal sound in the deserted thoroughfare – once a cacophony of rattle and hum – is the braying of lawyers and PR men in El Vino. Oh my Addison and my Steele long ago!

While wallowing in this lachrymose nostalgia recently, I decided to re-read the autobiography of G. K. Chesterton. My reverie was instantly shattered. 'I belonged,' he wrote in 1936, 'to the old Bohemian life of Fleet Street, which has since been destroyed, not by the idealism of detachment, but by the materialism of machinery. A newspaper proprietor in later years assured me that it was a slander on journalism to tell all these tales about taverns and ragged pressmen and work and recreation coming at random at all hours of the night. "A newspaper office is now exactly like any other place of business," he said with a radiant smile; and I agreed with a groan.' Journalism, Chesterton concluded, 'is [now] conducted as quietly, as soberly, as sensibly as the office of any successful moneylender or moderately fraudulent financier'.

It is simultaneously depressing and cheering to discover that the Golden Age to which one looks back with such yearning was itself regarded as dull and anaemic by a previous generation. Can it be that, in thirty years' time, old hands will reminisce mistily about the 1990s, lamenting with a wild regret the day when national newspapers moved from the Bohemian precincts of Wapping and Canary Wharf to the sober, sensible outskirts of Milton Keynes?

Girl Columns

ZOË HELLER

Most journalists will at some stage in their careers be handed back
the first draft of an article, with a request to 'put more of themselves'
into the piece. 'Let's hear how you felt about it,' the editor will say.
Or, 'I think we need a more subjective approach.' Or, 'Don't be
afraid to give us some first person.' Few journalists prove immune
to the flattering implications of such directives. They are not, after
all, being asked to do more arduous research, or carry out more
interviews, or think up a new introduction, or rewrite that boring
middle section. They are simply being asked to insert more of their
colourful, writerly selves into the copy. Very gratifying. For women
journalists, however, this sort of gratification carries hidden perils.

Historically, the role of the female newspaper writer has been to
leaven the serious (male) stuff of reportage and analysis with light
dispatches – news from the realm of the domestic, the emotional,
the personal. Even today, male newspaper editors are inclined, if
only subconsciously, to regard their female staff as the people who
soften the edges of the paper's main agenda. When a woman
journalist is invited to use the first person or inject some more
'attitude' into a piece, it is often a coded entreaty to beef up a
specifically female perspective. The request may seem innocuous
enough, but in taking such an invitation a woman takes her first
step away from the neutrality and freedom of being simply a writer,
towards the ghetto of writing 'as a woman'.

These days, most of the writing in the women's ghetto falls into
one of three categories. There is the good-humoured 'home front'
column in which a woman writes in a jolly, eye-rolling way about
her accident-prone kids and lazy husband. ('Mum – Johnny's stuck

a marble up his nose!') There is the stern comment piece, in which public affairs are examined from an admonitory, feminist point of view. ('When was the last time the Foreign Secretary changed a nappy?') And then there is the daffy 'girl' piece, in which a youngish single female confides the vagaries of her rackety personal life. ('Never try shaving your legs in a moving taxi.')

The last sub-genre enjoyed a great surge of popularity in the nineties – a reflection, no doubt, of the more general nineties vogue for 'personal narratives'. For a time, every British broadsheet had a jaunty female correspondent on its pages, providing weekly glimpses into her private affairs. The *Independent*, and later the *Daily Telegraph*, boasted Helen Fielding, the most famous exponent of the form, whose 'Bridget Jones's Diary' columns went on to become a best-selling book. The *Observer* had India Knight. *The Times* had Anna Blundy. The *Independent on Sunday*, and later the *Sunday Times*, had me.

The 'girl' columnists were distinguished primarily by the negligible attention they paid to politics, or indeed to any matter of social import. They dwelt almost exclusively on elaborate personal intrigues – indeed it was the frothiness of their chosen subject matter that earned them their diminutive 'girl' status. They all tended to an extreme and perhaps ill advised candour – regularly divulging details of marital breakdowns, sexual peccadilloes, depressive episodes, family rows and disgusting personal habits. The girl columns did, incidentally, have a male corollary. 'New lad' writing, typified by the sensitive blokeishness of Nick Hornby, sought to reclaim various masculine preoccupations and pursuits (football, beer, genial rowdiness) from the dustbin of male chauvinism. While it had a distinctly confessional streak, it was rarely as wincingly indiscreet as the girl prose – which is perhaps why it never took off in columnar form.

The (seeming) authenticity of the girl writers' revelations – the sense that a reader got of witnessing someone's real beans being spilt – was said to constitute a large part of the girl column's fascination, even when, as in Helen Fielding's case, the narrator was a fictional character. Their weekly revelations led readers to feel they 'knew' them, as TV viewers feel they 'know' their favourite soap stars. Much of the mail they received during their tenure – and all the girls got a *lot* of mail – testified to a following that was passionately – scarily – absorbed by their doings.

Scurrilous female confession was not, of course, a novelty in British newspapers – as far back as 1971, Germaine Greer had been writing sassy *Sunday Times* pieces about not wearing knickers. What was unprecedented, however, was the wilfully unheroic nature of the girls' self-exposures, their readiness to display themselves to unflattering and undignified effect. When Greer had chosen to lift her skirts and reveal her lack of underwear, it was to decry the antiquated practice of shrouding women's genitals (*Sunday Times*, 19 September 1971). When one of the nineties girls did it, it was merely to describe some excruciating incident in which her skirt had blown up and her bum had been bared. Where Greer had styled herself as a fearless Valkyrie, the girls gleefully presented themselves as comically ignoble ninnies.

Their columns retailed the sort of self-deprecating confidences that women often use to establish intimacy with other women: *Oh, you needn't be threatened by me – let me tell you about the time a tube of spermicidal jelly fell out of my handbag at the bus stop . . .* Personal humiliation was, in fact, *the* theme of the girl columns. (The humiliation took many forms, although for some reason falling asleep in a public place and waking to find that you'd been drooling proved to be one of the most persistent leitmotifs.)

The bravado with which the girl columnists revisited their own pratfalls and miseries puzzled a lot of readers. There seemed something contradictory and even suspect about avowing one's own folly and despair with such exuberance. Reading Bridget Jones brazenly extol the hopelessness of her love life had a strangely contrapuntal effect – like watching someone leap on a stage and belt out a show-tune about being shy. Indeed, when James Wolcott wrote an article for the *New Yorker* in 1996 decrying the outbreak of 'girlishness' in modern female journalism, he singled out this mixed tonal message as one of the more irritating aspects of the new girl writing. Wolcott was nostalgic for the explosive rage of seventies feminism

Polemicists such as Ti-Grace Atkinson, Germaine Greer and Valerie Solanas [author of the 'Society for Cutting Up Men Manifesto'] spurned the steady brush strokes of belletristic prose to spray-paint ideological graffiti worthy of the lavatory wall. Their underground spiels owed as much to Jean Genet as to any feminist godmother.

Sure, those warrior-chicks were a handful, but at least you knew where you were with them. By contrast, the kittenish girls of the nineties were troublingly all over the place – simpering and swaggering, telling you off, then rubbing up against your leg. The straightforward wrath of the tough nuts had been replaced with the tempery caprice of show-offs.

Some of these writers are gifted and amusing, but all cling to and fluff up an image of themselves that seems flirty and confrontational at the same time: flirtational. (Tell me I'm cute – or else.)

Quite so. The girl writers *were* flirtational. But the mixture of neurosis and confidence they displayed – that nervy oscillation between insecurity and bolshiness – was one of their greatest assets. The girl columns were not models of journalistic excellence; the quality of girl prose tended to be extremely uneven, but, at their best, girl writers achieved a refreshing, even startling, level of honesty. Part of that honesty lay in refusing to play either entirely tough or entirely timid – insisting instead on the confusing truth, which was a combination of both.

In one of Bridget Jones's diary entries, she described her indignant response to being told by her friend, Shaz, that she was not a feminist:

Could not avoid feeling hurt. Am feminist definitely. Believe in equality, give money to third world women's charity, have own job, independent life and home.

But another of Bridget's friends, Jude, offered the more convincing riposte:

Your feminist ideals do not encompass the need to be loved. And Bridget is prey to the influence of whatever society and media deem lovable.

Wolcott claimed (as many did) that the reason why girl writers were in such demand was that they were 'unthreatening' to male editors. In other words, their alleged 'post-feminism' suited the complacent misogynists who were running the show. In a similar vein, *Time* magazine explained the huge sales of the Bridget Jones book in Britain and America as a symptom of an anti-feminist popular culture which was intent on 'showing grown single women as frazzled, self-absorbed girls'. In truth, however, neither Bridget nor any of the other girl writers were anti- or even post-feminist. They were just candid about what imperfect feminists they were – how in spite of their aspirations to Amazonian independence, they did quite often cry over men, fret about their weight, and feel less than sisterly towards other women. The appeal of their writing lay not in some reactionary line they were toeing but, on the contrary, in their failure to toe any line very successfully. They were clearly nobody's role model and they were therefore free to tell it how it was. The fearless warrior-speak of the seventies for which Wolcott felt such nostalgia had doubtless been unnerving once, but after two decades of Virago paperbacks and *Guardian* Women's Page diatribe, such rhetoric didn't *épater* anybody much any more. It was the girls, with their candid admissions of female silliness, self-absorption and vanity, who seemed subversive.

In her final column for the *Observer* in 1999, India Knight took a bash at those readers who had attacked her, during her tenure, as a purveyor of solipsism and triviality:

The idea, apparently, is that reading some boot-faced old boiler droning on in the most embarrassingly (auto) didactic way about what we should think and why is valid and somehow important. Conversely, the argument goes, reading about the minutiae of someone's domestic life – of a life of which the author, unusually, has direct experience – is worthless and masturbatory: so much fluff, so much dross, so much space-filling (literature-wise, that's Jane Austen down the toilet then).

This was not the most elegant or winning of retorts. (The implied comparison of girl columnists with Jane Austen was particularly unwise.) But one sympathized with Knight's embattled tone. The ultimate irony of much of the criticism the girl writers received was that it tended, in its *bien-pensant* righteousness, to emulate the repressive gestures of male chauvinism. To attack women writers, as Wolcott did, for the lamentable lack of 'social dimension' in their work – for their failure to address weighty issues like 'late-term abortion' – was no different, in the end, from attacking women for their failure to write about housekeeping or napkin arrangements. In both cases, the attempt is to circumscribe the 'proper' areas of female interest. Why *is* a woman columnist honour bound to write about abortion rights? Why is any writer honour bound to write about anything in particular? No one has ever claimed that James Thurber's *œuvre* was diminished by his failure to address matters of foreign policy. Nor has anyone, for that matter, attacked Miles Kington for his inattention to the pressing male issue of prostate cancer.

But the problem of writing 'as a woman' is not *just* that you are inevitably burdened with the world's views on how you should represent your sex. With or without those views, your job is doomed to silliness, just as surely as if you had been contracted to write 'as a man' or 'as a Briton' or 'as a ginger-haired person'. Your femaleness clearly does not determine your stance on all subjects – in many cases, it may be entirely irrelevant to your view. But if your shtick is the 'female perspective', you are required to pretend that your femaleness is all – that every one of your opinions is refracted through the lens of gender. This, your editor is apt to remind you, is what you're being paid for. If you write a weekly column, you will rapidly find yourself having to manufacture womanly points of view in order to feed the yawning white space you have to fill. The business of what interests you takes a back seat to the business of fulfilling the demands of your woman-persona.

All column writing is prey to a certain theatricality. Charles Moore, editor of the *Daily Telegraph*, once observed that in order to write a successful column one was obliged not just to express an opinion, but to shout it. To establish a columnar identity, one *does* have to ham oneself up a little. But for writers in the women's ghetto, what this means, ultimately, is acting out a pantomime version of femaleness. Writing in drag.

As I write, the phenomenon of the girl column has passed its peak. None of the writers I have mentioned are still writing their columns and the main reason, I would venture, is that all of them grew weary of their restrictive girl roles. They may have started out having something new to say about modern femaleness, but having said it they were then obliged to say it over and over again. With repetition, the girl *Weltanschauung* soon lost any of its surprise factor. It hardened into formula and then self-parody. Candour was eventually replaced with a slightly cynical ventriloquizing of what the readers had paid to hear – a loop tape of comic twittering about boyfriends and periods. The girls had freed themselves from the duty to play noble viragos, only to find themselves chained to their Kooky Little Miss acts. 'This kind of column has a limited shelf-life,' India Knight wrote when she signed off. Yes, it does.

Writing 'as a woman' always winds up being a tiresome act – often as tiresome for the reader as it is for the writer. But the demand for women's columns – columns composed in a self-consciously female voice – is astonishingly hardy. One of the old liberal arguments for having them in newspapers is that they are said to provide an antidote to the chauvinism of a paper's invariably male-centric editorial. On the paper's bleakly masculine terrain, the woman columnist must be allowed to pitch her cosy tent of 'alternative' woman-centric thinking. Setting aside little spaces for women to purvey their *awfully important* woman-stuff is not an antidote to anything, of course. It is a textbook example of chauvinism at work. My advice to women writers: Don't Settle for the Tent. Even if the patronizing nature of the offer doesn't bother you, the deleterious effects that cute Women Korners have on your writing surely will. Gender writing is a deadening business. Wily women – Lynn Barber, for example, or Julie Burchill, or Catherine Bennett – won't touch it with a bargepole. They might write in the first person. They may even write about childcare from time to time. But they are careful never to venture into the grim camp of professional gender writers. Standing at the gates, they hear the

tired squawks and squeals from within and skip briskly away –
back to the wide open spaces and the simple pleasures of writing
as a human.

Reviewers I Have Known

A. N. WILSON

I never did understand why Alexander Chancellor, when editor of the *Spectator*, should have asked me to become the literary editor of the magazine. I had no experience of journalism. Perhaps this was his reason. One of my predecessors in the job, Peter Ackroyd, when he was about twenty-one, called on George Gale, then editing the mag at its Gower Street offices. Like so many young English literature graduates, he wondered whether there was any reviewing going. Gale scratched his head and didn't think there was. The young Ackroyd broadened his request. Would it be possible, perhaps, to write an article for the *Spectator* on some other theme? No, George Gale was very much afraid he didn't think this *would* be possible. A crestfallen young Ackroyd went down the stairs and came into the hall. As he was about to open the front door, Gale's head appeared over the banisters. He announced in his extraordinary gravelly voice, 'You could be literary editor if you liked.' Perhaps Alexander Chancellor, so different in all other respects from George Gale, appointed literary editors on a comparably capricious basis. I seem to remember that he eventually felt obliged to sack me from my job. This did not alter our feelings of friendship for one another, and by then I was hooked, fully able to understand Lord Beaverbrook's adage that he pitied anyone who wasn't a journalist.

It was less than twenty years ago, but what amazes me, looking back, is how completely Hacksville has altered. In many respects the journalistic world I entered was much the same as that of the nineteenth century – or even earlier.

Today, the word 'printer' means an electronic machine, not a human being. We have no printers, in the old sense; no galleys, no 'boys' running up and down flights of stairs with corrected proofs, no wise old men sitting beside the hot-metal presses and reminiscing through the night of Fleet Street in olden tymes. No Fleet Street. Journalism is now effected on computers. The editors and their executive staff are housed in soulless sub-American tower blocks miles down-river in parts of London which the rest of us never visit. The journalists themselves, scattered hither and thither, compose their copy on personal computers, and seldom if ever venture to London, certainly finding no cause to revisit their old watering holes. What mighty changes were brought to pass by the invention of new technology and by the arrival on the scene of Mr Murdoch! And all changes, one could say, for the worse.

No area of journalism has avoided the effects of the revolutions, least of all the literary journalist or hack reviewer. How things have changed, and how they have remained much the same, will be the subject of this essay. But first one must observe that one of the truly extraordinary things about the British scene towards the close of the twentieth century is that there is still so much comparatively serious literary journalism. Less so, perhaps, than in the great nineteenth-century days of the *Quarterly*, the *Fortnightly*, the *Westminster* and the *Edinburgh Review*, but still an impressive amount: the magisterial *Times Literary Supplement*, which in any one week produces a sprinkling of essays which one would like to be able to re-read in book form. The eccentric and much more mischievous *London Review of Books* continues to keep alive some of the qualities of the nineteenth-century radical journalism which inspired its founder, Karl Miller. And the indefinable *Literary Review* is in part a throwback to that mid-twentieth-century phenomenon, the 'little magazine' – one thinks of *Horizon, Encounter*, etc. – while being wholly *sui generis*. No one could claim that in a city which produced three such periodicals regularly, in addition to a host of smaller mags, literature is not catered for. And then there are the newspapers themselves, not merely the serious broadsheets but the middle-market tabloids too, which now give far more space to arts and books than was ever the case in the past. There is plenty of scope here, then, for the budding reviewer. Consider the fact that more books (for some mysterious reason) are published month by month than ever before, and you have a situation in which literary journalism should be flourishing as never before. Why is it, then, that I find myself bored by so many of the books pages of our worthier newspapers? Why do I have the sense that the big conglomerate publishers, with their publicity departments and their grinning 'publicity girls', have not-so-subtly transformed the untidy world of literary Grub Street into a branch of marketing? Why do I get the sense that many of the so-called literary editors in what was Fleet Street are foolish enough to allow themselves to be lunched, and in effect bought by publishers, rather than offering the reader balanced criticism of the wares on offer, alerting the potential book buyer to the rubbish, charlatanry and chicanery that flourish mightily as the commercial world of the Book and the Booker? It is no more than a hunch of mine. Perhaps I shall provide some sort of an answer to myself by musing in an undisciplined way on the twenty or so years since I started out as a reviewer of books.

Two thoughts, though to start with, before I allow my memories free play. The first is that all journalism – literary or otherwise – is much more a branch of imaginative literature than it is an exact science. Many newspaper readers make the mistake of hoping that these sketchbooks of the world which we call newspapers will provide a picture of How Things Really Are. But that is an illusion. The young Samuel Johnson had, as one of his earliest jobs in 1738, the task of reporting parliamentary proceedings in the *Gentleman's Magazine*. These were the days before reporters were allowed inside the parliamentary chamber, and so journalism depended on an eye-witness rushing from the public gallery and giving as good account as he could remember of what had been said during debates. But, as Boswell tells us, with the arrival on the magazine of the young scholar from Staffordshire, the 'speeches were more and more enriched by the accession of Johnson's genius'. It was soon discovered that an eye-witness was unnecessary, and that Johnson could provide perfectly plausible accounts of 'Yesterday in Parliament' without sullying his reportage by anything so confusing as actual memory. Much of the best, and by paradox much of the truer journalism comes to pass in a comparable manner even today.

The second preliminary point worth making – and one which applies, I suspect, much more to the 'literary journalist' than to those working in other branches of the profession – is that there is a sharp divide between those who wanted to go in for this line of business and those who have drifted into it *faute de mieux*. Very often, those who are best at it are in fact those who would never have supposed that they would one day be reviewers or literary editors.

When I was a young theological student at Oxford, half wondering if I had it in me to be a novelist or some other variety of 'writer', I recall being astonished when Julian Barnes confided in me his burning ambition to be a literary journalist. He was at the time reading for the Bar and working on the *Oxford English Dictionary* as a lexicographer: two eminently respectable and sensible ways of passing the time. How extraordinary, then, that more than anything in the world he should wish to belong to what he called – I recall the phrase vividly because I had never before heard it on anyone's lips – 'literary London'. I asked him what he meant by it, and he said that it was Martin Amis, a young Oxford graduate a bit older than me who, as well as being the son of the famous Kingsley, had made a bit of a splash by having an affair with Freddie Ayer's stepdaughter and writing a compulsively caddish novel about it; now he was deputy lit. ed. at the *New Statesman* (the lit. ed. was, I think, Claire Tomalin), and Julian thought that to be number three in this trinity would be very heaven.

Such a world was so far from my own that I could not really imagine wanting to belong to it. When I did capture a sense of its excitement, it wasn't from Julian Barnes, who sailed out of my ken after his ambition to work for Martin was fulfilled. It was, absurdly perhaps, when I some time thereafter read Thackeray's novel *Pendennis*. Those who have read the book will never forget the moment when the hero, Pen, and his friend Warrington are going through the Strand and pass by a newspaper office, which is all lighted up and bright. Reporters are coming out of the place, or rushing up to it in cabs; there are lamps burning in the editors' rooms, and above, where the compositors are at work: the windows of the building are in a blaze of gas. 'Look at that, Pen,' Warrington says. 'There she is – the great engine – she never sleeps. She has her ambassadors in every quarter of the world – her couriers upon every road. Her officers march along with armies, and her envoys walk into statesmen's cabinets. They are ubiquitous . . . Look! Here comes the Foreign Express galloping in. They will be able to give news to Downing Street tomorrow: funds will rise or fall, fortunes be made or lost . . .'

It is an inspirational chapter. Literally so, since many, many of the great journalists of the nineteenth and twentieth centuries were drawn to the Street of Shame by reading this book.

It is all over now, of course. Rupert Murdoch and the new technology, in an unholy alliance, brought Fleet Street to an end, and with it that concentration of journalists in one small part of London which made it all so very distinctive. Newspaper offices really were much the same (apart from the gas light being replaced by electric) as in Thackeray's day, right down to our own times, just as the taverns and bars where the journalists drank were much the same as in the century before Thackeray.

And though the reviewing and literary end of the profession was always a good deal less exciting than the reporting of wars or the bringing of news to the hot presses, which would effect the rise or fall of markets, it was not without its romance. You felt you were in touch with a very distinctively London literary past in those Fleet Street bars where, within the memory of some of the older journalists, Chesterton had blown in in his black cape, Belloc had got drunk and passed on his mantle to Beachcomber, and Beachcomber to Michael Wharton or to Ingrams. Ignorance alone, and snobbery, creates the atmosphere where some English writers think they are above journalism or distinct from it. In the great days of English literature, nearly everyone who was a name in 'literature' had also worked, usually prolifically, as a journalist. George Eliot started out as that Grub Street perennial, the Young Woman Who Isn't The Editor but in fact does all the work, subbing, commissioning reviews and sleeping with the editor of (in this case) the *Westminster Review*, when it was being edited by that rogue John Chapman. She was the first of many an archetype. Sonia

Orwell and the girls who hung around in the offices of Connolly's *Horizon*, or who are immortalized in Anthony Powell's *Books Do Furnish a Room*, would find her tale perfectly familiar. (She eventually ran off, in what would become the traditional manner, with a fellow reviewer, married of course. All this in the 1840s.) Much of Thackeray's best work is found in the articles he wrote for *Punch* and other periodicals. Dickens edited his own rag, *Household Words*. It is only perhaps in our own rather strange times that English writers should have supposed there was necessarily a distinction between literature and journalism. Highbrows or would-be highbrows were horrified by having to get their hands dirty with hack-work. To read John Betjeman's letters, you would suppose that nothing was more humiliating than having to review novels for the *Daily Telegraph*, but it was in such ways, until his prodigious success as a TV showman and poet began, that he kept the wolf from the door. Harold Nicolson's diaries are peppered with self-criticism for lowering himself by having anything to do with journalism. What a far cry from Samuel Johnson who, when he first approached St John's Gate, the headquarters of the *Gentleman's Magazine*, 'beheld it with reverence'.

My old friend Peter Quennell (one of Thackeray's successors as editor of the *Cornhill* magazine) definitely belonged to this twentieth-century breed of the unwilling literary hack. Sir Peter Quennell, as he became, looked like a figure from a vanished age by the end. His black Trilby hat and his dark-blue suits marked him out as the clubman he was. If you had seen him at the bottom of the stairs in White's, with a glass in his hand (whisky before luncheon, port afterwards), you might have taken him for one of the noble lords with whom he so enjoyed mixing. But he had no money save what he earned either as a book reviewer or as the author of those elegantly turned, if curiously unnourishing books, lives of Byron and Ruskin, studies of the eighteenth century in which he purported to be so much at home, and his sublimely beautiful but empty memoirs.

Like so many who have trod the paving-stones of Grub Street, Quennell had never intended to be a mere literary hack. As a schoolboy poet, he had attracted the attention of Virginia Woolf.

(Later he fell from her favour and he would quote, in rather mournful tones, her description of him in her diaries as 'an exiguous worm'.) He had assumed, when the Oxford contemporary of Graham Greene and Harold Acton, that he would be a writer greater than they – a mannerist poet, perhaps, a great aesthete, perhaps a novelist.

True, some workaday prose works came from his pen, but he was doomed, probably from some quite early stage in his life, to be someone whose life was determined by the need of that quick fix which journalism alone provides. He was deeply attractive to women. 'I love your badger hands!' Anne Rothermere would exclaim, in the days when he was her lover (before she divorced the great newspaper magnate and married the creator of James Bond, Ian Fleming).

Quennell was briefly employed as literary editor of the *Daily Mail*. He referred to the episode loftily, not displeased that his association with the great lady (née Charteris) should be known, but evidently weighed down by the ignominy of the task itself. He spoke very much as if being literary editor of such a newspaper was something of a joke – rather as if he had volunteered to fight for his own country and had served as a private rather than an officer. (He never did join up – his war work was fire-fighting, from which he was sacked for smoking on duty.) He said that the best weeks on the *Mail* were those when there was a Cup Final or a comparably exciting event in the footballing or cricketing world. Then the sports editor would demand, and get, the space normally allocated to 'books', and the lit. ed., responsible for writing, not merely commissioning, the book reviews would be spared both the chore of doing that week's work and the disgrace (as he loftily saw things) of seeing his name printed in such a popular newspaper.

Yet, like the Empress, he wept but he took.

He and his friend Cyril Connolly never, exactly speaking, had proper jobs. Unlike feebler journalists of a younger generation, they did not much go in for mortgages or owning property either. Quennell, five times married, never owned a house, preferring to live from hand to mouth, and from marriage to marriage, in flats or houses that were either rented or the property of his wives. 'I think I'm going to starve!' he once exclaimed melodramatically at the Sitwells' dinner-table, as he recounted how he had just been dropped, either by his wife or a literary editor or both. 'You aren't the sort that starves,' Osbert Sitwell replied. 'Now finish what's on your fork.' Looking at the cutlery in question, Quennell was compelled to admit that he had a forkful of grouse and a glass of excellent claret beside him. There was seldom a period of his life when this was not the case. Could someone who chose, as he did, to live by book reviewing manage to maintain such a style today? Quennell once told me he had started book reviewing in an era, not antediluvian in its remoteness, when Desmond MacCarthy was literary editor of the *New Statesman*. In those days, a young reviewer collected his payment on the day of publication. The cheque, Quennell told me, would pay for an evening at the Savoy Grill with a girl; even, if he struck lucky, pay for a hotel room with her afterwards. In the course of my own career so far as a literary editor and as an occasional book reviewer, I have often thought of this little economic statistic. It provides a vignette of a vanished age, a glory age of book reviewing when there were great literary editors – Desmond MacCarthy himself, or Ackerley, extending down in our own day to Terry Kilmartin, for so many years lit. ed. of the *Observer*, Karl Miller, who was lit. ed. of *New Statesman*, *Spectator* and *Listener* before founding the *London Review of Books*, Derwent May, the profoundly read ornithologist and novelist who was for many years lit. ed. of the *Listener* – and, best of the lot in my view, John Gross. Something happened economically in the middle to late years of the century. Some journalists are now paid huge sums of money, but they certainly aren't (unless I have been missing out on something for all these years) the literary journalists. Today if you reviewed a book for one of the smaller weeklies like the *New Statesman* or the *Spectator* and wanted to spend the cheque in a comparable manner, you would have to seek out something a bit less classy than the Savoy Grill, particularly if you had in mind the hope of a double hotel room afterwards. Paradoxically, if you wanted to live today as Quennell and Connolly lived in their day, you would have to be a reviewer on the much-reviled *Daily Mail*.

Quennell and Connolly, partly because of their bravado, partly because of their very considerable talent, represented the top end of the reviewing market in their day. There were always those lower down the pecking order. As I discovered when I myself became a literary editor, there was still a heroic band of the hacks of Old Grub Street pacing around London in search of a book, any book, to review. One such man, not untalented, had walked out of the headmastership of a grammar school when the Labour Party brought in comprehensive education in the 1960s. He had somehow thereby missed his best chance of a proper pension, and was reduced to a perpetual trudge round the offices of the *Spectator*, *Punch* and the *New Statesman*, and some of the Fleet Street papers as well. Sometimes one was callous enough to say, 'Nothing doing,' but most weeks one would give him a book, sometimes saying as one did so, 'It might not be worth a review, but . . . see what you think.'

This meant that one did not expect him to write a review, but that he could at least, on his trudge through Hacksville, turn down Chancery Lane and sell the book at Gaston's, the second-hand bookshop with specialized in review copies of books.

One of my predecessors as literary editor at the *Spectator* would insist on the publishers sending him at least three copies of any book if they wished to see it reviewed. One for the reviewer. One to be sold immediately to Gaston's. A third copy to be perused by the lit. ed. himself. If he liked it, he would keep it for his own library; if not, it would in turn be sold. Gaston's were said to have an arrangement with this legendary character whereby they did not even need to pay him cash, so long as they settled his enormous bills at El Vino. Thus the income tax inspector could be kept innocently unaware either of his reading or his drinking habits.

In the days of which I speak, book reviews were, by and large, written by professional reviewers, by journalists – if journalists of a slightly off-beam, eccentric, sometimes moth-eaten character. They were written by people who knew their trade and who, for the most part, needed the money. Nowadays, to judge from the literary pages of the newspapers, the Man of Letters (of either sex) is a thing of the past. Literary editors, no doubt leant upon by editors themselves or by the advertising departments, send out books to be reviewed by 'celebrities', by politicians, by media dons and TV pre-senters. Nor are there nearly so many 'regulars' in today's newspapers. In the old days you could reach for the Sunday paper and ask, 'What is Malcolm Muggeridge, or Harold Nicolson, or Raymond Mortimer reviewing this week?' Such brilliant essayists as this could make an interesting article out of almost any subject, and they would occasionally get round to mentioning the book in question. Now there are very few regular reviewers, and hardly any major figures in the world of literary journalism who are given the task of reviewing fiction. There is nothing in contemporary journalism to match the weekly fiction review which, rain or shine, Auberon Waugh used to write some twenty years ago in the *Evening Standard*.

It would be easy to see reviewers, if not as enemies of literature, then as very diverting rivals to it. Tennyson scornfully called Churton Collins, a literary hack of his day, 'a louse upon the locks of literature', and there are many figures reviewing today to whom the epithet could with justice be applied. If one were a purist, one would be worried more by the stylish, brilliant reviewers than by the harmless drudges. Who would not rather read Auberon Waugh than the latest novel which he was noticing? Who remembers the occasions for Virginia Woolf's sublime essays in *The Common Reader* series? – they all started life as reviews or review essays in *The Times Literary Supplement*. They are arguably the best thing, apart from her diaries, that she ever wrote. Certainly the great mid-twentieth-century reviewers, Connolly, Orwell, Muggeridge, Nicolson, Mortimer, Lambert, were always worth reading for their own sakes, regardless of the merits or otherwise of the book under discussion. Wasn't this a little hard on the author of the book, who might have hoped (vainly perhaps), having laboured to produce a history of the Spanish Empire, or a biography of Genghis Khan, that the reviewer would have done more than write a well-turned essay on the subject, with barely a reference to the book under discussion?

No doubt such a school of reviewing is unfair to the unfortunate publishers and authors of books. But it is not surprising. Of course we would rather read a well-turned review than a dull book. Many of us read fewer than fifty books a year but we must at the same time glance at hundreds of reviews. By the law of averages, there is nothing to stop a good journalist from writing a good review once a fortnight, or even once a week. That much more than one decent book per week is published in London defies belief. Yet, as anyone who has ever visited the office of a literary editor could testify, the London publishers are producing more and more books – hundreds of novels each week; dozens of biographies; travelogues by the score; histories by the dumpbin. Who will ever buy these books, let alone read them?

Certainly as a literary editor I was sometimes forced to remind myself that the primary purpose of a book page was to recommend the latest good books and, where necessary, to warn the public off pretentious or unreadable books which came over-puffed from the publisher. It was so tempting, instead, to fill the page week after week with essays by the best writers I could find.

When a reviewer has real panache one can almost wonder whether they need to mention the book at all. The most extreme example of this phenomenon was, in my experience, provided by the historian Paul Johnson. He is one of the most fluent writers in Fleet Street (somehow it seems appropriate to use this anachronism, for Johnson dates from the Good Old Days of journalism). Editors can always rely on him to produce 800 trenchant words of well-formed sentences and fluent paragraphs within an astonishingly short space of time. On one occasion, I telephoned Paul and asked him if he would review a book on (let us say) the American Civil War. I warned him it was a volume of some magnitude – over 800 pages – and I apologized for the labour in reading such a huge 'doorstopper', particularly since we needed the review fairly quickly – within the next fortnight. Game for anything, Paul Johnson boomed, 'Send it along, dear boy, send it along.'

Since it was necessary to make sure the book reached him in double-quick time, I asked my assistant Katie Campbell to send the book round by motorbike to Paul Johnson's address. I wondered how long it would take him to produce the review of this truly encyclopaedic and enormous work. A week? Not even Paul could do it in less time than that, surely.

The next day, as we sat together in the office, I mused aloud on this question. Katie put her hand over her mouth in the exaggerated gesture of one who had made a gaffe, and pointed to the book which was still on her desk. She had forgotten to dispatch it to La Maison Johnson. 'It doesn't matter,' I replied. 'Plenty of time. Send it round this morning.' But even as I spoke, the fax machine had begun to whirr into action, and 800 perfectly turned words on the American Civil War, with observant comments on the merits and faults of the book, had dropped into the in-tray. There was no reason not to publish this review. It was perfectly well balanced. I noticed, when the other reviews in rival newspapers began to appear, that the more judicious reviewers had all singled out for praise the very things that had appealed to the mighty imagination of Johnson. Like all really good journalists, Paul had somehow intuited the true nature of the thing under discussion. Journalism, as I began by reminding the reader, belongs to the genre of imaginative literature. It is not a branch of science. No self-important person who complains of 'bad' reviews – or who, come to that, objects to stories appearing about themselves in the news section – should forget this essential fact.

This does not mean, of course, that the authors of books do not, for the most understandable of reasons, mind passionately about the fate of their books. My failure to print a review of a (paperback reissue) of the book of a friend of mine when I was lit. ed. at the *Standard* inspired the author to phone me in a towering rage to wish most sincerely that I would roast in hell, a fate which he had thought would soon be mine. I did not resent his anger, since I have felt just such surges of rage myself when seeing the fate of my little books when being reviewed. If you are an author, there is nothing you can do about these feelings. The next time I saw my friend who had wished me in hell, we had a drink and a laugh about it. He had managed to get most of his bad feelings out of his system by expressing them. I am not Irish, as he is. I bottle up emotions and seethe. There is a blacklist in my mind of literary editors who have failed to give sufficient prominence to my books, or who have sent them to unsympathetic reviewers. And of course there is a blacklist of reviewers themselves. One can derive great pleasure from the misfortunes of these individuals, particularly if it is a misfortune one has engineered oneself. So irrational is an author's response to reviews that he can even hate favourable reviews if they are

29

ham-fisted or single out the 'wrong' aspects of the book for praise.

But though I, as the author of books, might develop obsessive hatreds of certain literary journalists, reviewers and editors, I am not so paranoid as to believe in conspiracy theories. It is sometimes said, and for all I know sometimes believed, that there is a coterie or a mafia called, to use that phrase of Barnes's, 'literary London'. These characters, believed to gather together in various Soho dives such as the Groucho Club, are all imagined to know one another, to scratch one another's backs, to give good reviews of their friends' books and to ignore the talent of those outside the charmed circle. I have to say that in all the time I have been reviewing, I have never come across much evidence of this mafia existing. In my time as lit. ed. for two papers I have only once allowed the sworn enemy of an author to get her hands on his book. This was when I gave Emma Soames a volume of Nicholas Coleridge's short stories to review. It was not done with malice aforethought, but you could say that it was a malicious act, since Coleridge, a magnate of Condé Nast, had just sacked Soames as the editor of one of his magazines. She gave him the treatment one would have expected and for a week or two it caused certain types of Londoner to gossip about it. Coleridge is a big, powerful man who, I believe, was undamaged by this squib. Soames is a great woman who has gone on to edit at least two other magazines since. I certainly committed a sin as a literary editor here, but I do not feel that it was a sin of the same order as, say, offering a serious novel by a full-time writer to his sworn enemy. Nor am I particularly aware of back-scratching in the world of reviewing, though it probably goes on. Certainly, at Christmas time, when papers publish the favourite books of the year by famous people, these individuals prove themselves to be shameless log-rollers. They choose one another's books like the literary luvvies they are. But I don't see much evidence of this sort of thing going on in the book pages of the newspapers. Among the weeklies, only the *Economist* now has anonymous reviews. Gone are the days when Oxford dons could review one another's books in *The Times Literary Supplement*, dipping their pens in anonymous poison.

I have sometimes been accused of being a savage reviewer myself.

In fact the number of hostile notices I have written could be numbered on the fingers of one hand – well, perhaps two. I am so soft-hearted that I always feel paroxysms of self-hatred and remorse when such reviews appear in print. Indeed when I said in the *Spectator* that I found Marina Warner a bore, her saintly godfather Lord Longford, a friend of mine, upbraided me so fiercely that I forswore reviewing for ever. Like most vows, this was one I broke, but I made it sincerely. I think I am fairly typical, in so far as when I was a young man trying to cut a dash I tended to be much crueller than I am now, as a bland middle-aged hack who knows how needlessly painful such barbs can be. Now when I feel shame about a review, it is because I have been dishonestly kind about books. I have lost count of the number of dull books I have hailed as masterpieces, rather than trouble myself to finish. No complaints, I have noticed, ever come from the author if you praise their book to the skies. If you read it three times and point out all the faults of a book, the author invariably accuses you of not having read it. If all the reviews told the truth, there would, most weeks, be a torrent of abuse for the mediocre talents of contemporary English writers and the almost non-existent skills of contemporary British publishers.

This, if conspiracies there be, is the great conspiracy which spoils literary journalism. It is the conspiracy to turn a blind eye to the decline of the book trade. As more and more and *more* books are published, the number of good books declines. The conscientious publisher's editor (nearly always now a freelance) is paid so little that if she (they are nearly always women) is to keep up with the numbers of books pouring from the conglomerate presses, she must cut corners and edit at speed. Most books now published should not have been published at all. Many of those which deserved publication deserved to be published on decent paper, without misprints, repetitions and errors marring the finished work.

The big capitalists who run publishing conglomerates – in some cases, the same as the big capitalists who own newspapers – could not care less about the quality of the books they are producing. All they care about is the cash flow, and to bring this in – to recoup the inevitable losses they incur in paying the authors in advance, often ludicrously over the odds – they have to publish fast, and have to publish too much. In the case of the truly gross overpayments, they have to secure maximum coverage or publicity for books. They will bombard literary editors with innumerable copies of the hyped 'bestsellers'. The booksellers and wholesalers are told in advance what the bestsellers are going to be. It is quite shocking to me to see how, more often than not, the literary editors go along with this commercially motivated farce, giving vast amounts of reviewing space, not to the genuinely interesting book, but to the book which has commanded the largest advance. The annual hype for prizes such as the Whitbread and the Booker is a similar example of the way in which capitalism dresses up as choice what has in fact been fixed and predetermined in advance. The judges on these occasions think they are free agents, but given the overwhelming numbers of books being produced, they naturally gravitate towards the ones that have been hyped.

The literary editor who could see through all this tissue of deceit and who was prepared (to use a vulgar but somehow inevitable phrase) to cut the crap, would be rare. To do the job properly would involve reading perhaps dozens of books each week. It is so much easier to let those smiling young women from Publicity at the big publishing houses make the decision on what should be reviewed. And, for reasons which are already apparent from the foregoing pages, most reviews are kindly.

So we don't live in a great age of literary journalism, even though we live in a period when there is plenty of opportunity for the aspirant journalist to try her hand at a review. My advice to her, though, would be to say: steer clear of the books pages. They're dead boring these days. If you want to make a name for yourself in journalism, learn the trade on a gossip column or a 'diary' and then make a pretty swift leap to some specialized branch of knowledge – become the health correspondent, or ask for some free travel and experience as a foreign reporter. If I had my time over again, I'd become a crime reporter and use the experience to write Simenonish *romans policiers*. For, as I now realize, from that moment my life was changed. It became immeasurably more interesting and amusing. Not that I for a moment regret the strange moment when Alexander Chancellor, then editor of the *Spectator*, rang me up out of the blue and asked me to be literary editor. That is the reason why I can hardly remember the fact that Alexander gave me the sack. I remember instead that he opened a door to an enchanted place, and for that reason he is one of my heroes.

33

Editors and Egomaniacs

HENRY PORTER

It was noon on a Friday, 26 January 1990, a time in the week when the editors of Sunday newspapers would normally be expected to be limbering up for the weekend. Instead Andrew Neil and Peregrine Worsthorne, then editors of the *Sunday Times* and the *Sunday Telegraph*, faced each other across a full courtroom where Mr Neil's claim for damages against Mr Worsthorne was being heard in an atmosphere of ill-suppressed glee. At least that was the mood of the journalists who had filled the press benches and public seats to hear the conclusion of a dispute which had smouldered since the previous spring.

In March 1989 Peregrine Worsthorne had published an editorial in the *Sunday Telegraph*, entitled 'Editors as Playboys', which took Andrew Neil to task for his affair with a woman named Pamela Bordes, who it turned out had been selling herself for £500 a throw. Neil did not know this during his brief relationship with Pamela Bordes, which was over by the time she was exposed in the *News of the World*, but Mr Worsthorne – now Sir Peregrine – argued that the fact that he had once dated her meant that he was not fit to be editor of a newspaper. As he later told the court, Neil was not in his opinion an *homme sérieux*. Instead of spending his time in nightclubs like Tramp where he was likely to be tempted by the unusually attractive *embonpoint* of a creature like Bordes, he should haunt the high tables of Oxford and Cambridge. He should shun all frivolity.

The case is still among the most comical ever to be heard in the Royal Courts of Justice. Quite apart from the hilariously ornate language produced by Sir Peregrine, it dramatically animated –

as well as any David Hare play could – the differences between Worsthorne's patrician conservatism and Andrew Neil's thrusting, edgy vision of New Britain. Neil was eventually awarded a near derisory £1,000 damages and costs, but by the end of the case the outcome seemed almost an irrelevance to anyone observing this comic spectacular. Naturally neither journalist saw the joke and for most of the proceedings they wore the concentrated, drained expressions of men taking part in high-stakes poker or bomb disposal.

And well they might. In an act of sublime folly they had left the safety of their newspaper offices and offered their reputations for the inspection of a jeering world. For the first time a case turned on the behaviour expected of an editor, which was extremely interesting because British newspaper editors have tried to preserve the fiction that they are not really public figures at all and that their lives are unworthy of scrutiny. Most successful editors like Kelvin Mackenzie, the former editor of the *Sun*, and Paul Dacre, the editor of the *Daily Mail*, tend to seek a lower profile than Andrew Neil ever did and avoid numerous television and radio appearances for this very reason. Anything they have to say is said in their papers and, if pressed by a trade organ for an interview, they are likely to talk leadenly about market share and the new contributors they have hired. This is the only thing worth writing about me, an editor will insist, gesturing to his new health supplement. Of course it is untrue but unless you are in the newspaper business and have experience of the wonderful egocentricity of editors – their demonic drive, their power for mischief and good, their determination to make the world conform to their view of how it should be and their restless absorption in the cycle of news-gathering and publication – you will have little idea how profoundly untrue it is.

Editors can be divided into two distinct groups. The first and largest consists of the shirt-sleeved, seat-of-the-pants technicians, all of whom tend to have risen through the ranks of sub-editors and section editors and generally have small experience of writing under their own name. This doesn't mean to say they can't write, it's just that a series of desk jobs in the office is generally a much easier route to the top. If you have talent and energy you can get there very quickly indeed. The late Lord (Hugh) Cudlipp, for instance, became editor-in-chief of the *Daily Mirror* at the astonishing age of twenty-three. Tabloid editors are usually drawn from this group because for one thing tabloids require a greater degree of technical skill in terms of getting the paper's pace, mix of stories and design right. A tabloid works on a highly developed formula, but if this is so rigid as to disallow novelty it will never sing. That's where the tabloid editor's wit, boldness and irreverence come in, although success is ultimately based on presentational skills, which simply cannot be faked. You've either got them, like Kelvin MacKenzie, or you haven't, like a number of former editors at the *Express* group. Equally, he must have a pretty visceral understanding of what's going on in his readership. This cannot be faked either, and if readers for one moment sense that they are being patronized or being taken away from their natural interests they will quietly seek a more sympathetic newspaper.

Where the technician relies on a sure eye and a sharp news instinct, the second type of editor sees himself as an altogether more rational creature who is happy to admit his technical limitations and occasional lapses of empathy. He is a thinker, he is likely to have spent most of his professional life writing and he is only at home in the broadsheet press. Because he has had little practice in writing headlines, laying out pages or re-configuring the sections of a paper, he will call on the technically gifted people among his staff, which may result in their influencing the character of his paper. This will not bother him unduly because he offers something supposedly much grander – leadership, a world view, an intellectual analysis of the state of the country, a moral compass. He has been chosen because of known political convictions and abilities as a propagandist, both of which have been advertised for years in his various columns. He is technically ignorant and regards the mechanics of newspaper production as not much more relevant to his job than the engine in his company car. In short he is the *homme sérieux* of Peregrine Worsthorne's vision, which is why Sir Peregrine should be unhesitatingly included in this category.

Perhaps surprisingly this academy of writers and commentators also numbers his adversary Andrew Neil among its members because he was principally a writer before he left the *Economist* for the *Sunday Times*. The former editors of *The Times*, Lord Rees-Mogg and Simon Jenkins, are also good examples, as are Charles Moore, editor of the *Daily Telegraph*, Will Hutton, former editor of the *Observer*, and Andrew Marr, former editor of the *Independent*. The last two had little practical experience before taking over their papers and it is significant that they were replaced by talented technicians – Roger Alton at the *Observer* and Simon Kelner at the *Independent* – who had both edited magazines and features sections for well over a decade before their appointments. Quite where Janet Street Porter, editor of the *Independent on Sunday*, fits into all this is hard to say because plainly she does not come from either of the two conventional groups of editors. This might conceivably be an advantage but on the other hand newspapers are very unlike TV in which Ms Street Porter has spent most of her career. An editor is much more than a presenter and has to work a great deal harder.

The division between the two groups used to be set fast and you could more or less guarantee that the types were confined to the appropriate format size – technicians and showmen to the popular press and thinkers to the broadsheets. But this has changed in the last thirty years, partly because of the growth in the number of tabloids, but also because the multi-section broadsheets require more technical understanding and marketing ability than they used to; perhaps less thinking too. The presentational wizard, therefore, the bubbling ideas man, the gimmick-crazed marketeer has moved into the ascendancy. For one thing proprietors find they're better at selling newspapers and for another they are likely to be more malleable on political issues. The exception among proprietors is Conrad Black, a kind of grand *homme sérieux* himself and the owner of the *Telegraph* group. He picks editors who share his conservative, eurosceptic views and at least look and behave like thinkers. While Murdoch terrorizes his editors on the phone at any time of day or night, Black ticks them off in letters to his own papers that are layered like *mille-feuilles* with subordinate clauses that are anxiously decrypted for signs of menace. The point is that he shows his editors a few degrees more respect than Murdoch and this is because he sees them in a different way. They are in some sense favoured reflections of himself.

Editors have become a more homogeneous group, which means that an individual can move from broadsheet to tabloid with no great difficulty. The reverse migration is rare, but this has a lot to do with the larger salaries to be found on the tabloids. Newspapers can make a great deal of money – even when hobbled by mad and bad managements, as the *Daily Mirror* and *Daily Express* groups were during the eighties – and editors are crucial to these profits, which explains their increasingly large salaries. Paul Dacre is the highest paid of the twenty national newspaper editors with a salary that is reported to have been set at over £600,000 after Conrad Black tried to lure him from Associated Newspapers. The rest are paid between £120,000 and £270,000. In 1998 the editor-in-chief of the *Independent* newspaper hired a sports agent to negotiate his package, a development which proprietors will not welcome, although they realize that the life-expectancy of a newspaper editor is commonly shorter than that of a dormouse. On average they last between two and three years in one job, although a few achieve longer tenures, or manage to slide from one editorial chair to another. Between 1977 and 1983 Derek Jameson achieved a run of three editorships – the *Daily Express*, the *Daily Star* and the *News of the World* – which defies the late Sir David English's axiom that an individual has at the very most one successful editorship in him.

Some would say that no amount of money compensates for the hellish distractions that are built into the daily editor's job. He leads an impossibly stretched life, the major part of which is spent doing anything but editing a newspaper. What follows here is – without exaggeration – a summary of his day. After a hasty reading of his own and rival papers the editor's day rapidly moves into a seamless round of meetings and conferences. At 9.30 a.m. the marketing director wants to know what is planned in the way of new supplements, names and serializations for the all-important circulation push in the autumn. Posters and TV advertising have to be settled within the next ten days, so decisions have to be taken now. That would be fine if there was plenty in the larder, but there isn't – the sensational exposé of New Labour's culture of backbiting has been sold to another paper. At 9.45 there is a meeting to discuss the new editorial computer system. The training programme and installation promise months of disruption, but the need for a new system is underlined at 11 a.m. when the old system goes down, trapping the next day's features section for several hours. Meanwhile there is an editorial conference to be held and the editor must find the inspiration to add the crispness and vitality (the proprietor's words) that were lacking in that morning's paper. There were mistakes in the first edition and already a businessman is threatening a libel suit if an allegation about his company's links with Iraq is not withdrawn. One hemisphere of the editor's brain rehearses the arguments he will present in the afternoon's budget meeting while the other wonders how he is going to keep the City editor and his prize female columnist, both of whom have been made attractive offers by a competitor. Just half a guilty eye is scanning the news list in front of him.

And so the day proceeds through meetings and phone calls – calls with government spin doctors, lawyers, distribution people, members of the board and finally the new proprietor, who cannot understand why his investment has not propelled the newspaper to the top of the charts. Each is demanding something of the editor – at the very minimum his time. There is an increasing sense at the back of his mind that nothing is being adequately resolved, and yet late in the afternoon a process of crystallization is taking place around him. Decisions are needed about the front page, the subjects of the editorials have to be chosen and the City editor's response to the legal complaint of the morning must be read. His juices begin to flow and for a brief three- or four-hour period he does what he is meant to do – edit the paper. The size and speed of the operation mean many important decisions will already have been taken by his executives, but he can sharpen, focus, emphasize and dump stories as the newspaper heads to the presses for the first time and then as it moves through each edition of the evening. This is when he puts his mark on the paper, but it takes flare and stamina at the end of a day that has been choked with administration. Still, there is nothing so intoxicating as being at the helm when there's a run of good news stories and things are falling into place exactly as planned. The energy comes from somewhere, and the rush of holding that first edition, a suspicion of dampness and a smell of the presses lingering in its pages, is unequalled in any work that does not involve kicking a ball into a net or performing in front of a live audience.

In the first few weeks of his job an editor is likely to go about with a barely concealed look of shock. The great pleasure in achieving his ambition has been quickly replaced by a fear that he – it is still only occasionally she – will never tame the beast, never gain the confidence of the staff, and so fail to engineer the specific reflexes required to make his paper distinct from the others. Many don't make the grade in the first year and then hang on, looking increasingly hunted, yet never quite bringing themselves to acknowledge what every member of their staff knows and probably the management too: they can't hack it. Why they fail is interesting. Some simply don't have the taste for riding the beast and then rather late in the day discover that they haven't got much to say either. A newspaper editor must be opinionated, if only to give his paper direction and identity. His views may add up to little more than a collection of prejudices, but they are better than no views at all, or an outlook which is just too reasonable or too damned nice.

Others fail because they never get to grips with the politics of the newspaper, or with handling the proprietor. A Murdoch editor, for instance, must calculate when to argue with the tyrant, when to fold, when to treat with undetectable solicitude and when to go on the offensive, which is sometimes the only option because, like all bullies, Murdoch takes notice of people who stand up to him. But the editor has to decide on the right response. Besides, this is not his only worry. Newspaper groups are treacherous places. Each is a court with one source of unchallengeable authority. Beneath this wheel are several editors and numerous circulation, marketing and advertising managers, all of whom seek to defend their own jobs by skilfully pointing out the failures of other departments. In these days of a shrinking newspaper market the editor's performance is the target of much bitching and he is well advised to develop an idea of which smiling suit is responsible for the worst of it.

If the novice editor survives the first few months, stabilizes circulation and does the usual jumping up and down to get himself and his paper noticed, he will begin to learn to take short cuts in his day – to throw out the new advertising agency when they're seeking to persuade him that a zany chipmunk character is the only way to induce people to buy the title; to ignore the marketing man who comes fresh from a focus group talking about young readers; and to tell the features editor that he may not upgrade his office car. He becomes more ruthless with his time and less careful with the feelings of his staff, which in any case he has lately discovered harbours a group of people who are bent on undermining him – not at every turn, but often enough to permit the occasional private smile of satisfaction on the subs' bench. It is a sport which is joined partly to test the editor's mettle but also to relieve the drudgery and disappointment entailed in certain newspaper jobs. To place a mildly insulting caption under a picture of one of the editor's friends, or to use a typeface or word that he has forbidden, provides a great deal of pleasure, particularly if the culprit can quote two conflicting edicts from the editor's office that excuse him.

One of the most difficult takeovers was in 1983 at the *Sunday Times* when Andrew Neil succeeded Frank Giles, a slightly inanimate gentleman editor. Giles had not changed the paper substantially since Harry Evans's regime, so when Neil was given the job by Murdoch he was determined to reform the journalists, whom he regarded as impossibly liberal, lazy and technophobic. The opposition was more open than usual and was led by Hugo Young, now chairman of the Scott Trust, who was then deputy under Giles and a leading political commentator. Young quietly inspired a sort of political resistance to Neil on grounds that the new editor represented the worst of Murdoch but was also a cloned Thatcherite. Eventually Young and several other senior figures took redundancy, but it was only after the move to Wapping, twenty-seven months into Neil's editorship, that he managed to jettison the majority of troublemakers and make the newspaper in his own image. A remark by one of the paper's executives at the time captured the level of resentment against the young editor, who was trying to wean his staff from typewriters. 'If he can't fuck it or plug it in, he's not interested,' said the man, throwing down a rejected feature on wildlife. Neil was indeed different. He had not the slightest interest in old Fleet Street and apparently no sentiment for the newspaper as the living, breathing organism of journalistic lore. He was the first of a new breed of editor who wanted to sell papers, cut costs, make money, seek out cross-media synergies and then at the end of the week write the government's policy. Whatever anyone said about him, there is little doubt that he grasped the enormous power that had accrued to editors and managements once the means of producing and distributing a newspaper had been seized from the unions by Rupert Murdoch. He used it just as decisively as his colleague Kelvin Mackenzie at the *Sun*. In different ways their newspapers came to represent the capering thuggery of New Britain in the eighties, although Neil was much braver than Mackenzie and genuinely carved an anti-establishment path for the paper. Both made huge fortunes for Rupert, who repaid them by luring them to jobs in his television empire and then contriving to make their lives wretched. However successful you are in News Corp, there can only be one star – KRM.

It is a truth, never seriously doubted by anyone who has worked in the proximity of an editor, that once he has served in the job for a few years his grip on reality begins to degenerate. The unhinging is due in part to the excessive preoccupation of an editor's mind, which churns endlessly with the business of the paper – with stories that have been missed, with the sharp practices of the competition, with the home news editor who must be replaced – but also with an insatiable appetite for novelty. All life is raw material for his publication and when it doesn't quite match his Technicolored expectations, he is liable to demand that his staff do something about it. Long-serving editors become convinced by a certain view or trend, gleaned during a rare passage through everyday life. One or two tiny, unconnected incidents are woven into an elaborate theory which calls for immediate ventilation in his newspaper. Politicians with suntans are untrustworthy; women who wear black tights are frigid; professional footballers are taller than those in the 1966 World Cup; Britain should become a dollar economy; suede shoes denote a tendency to lie. Whatever the insight, it is revealed at the editorial conference with great solemnity, at which point it becomes the priority of every executive who values his job to see that it gets into the paper. But in case the story does not materialize as the editor imagined it, there must be a way of his executives laying off responsibility, which is why the idea is often farmed out to a freelance. Freelances are advised to be alert after midday when these editor specials are being commissioned. In a rash moment he or she can agree to write an article which only a few people detained under the country's insanity laws would take on. Still, a journalist with sufficiently lunatic credentials is usually found, and indeed on the day I write this article a well-known writer has obliged the *Daily Mail* by advocating that Britain becomes a dollar economy.

Of course the main influence on the editor's mental condition is the power he exercises. As a matter of policy, editors deny that they have any power at all, although it is plain that they have great potential influence on national life – much more than most elected politicians. After several years in the job they get used to an attitude in their own staff which is at best indulgent and at worst fawning. You see this most obviously when an editor is placed in a live discussion programme on television. Suddenly deprived of the customary backdrop of compliant employees, he goes to pieces. If his views are challenged, he becomes petulant and shifty. And the jokes which have gone down so well at editorial conferences inexplicably fail to please the studio audience, at which point what is known in the stand-up trade as a 'flop sweat' ensues. Next day the editor returns to the soothing environment of his office, with several inches of editorial about sliding standards of television formed in his mind and a determination to nail the people who have made a fool of him. Perhaps this sensitivity has something to do with the isolation that an editor experiences. Cut off from normal life by the rigours of the job and surrounded by people who almost never tell him the truth, he is liable to form some very strange ideas about his own abilities and importance. In some ways he is only a little more in touch with the world than an abbot in a monastery.

Considering how much power editors have to concentrate the minds of their readers on an issue, it's surprising how little they use it and how uncreative they often are when they do. For the most part, tabloid editors content themselves with the pursuit of commercial goals and are oddly ill at ease when invited into Number 10 to discuss affairs of state. They prefer to take instructions about policy from their proprietor or even one of the government's news managers. Broadsheet editors think for themselves a little more and will be much better equipped to attend Downing Street chats. They may even have strong views about the single currency or the break-up of the United Kingdom, which they express with the vigour of those who don't have to take such decisions. But always playing at the back of their minds is the commercial imperative – what is going to go down well with the readership? Since the last British general election it has been interesting how newspapers have positioned themselves in respect of the European single currency, each keeping an eye on the developing opinion in their market. Newspapers are led as much as they lead these days. If you doubt this, consider the reversal of the *Sun*'s homophobic coverage during the exposure of two gay government ministers during the autumn of 1998. Or indeed the paper's equally swift climbdown on the criticism of the behaviour of Liverpool football fans after the Hillsborough disaster. Both were caused by an outcry from the paper's readership.

Editors have rarely been a courageous lot and it is probably true to say that in the nineties they have been even less willing to take on big libel cases or go against public opinion on matters of principle. Again, this is largely due to the commercial aims of newspaper managements, which feel uneasy when a campaign or a libel defence inconveniences the life of a paper. Andrew Neil's *Sunday Times*, already on a war footing with the Conservative government, revealed the links between British aid to Malaysia and a £1.3 billion armaments contract – a good story by any standards, but not to Rupert Murdoch, who called Neil to complain. 'It's the Great Andrew Neil,' jeered Murdoch. 'Not content with taking on one fucking prime minister, you have to take on two.' Neil believes that the story cost him his job and he is probably right. Quite apart from disliking the publicity Neil attracted, Murdoch prefers his editors to confine themselves to the casual destruction of celebrities, unless of course he ordains an attack on a government as part of a strategy of intimidation.

Murdoch reads the market better than anyone and what he understood a long time before most was the way that demographic developments in Britain, combined with a certain intellectual passivity, now required practically all newspapers to compete in the mid-market and therefore for mid-market material – show-business coverage, interviews, scandal, human interest stories, sports, health and fitness, and book chat. That was what the British wanted. It has reached a point where the distinctions between newspapers of entirely different pedigrees really only amount to their tone and the length of the articles they print. True, the comment sections, arts sections and City pages of the broadsheets still require greater levels of effort and knowledge, but the news and features agendas are pretty much the same in all areas of the market and there is even some sign that the tabloidization at the front of some broadsheets is beginning to affect their comment sections.

Editors insist that the reduction of choice, which of course is the end result of this dumbing down, has been the only way to deal with an audience that is less able or willing – one is not sure which – to make an effort to understand an issue or to get steamed up about an injustice. They have become obsessed with pleasing these readers whom they imagine to be constantly underwhelmed, which is all well and good, except that they have at the same time succeeded in narrowing the scope and reach of their papers. There are exceptions. The *Daily Mail*, which under the editorship of Paul Dacre became the gold standard for all middle-market aspirations, was confident enough to abandon its usual territory to cover the struggle for justice mounted by the relatives of the murdered black student, Stephen Lawrence. It was one of the most successful campaigns in recent years if only because it conformed to the rule that a campaign must have a definite goal which there is some hope of reaching. A newspaper that agitates to save dolphins or increase the number of acres devoted to deciduous planting is hopelessly misguided because there is no natural end to the mission – an editor can never declare that there are enough dolphins or oak trees in the world, which is what he needs to be able to do. That's the second rule of a newspaper crusade – only start one if you can be seen to win it and win it well.

More important than these considerations in the *Mail* campaign was that the Stephen Lawrence case involved a palpable injustice. Five young white thugs were believed to have got away with the murder of an innocent black man because of police incompetence. On the face of it the case was not a natural story for the *Mail*, but after Dacre had heard about the case, having met the young man's father, he devoted the *Mail*'s professionalism and energy to exposing the five suspects and the police. The suspects have not been put behind bars because they have already been tried and acquitted of murder, but the *Mail*'s energetic pursuit of the story did a great deal to prompt the public inquiry into the case and to cause the Metropolitan Police to campaign against racism among its officers.

It doesn't detract from the *Mail*'s achievement to say that it cost the paper very little money and effort to run the campaign and that there was virtually no risk attached to it. But it does underline how very easy it is to contribute to the life of the country if for one moment an editor like Dacre concentrates on a story which doesn't come out of a catalogue of ready-made mid-market journalism. That of course is where his imitators, both broadsheet and tabloid, make their mistake. They keep looking for a handbook, a guide to the G-spot of middle England, without realizing that occasionally you have to drag the readers into a story that they would never before consider reading. Good editing is about knowing when to do this.

Unquestionably the paper which has taken most risks in the last ten years is the *Guardian*, which began its run of important political exposés by naming the Conservative MPs who were prepared to take money in exchange for asking parliamentary questions favourable to Mohammed Al-Fayed. It then moved on to break stories about an extremely dodgy television documentary produced for Carlton TV and an irregular loan made by the former Paymaster-General Geoffrey Robinson to the then Trade and Industry Secretary, Peter Mandelson. The paper's most spectacular victory was against Jonathan Aitken, the former Chief Secretary to the Treasury, who took the paper to court over several allegations, one of which maintained that as a serving minister he had visited Paris to discuss an arms deal. Aitken very nearly won the libel action, but the editor, Alan Rusbridger, decided to fight to the end and at the very last moment evidence was turned up to prove that Aitken had not been accompanied by his wife to Paris, as he had insisted in his sworn testimony. Subsequently he pleaded guilty to a criminal charge of perjury.

Many argued that the editor's pursuit of Conservative politicians was politically motivated – an unforgiving prosecution of the class war by a member of the left-wing press. However it was finessed, this view of course sanctioned the corruption and seediness that had grown in certain sections of the Conservative parliamentary party. It also failed to acknowledge the large risks that Alan Rusbridger and his predecessor, Peter Preston, took to publish the stories – risks to their careers, the paper's reputation and its finances (the libel bill for the Aitken case alone is said to have been over £2 million). It suits few to say so, but their campaign, which of course also included the unseemly financial relationship between two Labour MPs, Robinson and Mandelson, contributed to the health of public life. It took courage to publish these stories, much more courage than the nasty little entrapments and bugging operations routinely practised by News International and Mirror Group Newspapers.

Is courage what makes a great editor? Well, partly. Whether he is from the league of gentlemen hacks or the regiment of turn-on-a-sixpence technicians, the editor must have it in him to defy the proprietor, the spin doctors, the pleas from Number 10, all legal advice and public opinion to publish a story that causes an almighty and nearly everlasting stink. He can't survive on this alone because frankly a lot of newspaper work can be rather slow. For those days he needs energy, optimism, political savvy, a good eye, curiosity, a love of reporting and facts, humour and – let us be candid – a monstrously large ego.

Stockholm Syndrome:
Journalists Taken Hostage

FIAMMETTA ROCCO

The journalism I like most is about people, which is why profiles
are always popular even when they don't really come alive. The
worst is the result of the twenty-minute, six-man, bus tour; the
non-interview granted to half-a-dozen reporters at once where
questions are scripted and non-scripted questions are forbidden.
And then there are the others: Tina Brown on how the divided soul
of David Puttnam helped to inspire the story of the two runners in
Chariots of Fire; Fred Dannen on the real John Demjanjuk, absolved
of being the Beast of Treblinka but just as evil; Alison Pearson on
the cold core of Martin Amis, or Henry Porter on Princess Diana's
last summer of love. What is astonishing about these pieces is not
that I should remember them, although some were published more
than a decade ago. It is that many of these subjects came to hate
the finished article and regretted ever having co-operated with the
journalist in the first place. Why does this happen so often?

Janet Malcolm, an American reporter who wrote a book about
the relationship between a journalist and his subject, begins *The
Journalist and the Murderer* with these words:

> Every journalist who is not too stupid or too full of himself to notice
> what is going on knows that what he does is morally indefensible. He is
> a kind of confidence man, preying on people's vanity, ignorance or loneli-
> ness, gaining their trust and betraying them without remorse. Like the
> credulous widow who wakes up one day to find the charming young man
> and all her savings gone, so the consenting subject of a piece of non-fiction
> writing learns – when the article or book appears – *his* hard lesson.

The journalist–subject encounter is often a troubled one, but it eludes scrutiny and remains one of the most ambivalent couplings in journalism, possibly because part of its troublesome nature is that neither side is ever completely honest about it.

Both sides enter into the arrangement for their own reasons. It is surprising how often a subject agrees to co-operate without fully thinking through the implications; the journalist too can remain remarkably ignorant of his or her true motives for picking a particular person to profile. Envy, fear, triumphalism are all powerful subconscious emotions that can affect how a journalist treats a subject and how well or badly the relationship will develop.

From the first handshake, the encounter evolves into a complex ritual that can escalate, even for the most experienced public figure, into a kind of co-dependence. The journalist needs the 'story', the closeness to the subject, the intimacy that will yield fresh insights. The subject, meanwhile, has needs of his own: above all to maintain the journalist's interest and stop him getting bored, and to persuade him or her that the *subject's* version of the story *is* the whole and only 'story'.

There are, of course, profiles that are written without the involvement of the subject. Some are very good. But even the best feel empty at the centre, echoing with that same hollow sound you get when you tap on the chest of someone with a new pacemaker. People are complicated, and the best profiles need the subject's help, not for what he or she will tell you in words but for the subtler, deeper and more irrational things that get conveyed in other ways.

One of the most interesting sentences in Janet Malcolm's book isn't actually in the book at all, but on the back cover of the British paperback edition which was published in 1998. Ian Jack, once the editor of the *Independent on Sunday* and no mean profile-writer himself, says: 'As a journalist, I did not feel good reading [this book] . . . but for the people who get written about, the story is an enlightenment and a warning.'

As it deepens, the relationship acquires some of the characteristics of a passionate love affair. Journalists rarely sleep with their subjects, but the bond is still intimate. The subject, especially if he or she is in the midst of a great crisis, may have no friend or relative who knows as much about what is happening to him or her as the journalist who is researching his travails for a profile. If the relationship ends abruptly, as it sometimes does on publication of the profile, the subject blames the journalist entirely. He absolves himself of all responsibility and relegates the journalistic encounter to the rubbish heap of love affairs that have ended badly and are best pushed out of consciousness.

But this particular relationship is not a love affair; its character-istics are more that of 'Stockholm syndrome', the psychological condition that describes the mutual dependence between kidnapper and victim. And the closer the co-operation between journalist and subject, the greater the danger. The deeper the Stockholm syndrome, the greater the sense of ultimate betrayal.

I had barely thought about this when I began writing long profiles myself in 1992. Reporters are drawn to this sort of work for different reasons. The more pompous talk about freedom of speech and 'the public's right to know'; the least talented talk about Art; the seemliest about earning a living. I was curious mostly. I grew up in a family with many secrets: love affairs, illegitimate children, divorces, remarriages. Trying to find out what was going on was the best defence against nasty surprises.

The story that a subject tells about himself is almost never the whole story. 'Why?' is the question I ask most often. What exists under the surface of this person that makes him fail, triumph, and even kill?

The subjects I choose follow no particular pattern. I quickly found I liked writing about powerful, driven people. I am terrible at actors, even worse at politicians. I write better about men than women. But what interests me most are people who have discovered that success does not protect them from catastrophe.

A prosperous man coats himself thickly in the lacquer of success so that no sliver of doubt or imperfection shows through. He smiles, he charms, he graciously squeezes your elbow. But he can also be a bore. Whereas a man who suddenly discovers that the edifice he has spent a lifetime constructing can no longer protect him can be angry and desperate. He is also a man who is thinking, reflecting, and adapting himself to change. To me, this man is more interesting and far more appealing. Whenever I read about someone like this, I see a little bubble forming above his head that says, 'Write me. Write me.'

Thus it was that in the autumn of 1992, just a few weeks before the separation of the Prince and Princess of Wales, I interviewed Prince Philip. I wrote about Maurice Saatchi as he was ousted from the advertising phenomenon he created with his brother. I watched Richard Leakey learn to walk again after losing both legs in an air crash, and for two years I followed a desperate Lord Brocket as he tried to avoid being sent to prison for fraud. Each piece took several months to research. I collected, in some cases, thousands of pages of documents and interviewed scores of friends, family and colleagues. I searched for nuances. At the end, I regarded what I wrote as balanced and fair, and I knew it added to the sum of what was already known about each man. But when my articles were published, every one of these men disliked what I wrote about them, and the accusation of betrayal was the loudest curse of all.

Over the years I have evolved a structure for each profile project. First I write to the subject, explaining what I have been commissioned to do and who I am. They are going to find out anyway, so they might as well find out from me first. I attach a list of people I want to interview, and I enclose a thick wad of profiles I have already written. No one can say they didn't know how I wrote about those who went before them.

As journalistic footwear goes, it's more Mary Janes than jackboots. To paraphrase Brad Pitt in *Thelma and Louise*, 'being interviewed by me doesn't have to be entirely an unpleasant experience'. Pitt, of course, was a thief as well as a seducer; journalists are both, but they cannot seduce or steal unless the subject somehow allows them to.

That 'somehow' is the subtext of the relationship that evolves between journalist and subject, the area both parties exploit, even if they do not fully acknowledge it, and which ultimately leads them to grief.

If a subject doesn't say no in reply to my letter, we meet to discuss the story further and to lay down certain rules. I am surprised how often it is the journalist who has to bring up the subject of ground rules: are interviews on or off the record, will they be taped, are quotes to be checked, does the subject insist on approving copy before publication? It is astonishing how many subjects refuse to take responsibility for establishing the ground rules themselves.

I have a few rules of my own. I do all my own research, even the most dreary bits like transcribing tapes; if you listen over and over to a tape, it's surprising how much you can pick up that you missed the first time round. I don't like paying for information. I always check quotes if that's the deal, and I never show anyone copy before publication. Ever. It leads to nothing but problems. Beyond that, anything goes. I try to be well-dressed, punctual, polite. I once dressed up as a flower delivery girl to get a look at the interior of someone's house.

If you are writing about someone who has a high public profile, much information is already publicly available. In addition to files of old cuttings and earlier interviews, company records, share deals, charity work, court documents and property records are just some of the many documents that are available to anyone who knows where to look. Far from being dusty piles of paper, these records, if you study them carefully, can tell you an awful lot about someone's personality.

Very little is known about Charles Saatchi's art collection and how it was financed; his holdings are in companies boxed within companies and the whole edifice is so complex it is difficult to estimate how much he spends and almost impossible to work out how much profit he has made. That is how he likes it, though he doesn't quite succeed at keeping it all under wraps. In a similar fashion, Jeanette Winterson, the author of *Oranges Are Not The Only Fruit*, has registered herself as a company and offsets everything she legally can, even the cost of dry-cleaning her clothes, against tax. A feisty writer who has twice visited critics at their homes late at night to verbally abuse them for what they have written about her, she is as aggressive in her finances as she is in dealing with critics or journalists.

To make the subject come alive on the page, though, what I want most is to know how and why he does things more than what it is he does; most of all, I want to know how his behaviour affects those around him. His unconscious actions tell me more about what sort of person he is and how he really feels than a million interviews.

In 1994, Richard Leakey, the renowned Kenyan palaeontologist, resigned as director of the country's wildlife service after a bitter political row. Leakey had had a terrible airplane crash six months earlier. Only his skill as a pilot saved his life and that of his passengers, but he lost both his legs. In a series of interviews in the hospital in Nottingham and later at the rehabilitation clinic in Roehampton where he learned to walk again and then later still at his home in Kenya, Leakey portrayed himself to be a victim of corrupt and venal politicians. He believed that his plane might have been sabotaged even thouh a 300-page report by two Cessna engineers proved the accident had been caused by mechanical failure, and that Leakey's terrible leg injuries were the result of wearing ordinary shoes rather than heavy flying boots. It's known as 'pilot's foot'.

Although he would not acknowledge this, it seemed that Leakey's own personality contributed as much to his downfall as anything else. His surgeon, Christopher Colton, told me the palaeontologist had given him three months to repair his crushed feet after the engine of the Cessna he was piloting caved into the cockpit as the plane nosedived into the ground. One was amputated. Colton said it would take a year before the second one healed, but Leakey replied he didn't have that long to wait. He ran Kenya's wildlife department as if it were an emergency room; he had to get back to work. If Colton couldn't fix his leg fast, Leakey wanted it amputated. 'In truth,' Colton told me when I interviewed him in London at the Royal College of Surgeons, 'Richard Leakey cut his own leg off.'

Now Richard Leakey is one of the most inspiring men I've ever met, but what continued to trouble me was how destructive he could be as well. People were frightened of him. At best, they respected him but I found no one who really liked him. His surgeon's words explained a lot about how Leakey behaves when he can't have things his own way. He'd rather not have them at all, and that goes for his job, employees, his brother Philip to whom he barely speaks, as well as his legs.

If you are a reporter, you can't force anyone to talk to you. So why do people agree? What do they hope to get out of it?

Subject and journalist both usually say that what they want is the truth. But that is a code word for other things: a flattering portrait, an attack on some secret enemy, or even a simple caress to their vanity. There is no such thing as objective truth in a profile. There are facts and then there is interpretation; like any biography, a profile is a work of the imagination. That is not to say you make it up. A journalist may go to great lengths to achieve a fair and balanced interpretation of events, but even he or she can't hide the fact that if you adjust the interpretation you change a story just as surely as if you substituted some of the facts.

Along with vanity, publicity or excitement, the subject chooses to co-operate with a profile writer for one reason above all: to influence or dictate the final outcome. But subjects often have very mixed motives, and many of them will go to extraordinary lengths to hide the extent of their co-operation.

I first realized Prince Philip might be interested in co-operating on a long profile about him when a royal press officer began calling some of my friends. I was summoned to a meeting at Buckingham Palace, where Prince Philip's private secretary told me my project would 'receive our blessing' provided I did not tell people they were involved. The Royal Family did not want it known that they ever co-operate with the press.

Prince Philip even gave me an interview. He proved rather terse, volunteering little in the way of answers even though the questions had been approved beforehand. But he allowed his friends to speak to me, and that was more valuable than any interview. What emerged was a portrait of a man abysmally neglected in his youth, tossed about between his German and English relatives, sent at the age of eighteen into the Royal Navy, where he invented the persona of Prince Philip we know now. His devotion to duty gave him the wherewithal to sustain his role as the Queen's consort, but it emptied him of what was needed to bridge the gap with his sons. The most revealing conversation I had was late at night by phone to Australia. Michael Parker had been Prince Philip's private secretary in the 1950s. 'I always wanted to see him put his arms around the Queen, and show her how much he adored her. What you'd do for any wife. But he always sort of stood to attention.' It was, in the end, a portrait of a sad man who had given his best to his country and his Queen. He hated it; this was not the version of himself he liked to have put across.

Similarly, Maurice Saatchi told me he never gives interviews. 'Maurice doesn't like his fingerprints on things,' his PR adviser, Sir Tim Bell, added. But Maurice did invite me out to dinner with him at the Connaught Grill, on condition that our encounter remain a secret. Saatchi, world-class adman, is clever, witty and charming. He is also extremely manipulative. In the winter of 1994, the gathering quarrel between Maurice Saatchi and the board of Saatchi PLC, of which he was chairman, was becoming so bitter it seemed it could only explode. Saatchi regarded himself as a victim and his opponents as stupid and malevolent troglodytes. What intrigued me was Saatchi's aggression towards the men who ran the company he'd founded. It made me wonder if in some way he actually wanted fire to engulf the company.

In the middle of my reporting on the Saatchi crisis, I suddenly learned through some corporate documents in Luxemburg that Maurice and his brother Charles had made more than £25 million out of one little business deal. The full extent of this operation, which had been dreamed up two or three years before the crisis, had never been fully disclosed to the company. But the timing was such that on the morning of the crucial board meeting that would vote on Maurice's future, news began to circulate among the directors that Maurice and Charles had been paid half that money just the previous week, in cash.

Maurice refused to discuss the deal when we met for dinner. Over Dover sole and a bottle of Chablis, I told him everything I had found out from public sources. He was silent but afterwards he relented a little, perhaps because he found it hard to hide how pleased he was at how things had turned out. Although he had signed a confidentiality agreement about the deal, he confirmed that my story was right and he added three crucial details that I didn't know.

He also told me at great length about how he'd been made a victim by the management of Saatchi. To Maurice, who regarded himself as badly treated, it was inconceivable that the news of this windfall might have generated dismay or even envy among his fellow directors. The deal had been with a potential client, and involved a former chief executive of Saatchi. Many of those on the board believed the money should have gone to the company. Every other board member I spoke to felt uncomfortable about the money, and one or two even said it was the final straw that turned them against their chairman.

But for Maurice, who lived expensively and had never been *really* rich, this money meant freedom. Never before could he have allowed himself the luxury of just walking away from Saatchi. The windfall freed Maurice to raise two fingers to the company. And he did. It was a gamble that called for blind destructiveness as well as ruthless self-confidence. Maurice had both, and he won.

My profile tried to explore how, behind the charm, the courtliness and the neo-Swifty glasses, there is a colder side to Maurice Saatchi's character – a totally implacable quality that he rarely allows to show through. I described in detail how Maurice and his brother had made their £25 million; he did not convince me he was a victim.

Maurice Saatchi often sends flowers and champagne to journalists. Indeed, one of the board's complaints was that in the year before he left, he had spent more than £5,000 on his floral offerings. I heard and received nothing from him after my article was published, but I came to know his true feelings when I ran into him at a party. Although nearly a year had passed, he still cut me dead.

If Maurice Saatchi had hoped I would portray him simply as a visionary dispatched out of ignorance by little men with no imagination, then Lord Brocket wanted me to be even more partisan – to take his side against the police, the judge and the prison authorities and blame his crime on his wife.

The facts of the Brocket case are simple. Desperately short of money, Brocket faked the theft of four valuable antique cars and tried to claim against his insurance. The recession was closing in, the bank was threatening to pull the rug from under his feet. Brocket Hall, in the family for three generations, was under threat. Think of the shame. Think of the children!

Seen in this light, Brocket's crime – from which he insisted he did not benefit personally – could be regarded even as heroic. But that would be to take the peer at his word, and to disregard the detail. I attended every court hearing of the Brocket case, and in the course of it I obtained nearly 3,000 pages of documents. The details of the heist were extraordinary. But even they were nothing compared with a file that I would never have seen had Lord Brocket not given his permission: the affidavits for the Brockets' divorce.

Lord Brocket married the American model Isa Lorenzo in Las Vegas less than twenty-four hours after he proposed to her. They were both engaged to other people at the time. It was not a good start. Although they eventually had three children, within weeks of the wedding both sought refuge in the arms of their jilted lovers, convinced they'd made a terrible error. As the financial pressures increased and Brocket became more and more preoccupied with his problems, his wife became addicted enough to pharmaceutical drugs that she began forging prescriptions for pethidine. When she was caught by the police, nearly three years after the so-called 'robbery', Lady Brocket told them the car scam had been her husband's idea.

The Hertfordshire police were, in fact, on the point of breaking the Brocket case through another source, but Brocket was (and still is) convinced he would have escaped prosecution had it not been for his wife. He wanted me to see the divorce documents to prove that his wife wasn't just a drug addict; she was vicious and mad to boot.

The file I was handed by a third party who kept it in a safe at his home contained many papers. Among them was a forty-page document known as 'The Book'. Because it contained quantities of lurid sexual detail, its existence was familiar to virtually everyone involved in the Brocket case, although very few people ever read it. I had known of it myself for more than two years, but I had never seen a copy. This was Isa's account of the Brocket marriage, a portrayal of pure misery. 'I can never go back to my husband again or I will die,' she wrote on the first page.

Brocket was furious that I used virtually nothing from 'The Book' in my article that appeared in the *Telegraph Magazine*. He regarded this omission as a sign that I took Isa's side in the matter, ignoring for a moment that no newspaper in Britain would have touched it. This was not the only thing he did not like about my article; indeed his complaints to Charles Moore, the editor of the *Daily Telegraph*, continued for nearly a year.

I was amazed he'd allowed me to see 'The Book' at all; whatever he may have wanted to prove against his wife, there was no getting away from the fact that he came out of it almost as badly himself. This small but telling incident illuminates a fundamental aspect of the relationship between journalist and profile subject. I now have a theory about it.

The whole encounter is a two-act drama, or rather a two-act drama with a prologue that establishes the rules and objectives, and an epilogue that represents publication.

In the first act, the journalist is the 'Listener'. Pen in hand, the 'Listener' is compassionate, attentive, and apart from asking the occasional question, imposes little of his own personality. This is a period of true joy in the relationship, when the journalist is getting the story and the subject basks in never-ending attention. Although the subject will have had his rights read to him in the prologue – perhaps more than once and even quite forcefully – he tends to ignore this in the first act. The 'Listener' probably rarely reminds him of the fact.

During the interval, there is a costume change. When the curtain rises, the 'Listener' has become the 'Writer' and may be quite a different being. The 'Writer' works alone, away from the subject. Partly because of this, but mostly because the subject would far rather the journalist remained the 'Listener', he fails to perceive that there has been a transformation. On the stroke of midnight, Cinderella turned back into a poor servant-girl. The journalist, who needed to become a princess to go to the ball, will always turn into the 'Writer' after the interval. The subject who fails to recognize that the journalist is really a poor servant-girl is the one whose dream of a flattering profile always ends in ashes.

Into Africa

CHRISTOPHER MUNNION

Cowering in a bloodstained corner of Idi Amin's military prison, I had cause, yet again, to ponder on my choice of career. Makindye was the charnel-house of Uganda's psychopathic dictator and in September 1972 business was brisk. Ugandan exiles had launched an invasion in the south, prompting Amin to unleash his ruthless thugs into the streets of Kampala to round up the usual suspects.

They included senior Ugandan police officers suspected of sympathizing with the rebels and, of course, the foreign correspondents who had been covering the brutal purge of Uganda's Asian community. We were arrested at gunpoint, bundled into a truck and driven to the dread Makindye prison barracks where, as we had heard, the nightly torture and slaughter of Amin's enemies, real and perceived, took place.

We soon learned how Makindye had earned its reputation. Our policemen cellmates were dragged from their impromptu prayer-meetings two by two to be sledgehammered to death in the yard outside. In those first hours we had no reason to believe our fate would be any different, but after a day or two it became clear that their intention was merely to knock us around a little and – this with marked success – to scare us witless.

I had been arrested with John Fairhall of the *Guardian*. A composed, gentle man, John fashioned an improvised chess set from our torn and masticated notebooks. Between protracted moves and to the accompaniment of screams from Amin's less fortunate prisoners, we would catch each other's eye and ask ourselves that age-old front-line question: 'What the hell are we doing here?'

In nearby cells, our colleagues, including such journalistic war-horses as Sandy Gall of ITN and the photographer Don McCullin, still shrapnel-scarred from his previous assignment in Vietnam, were asking themselves the same question. We had all competed eagerly within our respective organizations for foreign assignments knowing that a whiff of grapeshot and the adrenalin-rush of danger made for good copy, but a week in the Makindye hell-hole tended to focus the mind on a more philosophical approach to job satisfaction.

My own ambition to become a foreign correspondent had been fired in the 1950s by the swashbuckling approach to the coverage of Britain's hasty retreat from empire pioneered by Beaverbrook's *Daily Express* and its arch-rival, the *Daily Mail*. In those days both were broadsheets and their battalions of battle-hardened foreign staffers would get dashing mugshot bylines alongside copy littered with personal pronouns, which would start: 'I became the first reporter to reach the rebel headquarters . . .' or 'Bullets cracked over my head as I watched Moslem fanatics storm the palace of the pro-British monarch . . .'

At my bedside were well-thumbed copies of journalistic autobiographies, including that of the *Express*'s René McColl, a pioneer of the 'I was there . . .' school of foreign reporters. McColl, I remember, promised would-be correspondents their jobs would entail 'boarding airliners with blondes and disembarking with redheads'. In those days, air travel – as well as blondes and redheads – was regarded as the apogee of glamour.

My first foreign assignment was a trifle more prosaic. The *Daily Telegraph* sent me, by a Channel ferry reeking with vomit, to cover the activities of British football hooligans in Belgium. The Ostend policeman I approached for an interview failed to recognize your distinguished correspondent for what he was, cracked him over the shoulders with a long baton and urged him to return whence he had come.

Undeterred, I pressed my claim to each and every foreign assignment that loomed. In the 1960s the *Telegraph* had a large and distinguished foreign staff to fill its grey but comprehensive foreign pages. Better still from a young reporter's point of view, they were always ready to pluck a man from the home news staff for rapid deployment to a trouble spot as a 'fireman'. We would lurk close to the foreign desk, ensuring they were aware that we carried current passports and updated health jabs.

Such pestering led to a protracted stint in America – and my first sexual proposition as a foreign correspondent. Unfortunately, it came from neither a blonde nor a redhead. The *Telegraph*'s bureau chief asked me to cover a music festival in Florida. An internal airline strike obliged me to make the journey from New York by train to Atlanta where, the organizers assured me, they would arrange a lift. Sure enough, at Atlanta station a uniformed chauffeur carried a greetings board with my name on it. He ushered me into the back of a large black stretch limousine with tinted windows. Bloody luxury, I thought, introducing myself to my sole companion in the capacious rear compartment, a short, elderly, plump gentleman. He held out a limpish hand. 'Aaron Copland,' he said. Aaron Copland! Now my bluff had been well and truly called. I was to spend a four-hour car journey conversing with America's most distinguished composer. I desperately tried to remember some key passages from the *Bluff Your Way Through Classical Music* I had read on the train. We had not cleared the city limits when Mr Copland turned to me with a sweet smile and asked, 'Do you blow?' Bear in mind that I was desperately trying to think musically. 'Well,' I stammered, 'I did try the trumpet in the school band.' When he recovered from a near-hysterical bout of laughter and explained precisely what he had meant I broke the first rule of tradecraft and panicked, trying to open the door with the idea of making a jump for it. A colleague later advised me that the correct response would have been 'to close your eyes and think of Benjamin Britten'.

Sensing, perhaps, that musical criticism was not my line, the *Telegraph* foreign desk dispatched me to Aden, to one of those inglorious imperial epilogues where rival groups of Arab insurgents were fighting each other in between sniping at a hapless, hamstrung British garrison which was desperately trying to hold the line until the union flag was once again struck.

Here, at last, was genuine shot and shell and a chance to secure front-page prominence for my own 'I was there . . .' dispatches, in the *Telegraph*'s own more modest style, of course. My arrival in the steamy, shabby port coincided with the seizure by the Arab insurgents, in cahoots with the local police force and the rebellious South Arabian army, of the Crater district of the city. Britain's humiliation was my own personal triumph as it was by far the most dramatic foreign news of the period. Better still, the airport was closed for a few days so I had the story to myself.

The powers that be decided that Crater was not worth retaking as Britain was pulling out of the place within a few months. Colonel Colin Campbell Mitchell, C.O. of the 1st Battalion, the Argyll and Sutherland Highlanders, which had just arrived in the port, had other ideas. The unit had lost members of the advance party in an earlier Aden skirmish and tradition clearly demanded regimental honour be restored.

Mitchell, almost a parody of a British army officer, was as keen to cultivate the British correspondents as we were to stay close to a man we sensed was going to yield some excellent copy. The Argylls were under threat of yet more military cutbacks and he thought a good press might help. So keen was he to ensure we stayed on top of their every move that one memorable night, as the Argylls moved in to retake the Crater district, he insisted we accompany him on foot. As his men moved into position to take the main rebel stronghold, a fortified former bank building, we discovered to our horror that Mitchell had us ahead of his troops, pointing out with his swagger stick how the operation was about to be conducted, in full view of enemy machine-gun posts. Tony Carthew of the *Daily Mail* had arrived a little late. As he was furtively making his way through the shadows to catch up with us, he was tripped up by an Argyll corporal crouching in a darkened doorway. 'Who the fuck are you?' demanded the corporal. 'Carthew, *Daily Mail*,' whispered Tony. 'I'm trying to reach the colonel up the street.' The jock snorted in disgust. 'Well, tell the wee cunt that I'm the front line!' Crater was successfully pacified with no British casualties (not even among the press). Indeed, it became the safest place to be in Aden for the remainder of British tenure. Mitchell's bravado earned him the sobriquet 'Mad Mitch' and a brief reprieve for his regiment, but the fact that he had defied the political will brought a premature end to his military career.

It was during those long, dark nights in Aden's crumbling Crescent Hotel, the occasional mortar bomb hitting the roof and more frequent bursts of machine-gun fire from outside, that I got to know some of the headline heroes from my boyhood imaginings. Fleet Street's finest, like Peter Younghusband, the gigantic Afrikaner of the *Daily Mail*, and the legendary Donald Wise, an elegant David Niven lookalike who, improbably, interpreted foreign news for *Daily Mirror* readers ('Remember I'm writing for people who move their lips when they read, old boy'), spun hilarious, hair-raising yarns about the adventures and misadventures of themselves and their colleagues in the world's hotspots.

Most of their stories emanated from an Africa emerging chaotically from European colonial rule. Younghusband had rescued from a fate worse than death a *Baltimore Sun* opera critic who had strayed into Katangese rebel territory. The critic had passed out on the way to safety, so the ever-obliging Younghusband tapped out a graphic dispatch in his name and sent it to his newspaper. The bewildered *Baltimore Sun* man eventually came to, to find he'd been nominated for a Pulitzer for a story he had not written. Wise had just settled down to a morning aperitif when a shot rang out and a body thumped on to the pavement beside him from an upper floor. 'The first casualty of the Angolan war nearly landed in my beer today . . .,' he informed *Mirror* readers.

I was reminded irresistibly of Evelyn Waugh's *Scoop*. These characters had stepped straight from the pages of Waugh, who in fact had only run a light fictional brush over his own experiences as a reporter sent to cover the Italian invasion of Abyssinia in 1935. The impression that these old Africa hands were striving to outdo Waugh's outrageous characters was confirmed when I met W. F. (Bill) Deedes, just appointed the *Telegraph*'s editor after successful dual careers in journalism and politics. As a 22-year-old reporter on the *Morning Post*, Deedes had covered the Abyssinian campaign with Waugh, who had drawn on his young colleague's experiences to create his fictional hero, William Boot of *The Beast*.

I was still in my early twenties when the *Telegraph* offered me my first foreign staff posting. 'Africa, old boy . . . plenty of sunshine and some good stories . . . keep your head down . . .' Somehow it was typical of the wonderfully eccentric *Telegraph* of that time: send one of your smaller reporters to cover one of the larger continents. I did not complain, though. My first base was to be Salisbury in Ian Smith's rebellious Rhodesia, where the *Telegraph* maintained a spacious home with a few acres of grounds, a couple of servants, a tennis court and a swimming-pool. My brief from the foreign desk was deceptively casual: 'Cover the end of this UDI business, old boy, and then see what else is going on.' UDI was to last another fourteen years but there was to be little time to relax. I had emerged from a first dip in my pool and was giving instructions to my newly acquired domestic staff when a message arrived from London instructing me to drop everything and get to Nigeria immediately. The inconsiderate Ibos had declared the secessionist state of Biafra and civil war loomed.

The message from the *Telegraph* came clattering over the telex machine, then the most dependable form of communication. There were, of course, no computers, faxes or satellite links. Telephones throughout Africa were unreliable and erratic, and cable offices, when they were open, usually had to be bribed heavily to ensure prompt delivery. Our primary concern in those days was not so much to get the story as to get the story out. The correspondent's main preoccupation on arrival at any given dateline was to secure the most reliable means of communication with London, Paris or New York. A colleague of that era had calculated that we spent up to 70 per cent of our working time trying to 'file' – or transmit – our copy.

My telexed instruction from the foreign desk actually read: 'Assume you Lagoswards soonest procover situation onspotting warwise.' What E. H. 'Ricky' Marsh, the foreign editor, was telling me was to get to Nigeria right away and without debate to file graphic, front-line dispatches. The use of 'cablese', as this form of language was called, had originated in the days when the cost per word of sending a cabled message was formidable. Running words together with prefixes was one way of saving money. In the telex era there was no call to continue this subterfuge but correspondents and their editors had elevated it to an art form. Rather endearingly, it was still used in exchanges of messages by most newspaper offices well into the 1970s. John Ridley, an old *Telegraph* warrior, was a past master at using cablese to 'remind those desk wallahs of their station in life', as he put it. When his breakfast brandy was interrupted by an irritable cable from the foreign desk demanding 'Like soonest exyou when war outbreak likely,' Ridley paused long enough to tap back the reply: 'My balls unmade crystal.' Again London to Ridley: 'Like exyou one thousand words will Farouk survive query.' Ridley to London: 'No stop No stop A thousand times no stop.'

Lacking Ridley's panache, I Lagoswarded fastest, as per instructions, to cover my first African conflict. The first objective was to find the war. We knew that people were dying in their thousands somewhere out there in the jungle, but in the Nigeria capital the military government decreed that there should be no mention of any unrest, let alone Biafran secession or war. We were obliged to find our own way to the combat zones and take our chances. Port Harcourt, the sweltering southern town, appeared to be at one stage the epicentre of the fighting. It had fallen to the Biafrans but by the time we arrived it had just been retaken by the Federal forces, notably the 3rd Marine Federal Commando Division under the whimsical command of Colonel Benjamin Adenkunle, who revelled in the nickname 'the Black Scorpion'. This Sandhurst-trained pocket-sized tyrant was unimpressed by our credentials. 'You, the *Daily Telegraph*, the BBC and *Newsweek* magazine are all under my command here,' he barked. 'You will witness the rout of the rebels but do as you are told by my officers at all times.' On the road to Owerri as the massive Federal army machine stumbled and bumbled towards the Biafran heartland it was clear that most of Adenkunle's front-line officers did not know what to do themselves, let alone how to impart instructions to their ill-trained men. Those who had fortified themselves with some narcotic local weed were tempted to show off in front of the international press, particularly when the television cameras were in evidence. We quickly learned of the dark side of television's power.

On this particular trip, an ITN crew filmed a young Nigerian officer shooting down in cold blood a young Ibo captured by his men. The ITN men were horrified by the thought that the youth had been murdered to give them good footage but had been powerless to stop it. When the incident reached the ears of the Nigerian high command, the officer was arrested, court-martialled and sentenced to death. Adenkunle then press-ganged a BBC crew which had just arrived in Port Harcourt to film the young officer's execution. The condemned officer, bound to a tree and blindfolded, had heard the dread order 'Ready, aim . . .' when a young, nervous BBC sound engineer discovered his batteries were flat and interrupted with an involuntary 'Oh, shit . . . hold it!' As the grisly episode was being staged for television the execution was delayed for a few minutes to allow the BBC to change its batteries. (Ten years later in South Africa's turbulent black townships I was to see many similar episodes. Mobs of rampaging youths, most of them township gangsters given a political imprimatur to further the revolution, would become that much more violent once a television crew arrived on the scene. There was little my TV colleagues could do about it but it was clear to them that the presence of their cameras would frequently exacerbate the mayhem.)

So keen were the young Nigerian officers to impress foreign reporters accompanying them that they would take ludicrous and dangerous risks with their men. Again on the road to Owerri we suddenly came under a barrage of shellfire. By this time I was experienced enough to be the first to find the bottom of the deepest ditch. On this occasion I found myself clutched in the mud by the correspondent of a once-distinguished newspaper. That he was known as the 'African Queen' bothered me less than the fact that he had worn the same safari suit for at least three weeks. More infuriating was the realization that we were being shelled by our own side. Our guiding officer had, in his enthusiasm, led us to a completely wrong position, causing a Federal armoured unit to mistake us for rebels and open up. I could console myself only with the thought that I was obeying my last instructions from the *Telegraph* before I left Lagos. 'Like you upcheck British armoured cars Nigerian frontwise . . .' The incoming shells came from British armoured cars. I was able to confirm: 'Britshells confirmed personally frontwise.'

Foreign desks were notoriously unsympathetic to any danger correspondents may have faced in getting the story, particularly if it meant that the copy was late in arriving. 'Sorry about your leg wound, old boy, but we really must have earlier copy now that the printers are on strike again.' Herograms – messages from the office congratulating you on your dramatic, deathless prose – were few and far between. Worse, if a colleague from a rival newspaper managed a front-page, first-person account of some incident, you would receive a terse 'Why you unshot query' rocket from London. When Zanzibar erupted in bloody revolution in 1964, the *Mail*'s Peter Younghusband and his great friend and *Express* rival John Monks hired an Arab dhow to get to the island. The dhow skipper, alarmed by gunfire and screams from the shore, stubbornly dropped anchor a mile offshore and refused to go further. Younghusband, then young, fit and strapping, stripped down to his underpants and swam ashore, thus enabling the *Mail* to splash his account under a Zanzibar dateline with the introduction: 'Last night I swam the shark-infested waters of the Indian Ocean to the strife-torn spice island of Zanzibar as . . .' Monks, who had been obliged to file with the rest of us from mainland Tanzania, promptly received a message from the *Express*: 'Why you unswim shark-infested sea query'.

The same studied indifference to the man-on-the-spot's plight was the trademark of every newspaper's copytakers. These key men, now unfortunately a dying breed, were touch typists employed to sit in darkened corners of newspaper offices with headphones on, poised at any time of the day or night to record the off-the-cuff reports phoned in by breathless correspondents from all corners of the world. Not an easy job, given that telephone-line quality diminished in proportion to the intensity of trouble in any given country. Correspondents came to depend on them greatly, even knowing that as you came to the most graphic part of your dictated dispatch there would be a half-stifled yawn at the other end of the line and a bored inquiry from the copytaker: 'Much more of this, old boy?' If they were in a good mood, you might get some assistance. 'You realize you've split a couple of infinitives, old man?' There were occasional glitches. When Robert Mugabe unleashed his North Korean-trained troops of Zimbabwe's 5th Brigade against the hapless Matabele civilians in Bulawayo, I made the error, in dictating my copy to London every evening, of referring to 'Five Brigade'. On night four, the copytaker interrupted me. 'Forgive me,

Chris. I know strange things happen in Africa but why is this fire brigade going around killing people? Shouldn't they be putting out fires and rescuing kittens from trees?' To my mortification I discovered that the *Telegraph* had for three days run my stories with the 'notorious North Korean-trained fire brigade' running amok.

Such was the stuff of the journalistic apocrypha of that epoch. What distinguished it, perhaps, was the camaraderie among the old Africa hands, a deep comradeship born of shared gaol cells, under-fire fellowship and a common aim of getting to improbable places, speaking to impossible people and overcoming the frustrations of filing to London. Donald Wise's arrival in any given hotspot, for instance, was accurately described by a colleague as 'like opening a bottle of the finest champagne', such was his fizz and wit. Boozy late-night exchanges of yarns about broken marriages and complicated love lives helped. Rivalry, of course, was intense. The unwritten rule was that if a colleague secured a good story for himself, survived and managed to get it into the paper, then it was cause for yet another celebration and grudging congratulations – although there was always the danger of that dread message from London: 'Why your exclusive still exclusive query'. If two or more of the pack had a story and did not share it with colleagues it was an unforgivable carve-up.

Fiscal compensation – Fleet Street salaries on broadsheet newspapers were notoriously low until the 1970s – came with elastic expenses sheets, the manipulation of black-market foreign exchange rates and shrewd deals struck in emergency situations. For most correspondents it meant merely covering alimony and matrimonial lawyer's bills. For a few (including a couple of household-name television personalities) it resulted in the acquisition of splendid farms and sumptuous homes long before they were commanding six-figure salaries. Those were the days when newspapers were run by their editors, not by the grim-faced ranks of accountants who rule the roosts today.

The era came to its inevitable end with the rapid advent of laptop computers, mobile telephones, electronic news-gathering and instant satellite-linked communications. They, in turn, coincided with the newspaper revolution, the disappearance of hot-lead technology and its replacement by what some would argue is the more threatening tyranny of cyber-space domination of global information systems. Gone forever is the Errol Flynn school of foreign reporting with its swash and buckle, its larger-than-life characters and its cabled absurdities. Today's journalism is so intensely competitive that there is little time or scope for developing or expressing those endearing, individual idiosyncrasies that made the old Fleet Street such fun.

Let it be added hastily that the job is no less dangerous these days. Statistics show that world-wide an average of eighty journalists are killed each year in the course of doing their duty. Most have been photographers or television cameramen whose work demands their constant exposure to danger. They are obliged to wield equipment that can, and all too often is, mistaken for weaponry in the heat of battle. If journalism has any heroes, these are the men and women deserving of the accolades. Moreover, modern ordnance is far more lethal and unlikely to leave its victims sufficiently intact to boast of flesh wounds and narrow escapes in hackdom's taverns.

When live television newscasts showing Russian tanks moving on the Kremlin or smart bombs whistling past your correspondent's Baghdad hotel windows are beamed into people's homes around the clock, there has to be some amazement that newspapers bother with foreign reporting at all. Most British newspapers have, in fact, given up analysis and thoughtful interpretation of foreign affairs, preferring to believe that readers merely want stories involving Britons abroad. This parochial trivialization of foreign news must bring nostalgic lumps to the throats of old hacks who cannot help but romanticize the good old days when print journalism was king and the Wises and Younghusbands could exchange their 'Why you unshot?' cablegrams over long lunches in exotic corners.

And for those who might be misled into believing that those old hacks must have long since perished from some strange brew in some stranger bar, or from some stray shell perhaps, it is worth recording that Bill Deedes of *Scoop* fame is, at the time of writing, still reporting from the world's hotspots for the *Telegraph*, leaving a trail of exhausted younger colleagues in his charming wake, at the age of eighty-four.

Pinching Men's Bottoms Can Be Bad for You

PETRONELLA WYATT

When, in the mid-1990s, I first worked for the *Sunday Telegraph*, there was a story in one of the newspapers about a male hospital patient who had been sued for pinching a nurse's bottom. This gave the then deputy editor an idea. 'Let's see what happens when the boot is on the other foot,' he announced. It soon became clear that the part of the boot was to be played by myself. I was instructed to go to the Reform Club in Pall Mall, obscure myself behind one of its pillars and pinch the members' bottoms as they emerged from the club.

A photographer was on hand to make a pictorial record of my efforts. The results, featuring wide-angled shots of my legs as they hurried after scuttling middle-aged gentlemen, appeared on page three. The postbag that week was large. The editor was delighted. The reaction of other members of the journalistic profession was more muted. Auberon Waugh's verdict was, according to a friend, 'disgusting'. He told a mutual acquaintance that the story had demeaned both the newspaper and myself. The following week I was further demeaned. I was promoted.

If Helen of Troy's face launched a thousand ships, my career could be said to have been launched off a hundred bottoms. The story is a cautionary one. The surest way, these days, of starting a career in journalism is to make sure you are born a woman, particularly a presentable one. (I make no claims here, though, for myself.) Kaiser Wilhelm II suffered from what historians describe as an 'encirclement complex' – the fear of being hemmed in by his enemies. A male colleague of mine joked that he suffered from what might be called a 'Tootsie complex' – the fear that the only way his career would prosper might be via a sex change.

So wherein lies the caution? Beneficiaries of the fashion for women journalists will indeed enjoy a career. This is no guarantee, however, that it will be a satisfactory and fulfilling one – that is, along the lines that one had first imagined it. Early dreams of becoming a Clare Hollingsworth or a Rebecca West are for many female journalists unrealized simply because their physical appearance deems them, in the eyes of editors and features editors, better suited to other tasks. Being a certain sort of female journalist can be a blessing and a curse. A blessing because it undoubtedly opens doors; a curse because the doors frequently open on to a cul-de-sac.

There has never been such a demand from the rapacious media maw for women. This is partly because there are more newspaper columns to fill and more television programmes requiring presenters and pundits. Another, equally important, reason is that newspaper editors and programmers are continually instructed by management and marketing magnificoes to pursue female readers, preferably those under the age of forty. Women enjoy increasing spending power, and this makes them a rich target for newspaper advertising, both in the broadsheets and the tabloids. It is assumed by these marketing honchos and by many editors, unimaginatively and sometimes erroneously, that the way to hold the attention of women readers is to employ women writers. I say erroneously because, as we know well, a female prime minister encountered more hostility from her own sex than from the opposite one.

In the past, when women depended on their husbands for money, editors had no need for large female quotas. The few women journalists there were before the Second World War were employed on merit only, which required these females to be significantly better than the men with whom they competed for jobs. Literary females in those days, as Truman Capote observed, were seldom presentable. Look at Sheila Grant Duff, the 1930s intellectual and journalist, so often wrongly paraded as a great beauty. Then there is the fabled exchange that took place in the late 1920s between the writer and journalist Edna Ferber and Noël Coward. Coward to Ferber: 'You almost look like a man.' Ferber to Coward: 'So do you.' Indeed, genuine female beauties were regarded by editors with suspicion. In the parlance of the time, they were either 'fast' or idle. The two great Dorothys of American journalism, Dorothy Parker and Dorothy Kilgallen, were physically undistinguished in the conventional sense. Despite their obvious bluestocking demeanour, both recalled the difficulties they encountered in acquiring intelligent journalistic postings. For some time Parker was set to work writing captions for lingerie advertisements. ('Brevity is the soul of lingerie' was one of her more memorable thoughts on the subject.)

When these women became famous, no one would have suggested it was through anything other than grit and talent. This is as true of such female correspondents as Dorothy Thompson. Thompson, the daughter of a New York Methodist minister, began her writing career as a reporter in Europe in the 1920s. Later she married the novelist Sinclair Lewis. One can safely say that Lewis didn't marry her for her beauty.

Of course, as in any profession in which men and women were beginning to mix, there were occasional cases of the Hollywood-style casting couch – in other words, of pretty women trading sexual favours for professional advancement. Sheila Graham, the lubricious Los Angeles columnist, was better known, or at least known first, as the mistress of F. Scott Fitzgerald. The writer educated her in English literature and philosophy – an experience she recounted in the memoir *College of One*. It is doubtful whether without Fitzgerald's sympathetic patronage Miss Graham would have passed beyond lingerie captions.

The opening of careers to single women changed not only the complexion of journalism but the way in which women were hired. In the old days most women were driven, not to work, but to marriage by the intolerable conditions of life for the average spinster. She had no occupation to fill her days and no freedom to enjoy herself outside the walls of the family home. In the decades after the Second World War, however, if a woman had a good education she began to discover the possibilities of making an acceptable living as a member of the professional classes. Still attached to journalism was its half-mythical stereotype as the province either of rough men like Damon Runyan and Walter Winchell, or effete homosexuals. But the pioneering women journalists had endowed it with a new glamour. Hollywood films such as *His Girl Friday*, which featured Cary Grant as the editor and Rosalind Russell as his star reporter and former wife, convinced women that journalism was no bar to femininity and charm. (Russell was at that time one of the most attractive actresses in America.)

Many aspects of journalism appealed to women's liking for both glamour and intimacy. As Colette observed, it involves the verbal contact at which women are alleged to excel, making them adept at persuading subjects 'to talk' (profile writing and interviews are often seen as the female forte). It also afforded women in a world before mass contraception everyday contact with large numbers of single men. To paraphrase Dorothy Parker, if all the journalists in a newsroom were laid end to end I wouldn't be at all surprised.

What sort of journalists were these new women to be? No male hierophant was given a particular brief on account of his hair colour or the size of his pectorals, but as attractive women began to stream into newspaper offices for the first time, they were increasingly segregated according to age, shape and size. There is a natural early career stage for an attractive woman journalist on a national newspaper. This is a period on the newspaper's diary column, whether 'Peterborough' on the *Daily Telegraph* or 'Londoner's Diary' on the *Evening Standard*. During this period the woman will be tried out on what are known as 'soft' features, for instance writing up 'the Season', discussing the latest stay-up stockings and interviewing supermodels. If she shows too much aptitude for this, woe betide her short-term prospects. (Though if she shows none she may of course be fired.) Even Dorothy Thompson, having interviewed Hitler, was cajoled into writing a column on domestic matters for the American *Ladies' Home Journal*.

This sort of journalism is not what every woman aspires to pursue indefinitely. But it is still what a large number of editors believe to be her forte. Because of the increased numbers of photo-bylined features, or those illustrated pictorially, the attractive woman is preyed upon for her to continue writing them. A pretty colleague of mine with a serious interest in politics was sent time and again by her editor to Quaglino's restaurant in London to dress as a cigarette girl and then recount her experiences. I recall a similar feature that I was asked to write for the *Sunday Telegraph* which centred on a series of photographs of myself in different evening dresses 'making an entrance' into various London eateries. On another occasion I was asked to seek a post as a secretary, retain it for a week, and then compose an article on how I had been sexually harassed by my boss – whether I had or not. 'What is truth?' asked the jesting female features editor. Displaying uncharacteristic probity I turned the assignment down.

This sort of journalism is a hard rut from which to emerge. Whether or not she escapes from it depends on the good sense and tenacity of the woman involved, as well as the whim of the individual editor. One job women still have difficulty in acquiring is the editorship of a newspaper, especially a broadsheet one. Perhaps this is because proprietors, who remain male, feel more comfortable working with editors of their own sex, or believe that such a job is too time-consuming for a woman – who will eventually succumb to the lure of the family.

Yet it remains true that male editors are as capable of over-promoting women as of under-promoting them. (The editor's sex is not always the best indication of the attitude they will take towards their female staff, as some women are more inclined to regard their sisters with contempt and suspicion than men.) The next step for the young female writer is often something in politics.

Proceeding immediately from 'soft' features to the Westminster battleground can create difficulties. What do these women really know about politics? One almost suspects that women are assumed to be experts on splits simply because their skirts are. To be fair, Walter Winchell became a political columnist after writing a gossip column, but he had more than twenty years of newspaper experience behind him.

The promotion of green young women to political jobs none the less suits everyone for a time. It suits the editor because it illumines (aesthetically) his or her comment pages and prevents the paper from seeming old-fashioned or chauvinistic, two of the greatest sins in contemporary journalism. It generates publicity because editors are aware of the eagerness of television producers to use female pundits, especially attractive ones, on late-night programmes. I once heard a producer remark, 'Fetch me a blonde, but make sure she's right-wing.' Then, 'No, better have a brunette. Blondes tend to be too caring.'

But it is undoubtedly true that some women, understandably delighted at having been promoted so quickly, are soon left floundering out of their depth. The bylines on female columns appear to come and go more quickly than those on men's. Every so often a newspaper, sometimes the *Daily Mail*, sometimes the *Independent*, 'introduces' a brilliant new female columnist, only for her column and her to disappear nine or ten months later.

This is not to say that women are incapable of 'serious' political writing. On the contrary. Melanie Philips of the *Sunday Times* is an example of the eloquent focus of the educated female mind, though one sometimes suspects Miss Philips feels she must be duller than necessary in order to convince editors and readers of her seriousness. Polly Toynbee, though in my view wrong-headed on almost every issue, has none the less cultivated a lively and effectively discursive style – unlike others of her sex, who are prone to a sort of dire earnestness. But that too many mediocre women are rewarded with columns, while most men must still earn them over the years, is indubitable.

This discrimination in favour of females (both writers and readers) has led to the birth of the irritating 'lifestyle' column that is a hybrid of the diary and the conventional opinion article. Most Sunday newspapers now feel obliged to carry one, alongside a large photograph of the authoress sporting backcombed hair that resembles a large soufflé. Her brief appears to be to describe the domestic and sexual events of her week in as much boring and disgusting minutiae as possible. Men have recently joined this well-paid act, feeling obliged, perhaps because of their insurmountable gender disadvantages, to write in even duller detail.

These columns eventually run their course and the woman begins her mournful and unenviable journey from one newspaper to another, finally alighting on the pages of the *Mail on Sunday*'s *You* magazine, writing columns with such titles as 'Me and My Weekend'. She may on the other hand retain her column for some years because the editor regards her as he or she might regard an expensive racehorse just purchased. To sack or demote the columnist would reflect badly on their original judgement and wound their executive pride.

Of course it is possible to be both a very serious woman journalist and an attractive one, but even now few people are prepared to believe in the possibility. One male media mogul advised me never to wear lipstick as it would only lead editors to think of sex. Absurd as this remark may appear, while most newspaper editors remain male it has a grim truth to it. The well-groomed and intelligent female will often be labelled a token woman columnist or will have to live with the knowledge that her detractors are saying she is there as a result of her aesthetic value – or worse. This is a difficult tightrope to walk. One of the few women to have done it successfully is Minette Marrin, who writes a column in the *Sunday Telegraph*. The higher these women fly, the greater the jealousy and the greater the threat to their position.

There is the plain woman with a real and apparent gift. They are in the fortunate position of being admired for and judged only on their work. Nor are they dependent on the retainment of their youth and looks for employment.

These talented foot-soldiers do not escape abuse, however. They must become used to a different sort of hostile criticism. The social behaviour of women journalists rarely evades scrutiny, often of a condemnatory sort. If women writers are persistent they are labelled shrews, a description which male journalists have never had to bear. This is especially true of women interviewers (which is what I do for the *Daily Telegraph*). Women are socially and perhaps biologically programmed to be more accommodating in conversation and are therefore more often than men the victims of interviewees who imagine they can dodge or retreat because the journalist is female.

By this token it is very difficult for any woman doing a reporting job to do it properly and remain 'feminine' in the eyes of the world. Dorothy Kilgallen was forced to bear years of vulgar abuse from Frank Sinatra, who objected to her column disclosing his more questionable behaviour. The most frequent term used against such women is 'harridan' – 'loony left' or 'lesbian' harridan if they work for the *Observer*, or 'bitch' if it is for the *Daily Mail*. These are fine distinctions. She does, however, after many decades of toil, earn a grudging respect sometimes denied to her prettier sister.

There are of course allegedly serious women who are both plain and very dull writers. They interpret post-feminism as a negation of basic good humour. Jokes are anathema to them. These women give you page fright. They are not only paraded in newspapers but on late-night television programmes such as *Newsnight*, on which they talk incessantly and often incoherently about non-existent 'issues'.

It seems to me that most female columns are becoming duller. This is true of newspaper columns in general. It is partly the fault of editors. Editors of both sexes seem to want columnists to share the same views, or a consensus, as a genuflection to the alleged cultural and political uniformity of modern Britain. This is increasingly so since the New Labour dawn, or rather the New Labour yawn.

Originality can alarm editors as much as a strong ideology. You might argue, but what of such so-called 'controversial' columnists as Julie Burchill? Julie Burchill was successful not so much because of any strong ideology but because of the scatalogical language in which her opinions were couched; in other words, because she was 'streetwise'. (When Burchill moved her column to the *Sunday Times* this tactic failed dismally.) Many women columnists, particularly in the tabloids, seem to believe that a four-letter word is a substitute for a thought.

Discrimination in favour of women, while it undoubtedly exists, does not necessarily help them in the long term. In one sense it is better to go about it in the old-fashioned way and wait longer for your favoured job than to acquire it before you are ready (which happens to half of all female journalists), or never acquire it at all (which happens to the other half). The lesson for young women journalists is to write on subjects about which they have genuine knowledge, or at least an interest, rather than be driven along by editors pursuing their own cynical agendas.

The Slow Death of
Investigative Journalism

PAUL FOOT

Asked what they mean by the freedom of the press, most people say something like 'the freedom of people to write what they think'. The problem is that what most editors and most journalists think is usually predictable, craven and, worst of all, dull. Nothing wastes newspaper space more than columnists 'letting off steam', especially if they are billed as 'frank' or 'fearless'. There is nothing specially free about a courageous or fearless opinion which involves no courage or fear whatsoever.

A better definition of freedom of the press was expressed by three journalists who worked on the *Sunday Times* in the 1960s and 1970s and wrote a book about the Zinoviev letter. The author of this 'letter' was said to be Gregory Zinoviev, a leading member of the Russian revolutionary government who was expressing solidarity with the newly elected and first-ever British Labour government. The three journalists, Hugo Young, Stephen Fay and Lewis Chester, exposed the letter as a fake and mused on the ease with which almost the entire press of the time (1924) had been duped by the fake letter. They concluded: 'The newspapers of the time were in the most unfortunate sense organs of opinion, and provided an instructive example of the absurdity of the argument that the health of the press depends on the ability to reflect a broad spectrum of views. The health of the press, now as then, seems to us to depend on a simpler, more demanding function: its ability to find out and present facts.'

Young, Fay and Chester all worked for the *Sunday Times* of the 1960s and 1970s. In recent years this paper has become a bit of a legend for what became known, in a phrase which dates from about

79

that time, as 'investigative journalism'. The expression is often used by jumped-up bylined journalists who want to distinguish themselves from the common ruck. It is in itself a little ridiculous since all journalism worthy of the name carries with it a duty to ask questions, check facts, investigate. Moreover the legend of the old *Sunday Times*, its editor Harry Evans and its investigative Insight column is, like most legends, hideously exaggerated. Many, if not most, of the Insight columns were prompted by London middle-class obsessions (Was the antique trade a rip-off? Should Stansted Airport be built in the Essex countryside? etc.). But the legend is authentic to this extent at least: that Insight represented not so much freedom *of* the editor as freedom *from* the editor. The Insight column was put together by a group of staff journalists who decided themselves what subjects they would investigate and were given the freedom (plus the research and library facilities of a big and commercially successful newspaper) to get on with it. This delegation and spread of the decision-making process within the newspaper led to a spirit of independence and confidence through-out the staff, which explained a lot of the *Sunday Times*'s success. The quotation from the three journalists' book summarized the basic rule which guided the Insight team: that although it is almost always impossible to separate facts and opinion, most opinion worthy of the name is prompted by facts, and in the new 'investig-ative' journalism facts should lead opinion, not the other way round. The age-old problem of the relationship between fact and opinion was confronted again and again in his life by perhaps the greatest of British journalists this century, George Orwell. 'The more one is aware of political bias,' he concluded just before he died, 'the more one can be independent of it, and the more one claims to be impartial the more one is biased.' It is no good denying political bias – everyone is naturally and properly affected by it. The question is not how to disguise political bias but how to justify it. And the answer is by finding out and presenting the facts. Facts are the crucial stan-dard by which opinion can be judged. The central theme of Orwell's great satire *1984* is that whatever your opinion or your mathematical genius, two and two make four, and the ultimate obscenity of tyranny is to establish in the public mind that they make five.

The editor of this collection foolishly urges me to indulge myself in my own experiences, so here goes. In 1964 I came to London from Glasgow, where I had worked for three years in almost every editorial department of the Scottish *Daily Record*. I had been sent up there by Hugh Cudlipp, and was patronized everywhere as another toffee-nosed careerist sent up to pretend to get his fingers dirty before going back to London to sidle his way to the top.

Accordingly, I was brought down by Cudlipp to join a team on the new *Sun* newspaper, which replaced the old *Daily Herald*. The fashion set by the Insight team persuaded the then *Sun* editor to launch an 'investigative' page, called Probe. The imaginative idea was ruined by the man in charge of the page: a former city editor of the *Express* who thought of everything in terms of profit and loss. When I proposed a feature on capital punishment, which was about to be abolished under the new Labour government, he was immediately impressed. 'Find out,' he barked, 'how much money it would save – how much does an execution cost?' This form of control quickly smothered the Probe page. All four of us in the team resigned and went elsewhere. I was even offered a job on the Insight column, but turned it down because I was trying to finish a book.

Soon after I arrived in London, Richard Ingrams introduced me to a journalist who was already a hero, Claud Cockburn. Our opinions clashed immediately and sharply. However much he might prevaricate, Claud was still an old Stalinist. He still took his political line from Moscow, hated George Orwell, and found himself swimming rather sullenly against the rising revolutionary socialist current of the times with which I had been swept up. What bound us together was a passion for discovering and exposing awkward facts about British society in which no one seemed interested. In the 1930s Claud had produced a slovenly sheet called *The Week*, which constantly revealed disturbing facts about the behaviour of the richest and the mightiest in the land. In the early 1960s he gravitated naturally to *Private Eye*, founded in 1961, which was quickly selling more than *The Week* had ever done. Then and now, the *Eye* attracted all kinds of nutters with an axe to grind. What impressed me most about Claud was the time he would spend with such people, and how, more often than not, they had more stories than had all the Reuters and AP tapes put together.

'Listen to the loons,' was his first lesson. His second was that a single source in high places was worth a million official spokespeople. 'Never believe anything until it is officially denied,' was his immortal advice. Even more important was to find sources on the inside. 'Insurance,' he used to say. 'Find someone in insurance who trusts you and he will give you more stories than you'll read in all the newspapers.' I never did find that person in insurance (if he or she reads this, please ring me at the *Eye*). But I did discover quite quickly that a crucial part of a relationship between a source and a journalist is trust. The problem about the circulation of real information in our society is that people at all levels of it, especially the top, do not disclose even what they want to disclose. They are worried about their own position as the discloser. Only when they can be sure that they are safe does the information start to flow. It follows that, as far as the general flow of information goes, protecting the source of a story is more important than the story itself.

I joined *Private Eye* in February 1967, seduced by the juicy bait of two pages which I had to fill all by myself. Thirty-two years later I still recall the almost overwhelming sense of liberation when first writing for *Private Eye*. Off my back were the cloying hierarchies, the silly office intrigues and petty censorships which stifled so much writing in the official press. Into the bargain, these were exciting times. Jobs were safe, and sources were not afraid. Leaks abounded. The *Eye* postbag grew in size and quality. This 'investigative journalism', this piling fact on fact to present a picture of cock-up or conspiracy, was new and exciting. Not many people seemed to notice what I wrote (again and again real revelations sank like a stone: my articles about the Poulson corruption scandal which years later won me an award were greeted with profound indifference). But the mood among journalists and editors was emphatically in favour of more investigations, and more independent journalists to carry them out.

In 1972 I left the *Eye* to work for *Socialist Worker*, which I left in 1978, much downhearted that the revolution had not materialized. I drifted back to the *Eye*. One summer evening in 1979, Mike Molloy, editor of the *Daily Mirror*, appeared at my home and offered me a job on a special investigations team. I was not keen. I was spoiled by my freedom on the *Eye* to decide what questions to ask and what to write about. The thought of interminably competing for space on the *Mirror* bored me. Almost as an afterthought, Mike then suggested that I might have my own weekly 'investigative' space on the *Mirror*. This was an entirely different proposition, and, considering my political views and pedigree, a bold one. When it was confirmed, I could hardly believe my good fortune. On the day I went into the *Mirror* building in Holborn and was shown into a little office on the fourth floor, I sat there all afternoon paralysed by delight and terror. Delight that such an unlikely dream had come true, terror as to how on earth I was to find the stories to fill the page.

The answer, which now seems obvious but then was unheard of, was: from the readers of the *Daily Mirror*. It was Tony Delano, a friend of Mike's, who came up with a formula, which went on my *Mirror* page for fourteen years: 'If you have something you want me to investigate, ring me or write to me at the *Mirror*.' Popular papers had in the past provided 'action lines' to deal with complaints of the 'my gas fire doesn't work' variety, and pages of advice about personal or practical problems. But this was, I think, the first time a national paper had openly solicited information from whistle-blowers, grasses and finks, and provided a name (and a photograph) with which they could communicate. The caption led, inevitably, to a flood of letters and calls that had to be answered. Fourteen years later, when I was forced out of the *Mirror*, I was mocked for having two secretaries. These secretaries, and all the administrative back-up, were provided by an editor who had faith in his readers and in their ability to provide information, and was prepared to spend his resources on building that up. I reckoned that in those fourteen years I answered personally 150,000 letters and twice as many phone calls.

One story from those early years illustrates the *Mirror*'s commitment to facts even when they clashed with the paper's opinion. In the spring of 1983, a year after the Falklands war, I flew at the *Mirror*'s expense to Lima, Peru, to investigate the charge that the

Argentinian cruiser *General Belgrano* had been deliberately sunk on Margaret Thatcher's orders to stop a peace settlement put together by Peruvian diplomats. Late one afternoon, mainly by luck, I was granted an interview with a very senior official at the Peruvian foreign office who told me that a peace treaty had been prepared, printed and bound in red leather for signature by British, Peruvian and Argentinian diplomats; that a press conference had been summoned to announce the treaty, the withdrawal of all armed forces, the establishment of a United Nations force in the Falklands and the end of hostilities. The signing and the press conference was, said the official, called off at the behest of the Argentinians when they heard the news of the sinking of the *Belgrano*. I was shown the room where the treaty was to be signed, and I had recorded on tape the official describing the whole episode in great detail. It was fairly clear to me that there was powerful evidence that a peace treaty had been blown up with the *Belgrano*, perhaps deliberately. When I returned to London and wrote my story, Terry Lancaster, the *Mirror*'s able political correspondent, who had always been entirely supportive of my column, blew his top. 'We can't publish this,' he objected, 'it's an insult to the British forces who fought in the Falklands!'

A meeting was hastily convened in the offices of the chairman, Tony Miles. Lancaster put his argument fairly and passionately. I replied that I had reported what I believed had happened, and could justify every sentence with some document, tape or authority. In the end, with a few amendments, the piece was published on my page, without any editorial comment. The controversy about the Peruvian peace agreement has never been resolved. The House of Commons Foreign Affairs Committee, after long and detailed investigation, could not draw a conclusion one way or another. But at any rate, inside the newspaper, after what had been a rational and democratic process, fact had triumphed over opinion.

Despite (and partly because of) the election of a new Tory government that year, investigative journalism in the early 1980s was still in fashion. My friend Christopher Hird, who had been deputy editor to the former Insight guru Bruce Page at the *New Statesman*, took over as editor of the Insight team. David Leigh was winning awards at the *Observer* for his investigations into the activities of the prime minister's son and husband. But there were soon signs of a vigorous counter-attack.

In 1981, Rupert Murdoch added *The Times* and the *Sunday Times* to his *Sun* and *News of the World*. Almost at once, Harry Evans was transferred to *The Times*, and resigned the editorship the following year after a row with Murdoch about editorial independence. In the autumn of 1983, Andrew Neil was appointed editor of the *Sunday Times* in preference to two far more able and better-qualified in-house candidates, Hugo Young and Brian Macarthur. Neil's first act was to axe the *Sunday Times* Insight column and sack Christopher Hird. Neil explains in his book how the disbanding of Insight was part of his campaign against Britain's 'collectivist culture', but the key point was not the sacking of an individual for political reasons but the removal from the Insight team of its independence. The centralization of editorial control went on, and led in 1984 to the angry departure of Hugo Young.

But perhaps the most striking evidence of the approach of the *Sunday Times* to investigations was the Vanunu affair in 1985. Mordecai Vanunu, who had worked at an Israeli nuclear plant, approached the *Sunday Times* with information and pictures proving that the Israelis were manufacturing nuclear weapons. Even Andrew Neil could tell that this was a scoop of historic proportions. Prodigious efforts were made to check and eventually publish the story. By the time Neil published, however, he had lost contact with his source. Vanunu had been seduced by an Israeli agent who persuaded him to go with her to Rome, where he was attacked, knocked out, drugged, whisked off to Israel, convicted under secrets laws and sent to prison for eighteen years. The failure of the *Sunday Times* to protect its source, like the failure of the *Guardian* a year earlier to protect Sarah Tisdall, who had leaked them a document from the Ministry of Defence, was not just an outrage. It was a warning signal to anyone else who wanted to leak information. No one will ever know how many future whistleblowers decided to keep quiet for fear that they might end up behind bars, like Sarah Tisdall or Mordecai Vanunu.

In 1986, Murdoch, with the active support of Andrew Neil, moved his offices and printing from central London to Wapping in a co-ordinated, ruthless and eventually successful move to smash the unions. Though the print unions put up a stiff resistance, the smashing of the unions at Wapping was greeted by journalists in general with astonishing complacency. It was argued that strong trade unions in the press are not friends of press freedom, and the press is more free without trade unions. This complacency was partly responsible for the systematic smashing of trade unions throughout the press, so that at the time of writing only the *Guardian* and to a lesser extent the *Independent* still recognize and negotiate with trade unions.

My own strong view is that the smashing of the trade unions was part of the centralizing of control and bureaucratization in the press which have done so much to damage investigative journalism. The purpose of an organized union in a newspaper office is not just to look after wages, conditions and employment practices – or even to organize against the widespread nepotism and corruption in recruitment which is now commonplace in the national press. It is also to provide a centre where journalists can collect and discuss their common problems, including editorial problems, free from the management hierarchy. A recognized trade union adds to the spirit of independence inside a newspaper which is so crucial to successful investigative journalism. Andrew Neil's account of his role in the union-bashing at Wapping is not convincing, but the most interesting part of his book is his description of the disintegration of his own role as independent editor. As Murdoch, with the unions smashed, ruthlessly demanded – and took – more and more control, so the editorial freedom even of Andrew Neil was circumscribed.

These developments in the Murdoch group had been reflected at the *Mirror* long before Wapping. In my first five years at the *Mirror*, the paper was owned, as the *Sunday Times* had been, by a remote proprietor who kept his distance – in the *Mirror*'s case the IPC, chaired by Alex (later Lord) Jarrett. The editors ran the show, and their confidence in doing so was reflected, as it had been on the *Sunday Times*, in their willingness to delegate more and more editorial power to 'self-starters' like the Insight team on the *Sunday Times* and mine on the *Mirror*. Almost as soon as Andrew Neil took over at the *Sunday Times*, rumours started to circulate that the *Mirror* was to be taken over. When the unions went to Jarrett with a plan to borrow money to buy the papers for a co-operative, Jarrett replied that he would never sell to a single owner. In July 1984, he sold the lot to Robert Maxwell.

Some days after the takeover, Maxwell summoned John Pilger, the *Mirror*'s famous award-winning reporter, and me to the chairman's penthouse offices. He was full of praise and bonhomie. Humbly, he assured us that he would not interfere in anything we did. When I insisted that this pledge must be total – that he must keep out of all my operations even when he thought he had a story for me – he waved his assurance – 'Of course, of course.' I explained that this made the issue quite simple for me because I had my own space. 'Yes, Paul,' he said, sharply, pretending to joke, 'I regard you as a space imperialist.'

A year or so later, I was summoned again to discuss the renewal of my contract. Over champagne, and in front of my wife, and Mike and Sandy Molloy, he launched into a vitriolic attack on my column, saying it was 'all about shop stewards and criminals' and was not neutral or objective. I told him that if he wanted someone neutral or objective there were plenty of journalists out there panting for a page. I was not neutral or objective. I thought my job was to dig out facts to provide information for *Mirror* readers, for the people at the bottom of the pile, for the poor and the sick and the workers, etc., etc.; and if he wanted something different I would go elsewhere. He flipped right over at once, lavishing me with unctuous praise and renewing my contract. He sat there, almost wheedling, explaining his outburst: 'I'm sorry but I *can't stand* the thought of something going on in my newspaper over which I have no control.'

I hardly ever saw him again but I could not escape his brooding, toad-like presence squatting at the top of the *Mirror* building. I made out a list of people I knew were Maxwell's business friends and admirers, and stuck it on my wall. Whenever I planned an attack on any of them, I would ring them for a response. Every time, the effect was immediate. The outraged businessmen (or politicians, or trade unionists) would ring Maxwell's office and tell him to get me off their backs. He would ring the editor, Richard Stott. Stott and I devised a plan whereby, on each occasion this happened, I would tape-record the injured party's response, write the piece at great speed and get it 'legalled' (passed by the lawyers) before Maxwell's phone call. 'I'm sorry, Bob,' Stott would say, 'it's all been passed – there's nothing I can do.' We got most of the stuff published in the end, but how far we had come from the days of rationality and independence BM (Before Monster). The whole business of investigating, of digging out facts from reluctant company directors, civil servants or lawyers, was made much more difficult by the suffocating control which Maxwell imposed on his newspapers.

In the year between Maxwell's death in 1991 and the appointment at the *Mirror* of David Montgomery as chief executive, the *Mirror* editors ran their papers once again, and their circulations steadied. I was genuinely surprised to see how quickly the readers responded to the gross egomania of Maxwell on the one hand, and the rising confidence and morale in the paper after his death. It was almost as if the appointment in 1992 of Montgomery, engineered by the National Westminster Bank and Arthur Andersen, was a deliberate move to subvert the newspapers' ability to succeed without executives. In that year, incidentally, I felt my own investigations improved out of all recognition. I asked questions with much greater confidence that the answers, or lack of them, would be published.

Montgomery rampaged through the *Mirror* sacking everyone even marginally associated with the union and what he called 'the old *Mirror* culture'. This naturally included investigative journalism in general and my column in particular. To prove a little point about freedom of the press, I submitted a column cataloguing the revolting bullying of the Montgomery management, his share dealings and his colleagues' associations with Maxwell. The column was passed by the lawyers, but for the first time in fourteen years it was censored by the editor. Various attempts have been made since to restore investigative journalism to the *Mirror*. A typical effort is a weekly column, 'Sorted', which slid back into the old 'action line' tradition, seeking to 'sort things out' for the readers rather than inform them.

I am heartily suspicious of older journalists who hark back to the 'grand old days'. There were none such, and, in general, standards of journalism are likely to improve as time goes on. There is still a lot of robust reporting, especially about politics. The *Guardian* did for Hamilton, Aitken and Carlton Television. The *Independent*, freed from the dead hand of David Montgomery, is recovering some of its early zeal and is publishing strong stories. Even *The Times* and *Sunday Times* occasionally disgorge a gobbet of information. *Private Eye* still flourishes, utterly and genuinely independent. But the trend has been a gloomy one. The chief obstacle to investigative journalism in our newspapers and television has been the centralization of commercial power and editorial control. The proprietors have become more powerful and ruthless. Their editors, necks cricked from constantly glancing upwards, their judgement poisoned by years of what the *Eye* calls *arslikhan*, have become far more constipated, far less trusting of their colleagues, far more reluctant to delegate editorial power. The unions have almost all gone. Increasingly, sources are betrayed and opinions flaunted in space that should be taken up with reports and facts. The trend, no doubt, will change, but in the meantime let us hope that no one forges another Zinoviev letter.

Monarchs of Spin Valley

MICHAEL WHITE

'What did we decide? Is it to lower the price of bread or isn't it? It doesn't matter which, but we must all say the same thing.'
(Prime Minister Melbourne, March 1841)

Tony Blair or John Major, both pragmatic politicians to a fault, would readily have understood Lord Melbourne's exasperated warning to his cabinet as it grappled ineffectually with the problem of Corn Law reform. It was the single currency controversy of its day. Sleaze, Ireland, uncooperative colleagues (he nearly fought a duel over one reshuffle), taxes and trade unions, a dysfunctional royal family, Lord Melbourne struggled to master a familiar agenda, much as his successors would do. There again, Melbourne may not have known or cared much about bread prices. But, to judge from that famous quotation, he did grasp the importance of making sure that the Browns, Cooks and Prescotts of his day were all on message. Whatever the agreed line on bread was, they would all be expected to stick to it at the Dispatch Box and in the fashionable salons.

What Queen Victoria's prime ministerial confidant would not have understood, had he surveyed Westminster and Whitehall in the 1990s, is the voracious, round-the-clock demands of the modern media, or the obsessive importance which incumbents of 10 Downing Street now attach to the squashing or squaring of it. If such an improbable public official as Charlie Whelan had popped up at his elbow, explained that he was the Chancellor of the Exchequer's spin doctor, and offered his assistance ('I can fix that bread price story for you, Bill'), Lord Melbourne would have been puzzled and alarmed. Chances are that he would have had Charlie thrown into the street.

Victorian politicians, albeit usually at a distance, knew all about abusive, small-circulation newspapers with names like the *Ballot*, the *Penny Satirist* and the *Radical Reformer*, printed in alleys off Fleet Street. A few years before Trollope created a monster in Quintus Slide of the *People's Banner*, the great Duke of Wellington had been confronted with the kiss-and-tell memoirs of a lady friend. Declining either to appease or sue, he declared: 'Publish and be damned.' Melbourne himself was described by one journalist as 'an old, stupid, lame, ugly, toothless foozle'. Even in 1838 such remarks must have hurt. When they are picked up within minutes and piped into every home and traffic jam in the land by countless outlets of BBC radio and TV, including Radio 5 Live and rolling News 24, by ITV, Sky and the Internet, they also matter. CNN and the BBC's World Services carry them to Bogota and Brisbane.

And the broadcasters are just the hors-d'œuvre. Today's papers, regional and national, tabloid and broadsheet, would recycle the remark and turn it into 'Foozlegate'. They would then proceed to over-analyse its implications for civilization or, at the very least, discuss the government's chance of staggering on until Sunday, when the modern news cycle tends to change targets. One misjudged remark by the duty cabinet minister on David Frost's Sunday sofa and the whole thing takes off again. The process is as relentless as it is fickle, and, in its way, as competitive as those nineteenth-century sheets. If the *Penny Satirist* had claimed that Lord Melbourne tucked his shirt into his Y-fronts (a tabloid journalist called Alastair Campbell rendered such a disservice to John Major) the damaging canard might have taken years to reach John O'Groats. Today a Michael Brunson or Robin Oakley can make it arrive before lunch.

Enter stage left, right or centre-left, the spin doctor, one of the great comic inventions of the age. He – in the masculine world of Westminster politics it is always a he – is not a mere press officer, at hand to set out policy in a simple, even-handed fashion or passively field inquiries from reporters if they deign to ring. Such estimable officials still exist in all organizations which have a public profile and some accountability to customers, shareholders or voters. Some are brilliant, clever, helpful, funny. But they are as bicycles to a spin doctor's 1500cc Harley Davidson. A spin doctor is a press officer with an attitude, a PR man with a hot client, a marketing executive with a pitch. They can be found wherever there is a City takeover to be massaged, an Oscar nominee to be talked up or protected. Such spinners usually have fancy titles and work from large desks in big PR firms. But political spin doctors are a breed apart, the urban guerrillas of the trade, far more exposed to public notoriety than their slick commercial cousins. Their mission: the projection and protection of power.

The Collins *Millennium Dictionary* defines them thus: '(Noun. Informal), A person who provides a favourable slant to an item of news, potentially unpopular policy, etc. on behalf of a political personality or party.' Definitions vary, but the crucial element is always there. A spin doctor is proactive. He roams his domain, sometimes dubbed Spin Valley, restlessly seeking to interpret events and public reaction to them, to neutralize or forestall negative impressions and accentuate the positive.

It is, of course, an American expression. William Safire, erudite lexicographer and political pundit to the *New York Times*, notes that the verb 'to spin', meaning 'to whirl', has its origins in Old English. As a noun it is nineteenth-century, as in the spin on a cricket or billiard ball. The hint of deception is apparent. By the mid-twentieth century the term 'spin a yarn' had emerged, with its further implication that not all the hearer is being told is sixteen annas to the rupee. Doctoring has its own dubious connotations, as in 'doctoring the records' or the Broadway 'play doctor' who fixes a defective script. According to Safire's *Political Dictionary*, it was on 21 October 1984 that the two ideas were first welded together in English in an editorial in his own paper. Commenting on the televised presidential debate, the good, grey *New York Times* reported:

Tonight at about 9.30, seconds after the Reagan–Mondale debate ends, a bazaar will suddenly materialize in the press room . . . a dozen men in good suits and women in silk dresses will circulate smoothly among the reporters, spouting confident opinions. They won't just be press agents trying to impart of favorable spin to a routine release. They'll be the Spin Doctors, senior advisers to the candidates.

And spin they did. In the first TV debate that autumn ex-Vice-President Mondale had made President Reagan look old and unsure of himself. In the re-match Reagan was waiting for him. When Mondale moved back on to what he hoped would be fruitful ground the consummate actor joked, 'I am not going to exploit, for political purposes, my opponent's youth and inexperience.' It was corny, but it was enough. It shows he's still got grip, the spinners assured reporters. Americans awoke next morning to learn that a single one-liner had clinched Reagan's second term.

Note the capital letters, Spin Doctors. Within four days the term reappeared in lower case and gradually took hold. An irresistible word, it was imported into Britain during the Bush–Dukakis campaign four years later. As a Washington correspondent at the time, I may have been the culprit. But the *concept* had already arrived. By 1988, Peter Mandelson, a former producer on LWT's *Weekend World* (itself a very packaged and manipulated programme), had been Labour's director of communications for three years, imposing on Neil Kinnock's unruly party the new techniques, soundbites, focus-group polling, and spin. Margaret Thatcher had been looting Republican political marketing strategies since the 1970s. Her 1979 campaign was virtually an extended photo-opportunity designed to protect her from errors which might destroy her lead: all those calves, children and chocolate-factory visits were really TV with the sound turned down.

By this time Tory politicians had accepted that these things mattered. They knew that, if only Richard Nixon's handlers had persuaded him to apply a little Max Factor to that villainous stubble before debating with Senator Jack Kennedy on TV, he might have taken the White House in 1960. Labour took longer. If only Michael Foot had stooped to obtain the services of such a creature on that fateful Remembrance Sunday when he turned up at the Cenotaph in a duffle-coat. The offending garment would have been transformed into a symbol of the Labour leader's sensitive identification with Our Boys in the trenches. 'I'm surprised you of all people, Trevor, didn't know that all the troops wore duffle-coats just like that in World War One,' some Mandelsonian voice would have murmured in the ear of the *Daily Beast*.

How are such miracles of persuasion achieved? First and foremost, like most things in politics, by sheer physical stamina. The spin doctor is on the case in the small hours, scanning the first editions before bedtime in search of trouble. He is up early, with an eye on BBC breakfast news and an ear on the *Today* programme to see if yesterday's spin worked by establishing the framework of debate on his terms. Simultaneously he is barking orders on his mobile, then at his desk marshalling the day's line for ministers, officials and MPs. He holds his key meeting with senior co-conspirators when most reporters are still lingering over their first coffee. Later in the day the spin doctor meets the media enemy in ritual combat, in the basement press-room at Downing Street, at the Matignon in Paris, or in the west wing of the White House. He bullies, flatters, wheedles, tells lies when he has to do so, though he prefers to mislead by omission. So do his tormentors, who are not averse to throwing a highly selective account of a dispute at the spokesman, hoping to further foment ill-will. On one notorious occasion a misleading version of what Kenneth Clarke had said on Radio 4 was fed to John Major by reporters who had accompanied the prime minister to Tokyo.

Both sides are engaged in an ever more frantic fight to set the news agenda, its contents and parameters, its presentation and tone, to manipulate the other side and not be manipulated in turn. Picture the scene. A few minutes before 11 o'clock most weekday mornings when the Commons is sitting, twenty or so reporters drift through the Downing Street gates and down the steps at the side of London's most famous jerry-built terrace. They represent the main TV stations, the wire services (notably the Press Association and Reuters), the evening papers – almost on deadline in cities up and down the country – and most of the national dailies.

Until John Major's day they went through the front door and perched on the arm of the press secretary's sofa. Now they sit on rows of stackable chairs in a gloomy basement like social security claimants. Which, in a way, they are. On the dot or at 11.02 or 11.05, the prime minister's press secretary sweeps in, followed by up to eight press office colleagues who also need to learn what the day's line is. A veil of secrecy hung over these occasions twenty years ago. Political correspondents would talk airily of 'sources close to the government' or 'informed sources'. But the pace and pressures were also much slower. In those days the spokesman, a soft-spoken Scot called Tom McCaffrey during Jim Callaghan's tenure from 1976–9, rarely engaged in what could be called spin. Sir Tom, as he later became, set out the government's case and if, next day, it was not reported quite as he had hoped, he might register a mild reproach. Certainly there would be no denunciation of 'bunkum and balderdash' (copyright. Bernard Ingham), no 'complete crap, C-R-A-P' or 'G-A-R-B-A-G-E', terms favoured by the Blair spin machine, or 'bollocks', which was Charlie Whelan's denial formula of choice. There would be no mocking abuse heaped on a colleague's story in front of the 11 o'clock lobby, no menacing phone calls to reporter, his editor or BBC producer, no threats of non-cooperation or complaints to the proprietor. Yet in theory the system is more open now. After the hostilities of the late Thatcher years John Major initially made it more so when he conceded the right to source the spokesman's words to 'Downing Street' or 'the prime minister's office'.

Under rules devised by the Cabinet Office when Tony Blair became prime minister this has gone further. Lobby briefings are now on the record. *The* spokesman, or his deputies – to be designated '*a* spokesman' – may be quoted directly, though not by name. Nor can he be filmed by the TV cameramen who are on permanent duty on the pavement outside Number 10 and would love a warmer billet from which to provide the day's video-wallpaper that accompanies the TV reporter's two-minute spot.

That change will come eventually. It may have arrived by the time you read this if Downing Street judges it to serve its own best interests to put the official spokesman on camera to speak directly to the voters, Washington or Bonn style, instead of being filtered by what Blair loyalists call a jaded and cynical press. However, if Washington's 'open' system is a guide, it will not stop hole-in-corner briefings, a long way off the record. It will merely encourage aspiring Paxmans on both side to play to the camera.

In any case, media narcissism and the post-modern passion for deconstructing such transactions have ensured that the spokesman is famous regardless of the mandarin rule. Let us call him Campbell Alastair, not his real name, I stress. He proceeds to provide routine details of the prime minister's day. On a typical day Tony Blair may already have breakfasted with CBI leaders or visited a school in the East End to provide TV pictures that accompany a plea for higher standards. He could be meeting the German, Irish or Israeli foreign minister before lunch (though foreign dignitaries have been heavily weeded out of the Blair day). He may lunch at his desk a sandwich or pizza perhaps (Number 10 lacks a canteen) and chair a cabinet committee. No details of either are provided. At six he *may* see the Queen, usually on Tuesdays, then dash up the M1 to Luton to make a speech on welfare-to-work. Copies of his text will be available later, though Mr Alastair may help the evening papers or broadcasters with early deadlines by providing the important quotes. Even that small service helps to dictate the way the message is delivered. If the full text turns out to be hedged with cautious caveats, it is often too late to do much about it. At Question Time the prime minister can deny over-enthusiastic headlines. 'Taken out of context,' he can assure alarmed backbenchers.

Of the all-important but informal ministerial bilaterals on Mr Blair's cream sofa the scribblers hear nothing at the 11 o'clock briefing. Such meetings, not the cabinet, are increasingly the essential mechanism for decision-taking and reporters only hear about them by luck or by leaking. But Mr Alastair does not ignore the cabinet colleagues. That George Robertson initiative on the Euro-fighter and Clare Short's important written parliamentary answer ('Number 65') about aid policy will get a mention at the 11 o'clock. Ever since that ambitious media-manipulator Neville Chamberlain first appointed a civil servant, William Steward, as his official press officer there has been tension between the role of spokesman for the government as a whole and spokesman for the prime minister.

Number 10 has no huge bureaucracy. Publicity is one of the weapons at its disposal as it grapples with ministerial recalcitrants. It can use the media to galvanize public opinion behind a policy or person. The task is always delicate, not least since jealous colleagues are always ready to attack the media messenger, as 'too big for his boots', or over-mighty, deputy prime minister in all but name.

Mr Alastair does attend cabinet, the first press secretary to do so. That fact grossly inflates the press secretary's role. He is not a policy-maker, but he acts as a useful lightning rod. When Bernard Ingham dubbed Margaret Thatcher's ministers 'Mona Lott' (Francis Pym) and 'semi-detached' (John Biffen) it caused unease among lobby correspondents, a feeling that it was not the spokesman's job to attack cabinet members. In the late eighties those tensions led to a boycott of the twice-daily lobby briefings by the *Guardian*, *Independent*, *Scotsman* and *Economist*. Biffen got his revenge. He memorably described Sir Bernard as 'the sewer, not the sewage'.

Mr Alastair knows the pitfalls. It is not easy. When reporters ask (as they often do) if the prime minister still has 'complete confidence' in Peter Mandelson, Geoffrey Robinson, Ron Davies, Harriet Harman, or Glen Hoddle, a straight 'No' is never the right answer. 'Yes' can also be dangerous, as in 'Blair Backs Robinson in Offshore Trusts Row' or 'I'm Right Behind Ron, says Tony'. So he obfuscates, fudges, makes jokes or bores for England, anything to steer the pack away from Trouble. Being directly quotable, as previous press secretaries were not, simply raises the stakes. Sometimes a pause or smile is eloquent enough to convey a meaning. It is often clear that Mr Alastair does not share the boss's enthusiasm for Lib Lab co-operation, but not a hint of it can be heard on the tapes which routinely record his briefings.

Such sparring is the small change of the daily joust, the 'gaggle' as it is called in the Clinton White House. Books on the subject confirm that the culture is much the same in both countries and most of the material pretty dull. Reporters test their own theories or each other's last story, they query policies and that ambiguous phrase in last night's speech in Dudley. They tease Mr Alastair or his deputy, try to wind him up. In return they are soothed or abused, though Mr Alastair rarely attacks New Labour-courted papers like the *Sun* and *Mail* directly. The *Financial Times*, *Guardian*, *Telegraph* or *Independent* are easier targets. The BBC is the easiest target of all, as it usually is under the Tories, a large, publicly funded barn door.

Sometimes the technique works. Anyone who has seen Sir Bernard Ingham on TV knows his style. Occasionally voters also catch a glimpse of men at work. During the 1997 election campaign, Peter Mandelson took offence at the *Daily Telegraph*'s role in promoting a Tory attempt to revive the 'Labour tax bombshell' scare which worked so well in 1992. Spotting the paper's political editor, George Jones, entering the morning briefing at Labour HQ on Millbank, he started clapping. 'Stand back. Applause, applause for George Jones, straight from *Newsnight* and [Tory] Central Office,' Mr Mandelson called out. Jones stormed off and wrote an article about the incident next day. Mr Mandelson, ever adept at getting under journalists' skin, melted away before the TV cameras had time to focus.

Campbell knows his boss's mind without having to ask. They are virtually the same age and have sprung from similar backgrounds, provincial middle-class, Oxbridge meritocrats. Inexperience of office bound them together in May 1997. Campbell can be charm itself. Yet there is also a chippiness about Mr Blair's spokesman which is absent in the prime minister himself. He comes across as much more Old Labour, more puritanical, less comfortable with wealthy supporters to whom the prime minister is drawn. Though a vet's son and Cambridge modern languages graduate, Campbell sometimes gives the impression that he was forced to leave school and go down the pit at sixteen. He is not merely a tabloid man, he is actively disdainful towards the broadsheets with their residual notions of balance and objectivity. That is one reason why his pleas to the media to address 'the real agenda', not the trivia, often fall on deaf ears. Everyone remembers Ally and John Major's Y-fronts. On good days he recalls his journalistic career as 'the days when I was only a part-time propagandist'.

Campbell's metamorphosis from Fleet Street drunk to disciplined, driven disciple tempts one to ask if social dysfunction goes with the job. Joe Haines, who also had fights with the lobby on Harold Wilson's behalf in the 1960s and 1970s, could also be chippy. The ex-communist trade-union official, Charlie Whelan, is a lovable Cockney self-caricature, the man who provided Gordon Brown with a warmth (and a focus) sometimes missing from the dour chancellor's public image. He did so with the knuckle-duster, not the velvet glove preferred by Peter Mandelson, who brought clear, strategic thinking to Labour campaigns. 'Peter is the first person I would ring if World War Three broke out. Other people would ask what we should do. Peter would say we must do this, this and this,' Blair once confided. But on a bad day he could deploy those talents with all the manipulative skills and emotional maturity of precocious six-year-old: 'I'm not going to speak to you again, not for three weeks.'

It sounds more fun than it is. By its nature most spinning is dull. Most government policy is dull; most ministers are not Mo Mowlam, with her fetchingly informal charm. The Competition White Paper may be important (it is important!), but it cannot easily compete with page 3 girls or Chris Evans taking Gazza on another binge. Newspapers compete in a shrinking market, in societies where politics has been dethroned as the major determinant of people's lives, and they have abandoned their past commitment to routine political reporting and deference to the people's elect. Their appetite to devour the powerful grows. Spin doctors know this. Their job is to make the sexy unsexy ('Robin is doing a very good job over Kosovo') and the unsexy sexy. In late 1998 Mr Alastair actually inserted such a phrase into a dull Blair speech in the City. It worked! 'Blair Says Sound Public Finance Is Sexy,' declared the *Daily Mail*. Mr Alastair's contempt for the success of that cynical device was palpable and curiously reassuring.

Yet once in a while the twice-daily ritual briefing (as every media studies student now knows, they are repeated at 4 p.m. in the lobby correspondents' room in the Gothic towers of Westminster) takes off as an event. It is confirmed in Rome that Mr Blair did speak to his counterpart, Romano Prodi, about Rupert Murdoch's plans to buy into Italian TV, something the Downing Street spokesman had sidestepped twenty-four hours earlier. Had Mr Blair intervened? No. 'That's crap. If he had a conversation at another head of government's instigation and this conversation was private and confidential, then we do not brief on that,' snaps Mr Alastair. Ill-tempered exchanges follow for three days until Mr Murdoch himself confirms that he had sought information like 'any British business needing help'.

As with other controversies, what had previously been 'a complete joke' now turned out to be true. A similar pattern ran through the Formula One/tobacco sponsorship row, involving Bernie Ecclestone's £1 million (a sum initially dismissed by Labour spinners), and the circumstances of Ron Davies's resignation, when Mr Alastair professed himself as baffled as to key details as reporters were. Next day it transpired that the 'salient facts' he had shared with the media should have been distinguished from less salient gossip provided by a senior policeman – and subsequently unearthed by the press.

Trivial stuff perhaps. But much of the style of a government and the character of its leaders is defined in such terms and always has been, long before TV tempted Tony Blair to do headers with Kevin Keegan or William Hague to wear a baseball cap on a water slide. Napoleon got David to paint him, Ronald Reagan simply got on a horse for the cameras. When, early in 1999, the populist in Mr Blair prompted him to tell ITV's Richard and Judy show that the England football coach should probably be sacked for his remarks about the disabled (he would have ducked their questions on the euro) the spinners insisted his words had been taken out of context.

That is the oldest, lamest defence in the book, no stronger for often being half-true. But even that has its uses. In the same month, the Taoiseach, Bertie Ahern, wanted to help the Unionist leader, David Trimble, win a crucial vote in Belfast. So he gave a tough-talking interview about the need for the IRA to start decommissioning weapons to the London *Sunday Times*, calculating that the paper would put a further pro-Unionist spin on the story. When Sinn Fein erupted, Ahern was able to repudiate the *Sunday Times*'s headline and interpretation. Trimble won his vote. That was the insider gossip anyway, a virtuous example of media manipulation which takes into account the prejudices of the recipient of a favour, in this case an exclusive interview. There again, it may simply have been hindsight. There are times when a spin doctor claims credit at teatime for a headline he was disowning at noon. Failure is an orphan, but a successfully planted story has a large family.

For the spin doctor is not idle when he is not crossing swords with the political editors of the BBC, Channel 4, the *Mail* and the *Sun* over the daily surge of events at the twice-daily lobby. He is anticipating and planning events yet to come and how to shape them to the government's purpose. Working closely with policy-makers (an established trend which the Blairites have accentuated) he will ensure that the prime minister visits a school the day before David Blunkett announces performance-related pay for teachers. He may arrange to leak key passages from the premier's speech – Mr Blunkett having wisely agreed to share his big day – to a pro-education newspaper, perhaps via an obliging political correspondent or (if it is a bit technical) the education correspondent. He may just tell an aide to tip off the *Today* programme, always a useful media bulletin board. If the prime minister has made an important speech or, for old times' sake, a statement to the Commons, his spokesman may ring around selected political reporters – his tormentors a few hours previously – to make sure they understand the line. They may understand all too well and happily run with it because it goes with the paper's editorial grain. The *Sun* famously turned on a sixpence and backed the Greenwich Dome after BSkyB took a strategic decision to invest in the project and/ or in its then patron, Peter Mandelson. Or a reporter may decide to ignore the official line because 'I can't get pro-European stories into the paper.' Or because the spinner spun the story exclusively to the *Daily Mail* yesterday. Or because he or she believes the line to be at odds with the known facts.

But there is always a trade-off. When a newspaper or a reporter asserts their independence of the system, the system pays them back. The 6.30 phone call goes elsewhere, the tip off that a rival has an important exclusive (the spinners may want to wreck it by planting their version elsewhere) does not come. The interview with the boss goes to another channel. 'That newspaper is totally biddable and manipulative,' I once heard Peter Mandelson complain about a Fleet Street broadsheet after it had printed unsceptically a spoon-fed story of which he disapproved. In the long battle between Mr Mandelson and Gordon Brown to be Tony's Best Friend, the then minister without portfolio, no slouch at manipulation himself, had used those same biddable qualities many times. Such is politics. The consolation for exclusion is that fellow MPs, officials and the long-suffering reader can usually spot the prisoners of spin. 'We all know where that tale came from,' MPs will explain in Annie's or the Strangers' Bar. 'He/she is one of Peter's mates.' Or Charlie's, or Alastair's.

Reporters are all prisoners sometimes, because all benefit from the complicity which is always on offer and sometimes just what newspapers think their readers need. As the long years of Conservative rule slowly crumbled and Thatcherism gave way to a less charismatic regime, Labour's increasingly effective assaults upon the government were good copy. The cruel imbalance, a total reversal of the situation in the early eighties, was reinforced by both personnel and technology.

This time it was Labour which had the computers and the 'Excalibur' software to track down every contradictory utterance by the Tories. Bernard Ingham was replaced at Number 10 by mild Gus O'Donnell, an excellent Treasury economist without a jugular instinct, who was followed by a diplomat, Chris Meyer. A more combative figure, Meyer was disinclined to blot his copybook by over-zealous partisanship for a flagging regime. He is now ambassador in Washington. A succession of spinners at Conservative Central Office failed to make up the deficit. Against them were arrayed Messrs Mandelson, Campbell, Whelan and the Zapata-moustachioed David Hill. Now a lobbyist with a big desk, then Labour's communications chief at party HQ on Millbank, the unflappable Hill is proof that successful spin doctors can be utterly normal people. He might have claims to have been Labour's first spin doctor on the strength of the zealous promotional work he did for Roy Hattersley in the late seventies when the young cabinet minister was tipped for greatness. But that honour must go to John Harris, now Lord Harris of Greenwich, who did similar wonders for another ex-future leader, Roy Jenkins, a decade earlier.

Election campaigns and the months which precede them give the voters a chance to see the spin trade in near daylight. They stand at the back of press conferences, watching their elected masters parry media questions, signal warnings and wait to pounce on dissidents. It is what they do most Wednesday afternoons behind the press gallery at Westminster after the weekly Blair–Hague tussle at Question Time. William Safire's description of the post-debate technique in 1984 will serve very well, except for those silk dresses.

Nicholas Jones, the energetic BBC political correspondent (brother of George) who is a three-book historian of spin, lovingly chronicles every twist in Labour's presentation of its pre-1997 economic plans. The size and scope of the windfall tax (usually one for the *FT* or the posh Sundays) ran for months. Not so Gordon Brown's commitment to stick to Ken Clarke's spending plans for the first two years. That was an unexpected Sunday-for-Monday coup. Mr Brown's economic adviser, Ed Balls, turned up in person at the press gallery at Westminster, a rabbit-warren of offices below Big Ben, and successfully talked the story into the page 1 splash at all five London broadsheets. Even that feat was topped next morning when the shadow chancellor appeared on the *Today* programme, ostensibly to discuss those reports. Towards the end of the interview he also announced that he would not raise Middle England's income tax rates if Labour won the coming election. With one economic speech the spinners had dominated the front pages and the news bulletins for two days before the speech was even delivered. That is spin.

Blair and Brown had been engaged in shadow-boxing over the 50p-in-the-£ top rate for months, with Charlie Whelan encouraging some reporters to think that his man, Gordon, was determined to press ahead while others (sometimes Mr Mandelson) repeatedly told their media mates that Tony was equally determined not to risk a repeat of Labour's tax-and-spend disasters in 1992. Fleet Street journalists and their editors pay higher-rate tax. The interest was huge and persistent. Yet at the end of the day it may just have been a put-up job to sustain interest or to heighten the impact of the 'no change' decision when it eventually came. Even now, few people outside the loop are certain.

That too is spin of a high order, manipulating both events and perceptions. But it was achieved at a price. When Mr Alastair nowadays complains about negative, rottweiler journalism and the pack mentality, he should know. Though always a 'part-time propagandist' in his *Mirror* days, he was part of it before he joined Blair. Younger reporters at Westminster are Alastair-inspired, if not trained. When they are not happy to embrace Downing Street's agenda they are happy to take great lumps out of it. Shorter attention spans and the current fashion for adversarial journalism means that the nuances of social security reform can easily get lost. 'Welfare: the Crackdown' declared the *Mail*'s splash headline on the morning before Alistair Darling unveiled his modest plans in early 1999. Why? Because Blair had written an 'exclusive' tough-talking article for the *Mail*. That is spin as well, though in this case the Danegeld failed to keep the *Mail* on side. Next day the paper denounced the package.

In one sense there is nothing new in all this. In his *Brief History of Spin*, a BBC documentary in 1997, the Oxford historian Felipe Fernandez Armesto awarded an honoured place to Maecenas, who helped the Emperor Augustus win and hold power. Genghis Khan also had a man, Changchun, to soften the rough edges of his image as an international statesman. 'He loves kids as well as horses, does Genghis, Trevor, honest he does. Dotes on his grandchildren whenever he gets to see them. But don't ask him about it, he's touchy about his private life, Trevor.'

Yet that misses the point and potency of political manipulation in an age of 100-channel TV and mass marketing, where the difficulty of sorting fact from fiction, illusion from reality, becomes steadily more difficult. What the American analyst Daniel Borstein dubbed a 'pseudo-event', one staged wholly for the benefit of the press or TV, has spawned a vast industry since the Second World War. The consolation for voters is that the balance of evidence suggests that the spin patrol cannot sell a hopeless, inadequate or dishonest candidate or policy for long. In a half-functioning democracy you can, as it were, spin some of the media all the time, all of the media some of the time, but not all of the media all of the time. And the evidence suggests that voters wisely mistrust both sides.

So anxious citizens, fearful of manipulation, should look to spin's failures as well as its successes. The price of being too clever by half can often be immediate. Unable to place Mr Brown's speech on equality on page 1 of the *Guardian* (the Israelis bombed a refugee camp on the same day), Mr Whelan over-egged it for the *Times*. The threat to abolish child benefit for sixteen-to-eighteen-year-olds made page 1, but aroused premature opposition. The policy is yet to be implemented. The boisterous Mr Whelan, 'Lord Bollocks' to some admirers, has gone, a marked man since he stood outside the Red Lion pub in Whitehall trying to spin away the headline on another *Times* report about the euro which went further than was convenient at the time. He had set up the story himself. Peter Mandelson, the prince of spin, has also retired hurt, victim of a miscalculation on that Notting Hill home loan against which he would instantly have warned any colleague wise enough to consult him. David Hill has taken Sir Tim Bell's shilling, and none of the bright young men surrounding William Hague have yet sold him to a wary public. Alastair Campbell alone survives, Monarch of Spin Valley. His combative and wide-ranging role in the public relations battle during Nato's war for Kosovo served both to raise Campbell's reputation and make new enemies. In July 1999 his public attack on the 'sneer squad' at home and on media suscept-ibility to the Milosevic 'lie machine' in Belgrade made valid points. But it also served to illustrate the prickly and intolerant side of the Blair regime, its instinctive authoritarianism. In the very same week Tony Blair had chosen to pick an ill-judged fight with the British Medical Association, the latest enemy within for a regime which felt itself short of worthy, self-defining foes. The Downing St spokes-man's assertion that 'in the face of an aggressive media you some-times need aggression in return' could easily be turned on its head. With Mandelson consigned to the shadows, it had become a lonely position at the top of the media heap and, increasingly, a vulnerable one.

How to Claim a Camel on Expenses

ANONYMOUS

The 'five Ws' young reporters need to know before they write their stories are Who? What? Where? When? and Why? Ian Hislop and Nick Newman wrote a sketch for the *Spitting Image* TV show in which the journalists – three pigs in felt hats with 'Press' cards in them – gave this cliché a satirical twist. Their porkers cried, 'Whose round is it? What are we havin'? Where's the pub? When's it open?' and 'Why don't we have another one?' *Private Eye* had established a journalistic stereotype with their omnipresent and frequently 'tired' correspondent, 'Lunchtime O'Booze', whose idle, nostalgic conclusion to all stories was, 'One thing is certain . . . nothing will ever be the same again.'

Expenses – 'exes' – aren't what they used to be. Papers in the 1990s are lean, mean, money-making machines. No turn-of-the-century management would tolerate – as the 1960s *Express* did – a reporter who, after being found lying in Fleet Street by his editor, piously told his employer, 'I may be lying in the gutter but I am looking at the stars.'

When I arrived at the *Sunday Express* in 1964, the chief reporter, Peter Vane, took me aside and asked to see the first week's expenses I had submitted. Peter was a handsome, gentle, smartly dressed giant with one hardly-worth-mentioning style solecism: hipster trousers tethered beneath a great paunch. He had served in the Royal Navy, and was an experienced journalist who had been the *Sunday Express*'s correspondent in New York in the 1950s. He was always kind and helpful to younger journalists but his expression darkened as he studied copies of my expense sheets, noting items such as 'Bus to West End area, plus return, two shillings', 'Tea, sixpence', and 'Use of public phones, two shillings'. Sighing heavily, he said the exes would not do.

Alarmed to think I had been unmasked as an embezzler after barely a week, I told him the exes were totally accurate. I had made a point of recording all my expenditure while out on stories and writing it down in a special notebook. I agreed the list went on a bit, but I'd had a busy week. He studied me without comment and my unease grew. I began to think not only of being sacked but of being prosecuted for fraud, with sarcastic barristers asking if there was anyone who could vouch for my taking a Number 11 bus from Fleet Street to Sloane Square . . . *No? How unfortunate. Never mind. No doubt you retained the ticket? You didn't? Oh dear . . .* I told Peter I'd be happy to delete some of the journeys and cups of tea in the interests of keeping the management happy. I'd no wish to upset the apple-cart with my free-spending ways . . .

Peter inspected my face carefully, like a poker player assessing his opponent, and smiled faintly. Evidently satisfied of my sincerity, he then told me the expenses were far too low and badly composed. Rule Number One: 'Never travel by bus while on *Sunday Express* inquiries. Always take taxis.' This wasn't extravagance but a question of credibility. If the public thought *Sunday Express* staff reporters traversed London by bus, confidence in the paper might be shaken. Likewise, charging for cups of tea was a terrible mistake. Journalists from the *Sunday Express* on important inquiries did not lounge in Joe Lyons drinking tea among women shoppers. Over the course of a day's inquiries, where time allowed, they had breakfast, morning coffee, lunch, afternoon tea, dinner and sometimes 'late supper plus refreshments'. (We never referred to 'drinks', far less 'alcohol'; it was always 'refreshments'.) He would provide all the figures the management allowed for each repast as well as the range of tips the management considered acceptable.

Now he came to the matter of entertaining contacts. He was disappointed to note that my otherwise exhaustive expenses did not include a lunch, a dinner or 'refreshments' to 'contacts' (always 'contacts', never 'sources' or the even more explicit 'informants'). I did not seem to have spent any money on anyone other than myself. This gave a poor impression. *Sunday Express* reporters were expected to look after those who provided vital information. We were in our way goodwill ambassadors for the paper and, if a receipt was retained, the cost of such entertainment was always reimbursed by an understanding management.

Could I drive a car? Yes. Then get one, he said. A mileage allowance could be charged which covered petrol and general running costs. Make sure it was a car, not a scooter, he said, mentioning a colleague suspected of charging car allowance while swerving around London on a second-hand, 100-miles-to-the-gallon Vespa. Peter grimaced with distaste at the thought of a *Sunday Express* man astride a Vespa while on inquiries.

Ideally, exes should reflect the cost of being a sophisticated man of the world who might over the course of a single day be expected to interrogate a duke or a dustman, or provide high tea for a famous actress. Peter produced for me a model expense sheet – what should be charged for, how much for each and the total I should endeavour not to exceed. It was around £12 a week, three times more than I'd charged, and doesn't sound much now. But it was more than half my take-home salary then.

Had I continued secretly to languish in cafeterias, and use buses, while charging for the full complement of meals, no doubt in time I might have become prosperous. Perhaps there were colleagues who did this secretly, although I never heard of one. Instead we lived up to our exes – riding in taxis, lunching and otherwise entertaining contacts. This is not to say all of the exes we charged were genuine, but an unwritten code – policed by the chief reporter and the news editor – ensured that most fiddling was small-time. Those caught falsifying bills were sacked. They got no protection from the National Union of Journalists, though it was then at the height of its powers. An Oxford-educated political writer was fired after being accused of adding to his expenses after they had been cleared by the signature of editor John Junor. A gossip writer was shown the door after altering the sum on a restaurant receipt. A reporter specializing in religious matters was sacked – 'unfrocked', said guffawing colleagues – after sending all his Christmas cards, including one to the editor, via the *Sunday Express* post room. A political expert was rumoured to claim luncheons via false restaurant receipts while using the money to consort with whores at King's Cross, but he took care never to be caught. Having exes was seen as a privilege not to be abused.

We were not highly paid. In contrast to printers, we were poorly remunerated for unsocial hours and high-pressure work. Exes also served as a bonus. Journalists seen as lazy had their exes cut without appeal. The management knew that large amounts of money were spent on alcohol but it was accepted that reporters on the road, filing from the location of a big story, had to wind down and amuse themselves somehow. We weren't expected to sip a mug of cocoa in a boarding-house and retire early. Even at scenes of great tragedies, there was often great conviviality after first editions had gone. I remember complaints from the burghers of Merthyr Tydfil about journalistic carousing after the 1966 Aberfan disaster nearby. The Red Cow Inn resembled a bar in Sauchiehall Street, Glasgow, on Hogmanay night.

The subject of exes both amuses and angers journalists. We laugh about some extravagant claims but become indignant over those who are seen to be abusing the system. There are no cut-and-dried rules about what is acceptable, or otherwise, but generally the exes of busy, productive, on-the-road journalists are considered more legitimate than those of office-bound colleagues. Foreign correspondents, or journalists on overseas assignments, were granted the greatest leeway. When the *Daily Express* was Fleet Street's pace-setting paper, it had a much envied team of foreign correspondents who were thought to have the most generous exes. They travelled first class, wore Savile Row suits and often seemed more substantial figures than the politicians and diplomats with whom they mixed. When in the 1960s the *Daily Express*'s suave René McColl met George Wallace, the governor of Alabama, his piece began with a passage about how the dapper segregationist inspected his fine silk tie, asking where such a stylish adornment could be obtained. 'Jacques Heim, Paris,' Mr McColl informed him. It was said that when the *Express* accounts department queried a very large bill for 'local transport' during a Middle East military contretemps, the correspondent involved explained that he had hired a 'racing camel' and the final cost included its burial after the beast had rendered magnificent, heart-bursting service to the paper. Some foreign correspondents on big papers contrived to live on their exes and bank their salaries offshore. One famous *Express* figure was said to have transported a racehorse to New York on the *QE2* and when this item of expense was queried by the management he replied that the animal was a much loved family pet. Another is said to have bought a vineyard in South Africa after he was made redundant, doubtless with the help of his exes.

The *Express*'s Brian Vine – a legendary figure who conducted the operation to find Great Train Robber Ronald Biggs in Rio de Janeiro – was for years the kingpin of Fleet Street's Manhattan press corps. A plump, expansive figure in handmade suits, silk shirts and extravagant ties, monocle-wearing Mr Vine kept an apartment in mid-town Manhattan, a house on the tip of Long Island and another property near Palm Beach, Florida. He wore Gucci loafers, drove an enormous Cadillac and considered himself almost a consul-general in New York for the *Daily Express*, as it was then. Economy measures meant little to him, except as a fit subject for jokes. He once told the *maître d'* of the 21 Club, a fashionable dining venue: 'I should like your finest table and your smallest bill.' To other restaurateurs, he would say: 'Bring me your wine list and no cheap stuff, mind!' Keeping Mr Vine in Manhattan was an expensive proposition, but it was worth it. Even rivals conceded he was the best there was – shrewd, energetic, fearless and yet so authoritative that Britain's consul in Rio had calamitously taken him for a Scotland Yard commander during the Ronald Biggs arrest fiasco.

When the *Daily Express* was taken over by a builder, Victor Matthews – later ennobled for his services to the Tories – the atmosphere at the paper changed. Lord Matthews – as he became – considered journalists no different from any other kind of employee and was mystified by their expensive culture of wining and dining. When a well-wisher sent him a copy of a New York magazine carrying a story about his New York correspondent, Brian Vine, his mystification turned to anger. Mr Vine informed the magazine that his paper was now owned by a Cockney businessman happy to retain his expensive services. The impression created was that Mr Matthews considered himself fortunate to have such a distinguished viceroy in Manhattan. The new *Express* proprietor read the piece with growing astonishment and anger. Finally he cried, 'Brian Vine? I've never heard of him!' (This was quite possible. Mr Matthews had asked 'Jack who?' on being introduced to the *Evening Standard*'s famous cartoonist 'Jak'; he had also indicated to the paper's equally celebrated theatre critic, Milton Shulman, that he had never heard of him but was happy to accept editor Charles Wintour's assurances about his stature in theatrical circles.) The New York magazine profile was a serious gaffe by Brian Vine. He was brought home to an undefined position on the paper and left to join his old friend and colleague Sir David English, editor of the *Daily Mail*. Impish Sir David – no slouch on the exes front himself while a foreign correspondent – anointed Mr Vine managing editor, traditionally the executive who vets expenses.

Working as a journalist abroad is always expensive. There's never time to research the most cost-efficient way of travelling. When I was hauled away from a Hollywood party with photographer Paul Harris and a colleague from ITN after our London offices had said there had been a huge earthquake killing thousands in Mexico City, we found all scheduled flights cancelled and had to rent a private Learjet. Since the plane didn't have the range to make Mexico City without refuelling, we landed at a small Mexican city *en route*. Once refuelled, our pilot proffered his fuel credit card. It was refused and an argument ensued. Harris, the ITN man and I got out of the plane. Armed Mexican police and their vehicles now circled the jet. The pilot pleaded with refuellers to get on the phone and validate his card. No dice. They wanted part of the sum in hard cash. Obviously it was a scam. The atmosphere of menace was not lightened by Paul Harris remarking loudly, as if the locals could not understand what he was saying, 'What you've got to remember about police in Mexico is that they don't get salaries as such. They get a uniform and a gun and the rest is up to them.' Finally we had to open our wallets and spread cash out on the wing. A couple of hours later, after reluctant controllers had allowed us to land at Mexico City, there were other unusual expenses. All of us were in evening dress, having come straight from a party. While Harris and I weren't too fussed about touring disaster scenes and overflowing hospitals in tuxedos, the ITN man didn't think he could present his report to camera in a frilly evening shirt.

A newspaper's politics didn't have much bearing on exes. Journalists at the Labour-supporting *Daily Mirror* during the 1970s and 1980s were accustomed to very high levels of exes. The accounts department near the top of the paper's building on Holborn Circus was known as 'the bank in the sky'. Writers queued with 'advance' chits to withdraw spending money. They'd later cover these sums in their exes. It was an imperfect system from a managerial point of view. Those who'd withdrawn money tended to pad their exes so that they didn't end up in debit. Some annual social events – the Derby, Royal Ascot and the Cannes Film Festival among them – were covered extravagantly by the *Mirror*. Editors would join writers and photographers, tables were booked in the best restaurants and there was dusk to dawn carousing. Royal tours abroad were also marked by great extravagance. One royal reporter paid for himself and a local British diplomat travelling with the royal party at a brothel in Acapulco. This was considered money well spent. The diplomat could not have been more helpful subsequently to his press travelling companions.

At the turn of the century, exes aren't what they were. Journalists are better paid now and most managements are intolerant of padded exes. Some are very nitpicking about what are justifiable ones. A *Daily Telegraph* foreign correspondent had his newspaper bill queried recently, although when working abroad it is impossible to function without studying the local press. Increasingly, newspapers are owned by business conglomerates and the emphasis is on tight costs and profits. Lord Beaverbrook's famous remark to a Royal Commission, 'I run the *Daily Express* for influence, not profit', would be unthinkable now. Who would have dreamed that the *Daily Telegraph*, once a family-owned Tory paper, would share a Docklands skyscraper with the Labour-supporting *Mirror*; and that the latter, notwithstanding its lofty new HQ, would no longer run a bank in the sky? Once it was unheard of for journalists to eat sandwiches at their desks, but now it's the norm. This was seen as a tragic development by the late *Evening Standard* cartoonist Raymond Jackson ('Jak'), who could not function without regular refreshments. His office fridge was stuffed with Dom Perignon champagne, his lunches often lasted until 5 p.m., and in the evening he was conveyed around London nightclubs in a hired car, occasionally accompanied by an eclectic collection of bibulous friends which once included the novelist A. N. Wilson and a group of trained assassins from the SAS. Sometimes his guest was his proprietor the 3rd Viscount Rothermere, who was accepted for membership of the actors' Soho drinking club early one morning on the basis that he would play the saxophone he'd recently acquired. Jak would cry 'Order! Order!' as the evening degenerated, but it was the disorder created by tipsy journalists that he loved most of all. The office, of course, picked up the bills.

His regular lunching companion, columnist and ex-editor Sir John Junor, considered Jak's energetic, office-sponsored entertaining utterly necessary. But Sir John tended to be a little more careful with his own exes. He liked to say, 'Never give your guest a sniff of the à la carte menu. Always tell them firmly, "Well, the set lunch looks fine to me."' He checked all bills carefully, refusing to return to a favourite haunt at which he had his own table after accusing a waiter there of bilking a friend of his, the comedian Eric Sykes. But he didn't take penny-pinching too far. He once summoned a travel correspondent who'd listed 'a half-carafe of rosé' on his exes and told him, 'Lewis, no one in their right mind orders half-carafes. And only pooves drink rosé.'

Jak liked to justify his jollifications by saying he had to get out and about among people to see what they looked like, how they behaved and spoke. This was his way of tuning in to the London *Zeitgeist* and he often included the names of his favourite haunts in cartoons. He deplored the modern tendency of journalists to be office-bound, living vicariously via a computer screen. Since the great Docklands diaspora of the 1980s, journalists don't see so much of their rivals, and that's a pity. Having to face one's rivals often kept journalists honest.

How could you face the jeers in El Vino if you'd written palpable nonsense that morning? Besides, you see stories when you are out and about. It is a very poor diarist who lunches at the Ritz, the Garrick or the Ivy and fails to come away with a usable paragraph.

The previously mentioned Brian Vine was in Annabel's nightclub just prior to the Duke of York marrying Fergie. Brian and his merry companions were joined at the bar by Diana and Fergie, who had dressed up as a policewoman and a meter maid to gatecrash the Duke of York's stag party. A great scoop and a capital justification for roistering on exes. Except for the fact that Mr Vine and his friends were so well refreshed they did not recognize their new WPC companions.

Dumbing Up

PEREGRINE WORSTHORNE

Shortly after World War Two – as we have come to call it – the Newspaper Publishers Association persuaded the *Glasgow Herald*, then as now Scotland's leading newspaper, to introduce a two-year training scheme for Oxbridge graduates who wanted to become professional journalists – then, unlike now, a very rare breed – and it was my good fortune to be chosen as the first guinea-pig. But not once throughout the whole two-year period was I allowed to write a single sentence of my own. Instead the job consisted exclusively of sub-editing the writing of others – i.e. checking, and if necessary correcting, their facts, their spelling and their grammar. Even that description somewhat aggrandizes the nature of my task. For at least the first six months it consisted of nothing more – apart from making tea for the other subs – than copying out from the *Radio Times* BBC programmes, the weather reports from the Meteorological Office, the tides and lighting-up times, details about the moon, the sun and the stars and, if I was particularly unlucky, the cattle market prices, all of which duties, as an aspiring foreign correspondent, I found somewhat *infra dig*.

After a few months, faced with such tasks, my concentration began to falter, and there would be letters from readers complaining about having been badly misled about one or other of these by no means unimportant – as I am now prepared to recognize – matters. A particularly large postbag arrived after I had mixed up the time of *Itma* – then the favourite Light Programme comedy series starring Tommy Handley – with that of *Music While You Work*, another Light Programme regular. Needless to say the chief sub-editor, Mr Andy Anderson, a splendid Glaswegian autodidact – who had never disguised his scepticism about the possibility of trying to turn graduates into proper journalists – had his worst suspicions confirmed. Not that this worried me unduly. For in my arrogance I saw no reason at all why clerical proficiency should be regarded as an important condition of journalistic promise. One might well expect some future virtuoso pianist to concern himself with misprints in a concert programme.

Eventually, however, this cavalier attitude to accuracy got me into trouble with my high-flying immediate superior, Alastair Hetherington – who went on to become a legendary editor of the *Manchester Guardian*. Too busy one evening subbing next day's lead story, he had farmed out to me, as a great privilege, the Birthday Honours List. This meant having to check the respective ages of all the new Barons and Knights by looking up their dates of birth in *Who's Who*. Even this piece of research, I am ashamed to say, proved beyond me and I got some of their ages a year out, as Alastair Hetherington furiously pointed out when I came into the office the following afternoon. But instead of apologizing I tried to laugh the matter off. 'So long as I have made them a year younger than they are, we can at least be sure the new Dames won't complain,' I joked. This was too much for Alastair. 'Unless you learn to take accuracy more seriously,' he intoned, 'there will be no future for you in journalism.'

Time to move on, I concluded. Fortunately, before going to the *Glasgow Herald* I had applied to *The Times* for a job and been told to try again in two years' time after completing my apprenticeship in Scotland. Defying Alastair's prediction, this is what I did and was again lucky enough to be taken on as a junior in the foreign subs' room, where I spent another year without being allowed to write a word. But quite early on in my time there my cavalier attitude to accuracy again got me into trouble. One night I was asked to check the spelling of all the Arabic names of members of the Sudanese government, which it was the custom then of *The Times* to give in full – something they don't bother to do nowadays even for the British government itself. 'Get advice from the professor,' the chief foreign sub-editor, Mr Holmes – as he was universally known – advised, which was easier said than done, since on reaching the

specialist corridor on the floor above I found that there were five
different professors to choose from and, without knocking on every
closed door, no way for me to know which was the relevant one
for my purpose. As it was, even after locating the Arab specialist,
Professor Rushbrook Williams, I still managed to misspell the name
of the junior minister of posts, an error soon pointed out by a senior
ex-official of the Sudanese civil service – with the likes of whom
the *Times* readership was then richly endowed.

In disgrace I was called before the editor, William Casey – until
then only an august and distant presence – who gave me much the
same message, only more politely and gently expressed, as I had
been given only a few months earlier by Alastair Hetherington. His
way of putting it went like this: 'Dear boy, *The Times* is a stable
of hacks and a thoroughbred like you will never be at home here.'
Those were the good old days when even a rebuke was dressed up
as a compliment. Unfortunately, as I learned later, this was his
routine circumlocution to all aspirant journalists from Oxbridge
who were judged to lack the necessary gravitas about matters of
fact. Apparently he had used the same language to sack another
such just down, with a starred First in Classics, from Balliol, who
had failed to notice a solecism in the Archbishop of Canterbury's
regular Easter sermon.

In those days, of course, *The Times* was prized all over the world
as the international paper of record. So its obsessional concern
about accuracy was quite understandable. Its readers cared desperately about these details – as if their lives depended upon them, as
indeed in some cases they well might have. Legend had it, for
example, that in the nineteenth century a war between Britain and
France had nearly broken out because of a mistake made in a
dispatch from the Paris correspondent. *The Times* in those days
was not read for entertainment, or to pass the time, but rather for
essential information needed by the then governing and administrative classes to carry out their official duties. How seriously *Times*
colleagues took this responsibility is well illustrated by an exchange
I had with one or two of them at about this time. Apparently the
chair in the subs' room I was sitting in had a few years previously
been occupied by Graham Greene, already a well-known novelist,

whose time there had been given over entirely to checking the stories of others rather than in writing any of his own. 'Was that not a waste of his talents?' I had naïvely inquired, only to be told, in no uncertain terms, that the last thing a serious newspaper like *The Times* wanted on its staff was 'a famous writer of fiction'. I rather doubt whether today's editor would take the same view. More likely he would put an enormous box on the front page announcing 'Top Writer joins *The Times*' in type only marginally smaller than if Graham Greene had been a woman.

Which brings me to my point. The most important qualification for being a journalist when I began fifty years ago was not an ability to write. That was even a disadvantage or a liability, since literary facility could so easily tempt a journalist into embroidering the tale which needed, above all else, to be told plainly and unvarnished. Nor was it only literary facility that aroused suspicion in those days; so also did any tendency towards intellectual sensationalism – i.e. a fondness for paradox, for turning arguments on their head so as better to make a point. Intellectuals, therefore, were frowned upon as well as writers, and not only by *The Times*. For when I went to the *Telegraph*, which was then owned by Michael Berry (later Lord Hartwell), as a leader writer I ran into the same attitudes. There too viewy young men were very much discouraged, particularly if their views were radical. Of course this was partly because the *Telegraph*, then as now, supported the Conservative cause. But another reason, just as important, was that all the quality papers of those days, including the Liberal-minded *Manchester Guardian*, felt a real responsibility for not rocking the ship of state.

Recently I heard Alan Rusbridger, today's *Guardian* editor, say in a public lecture that 'the exposure of corruption in high places is at the very centre of what good journalism is about'. Fifty years ago, no quality newspaper editor, even a radical one like C. P. Scott, Rusbridger's great predecessor, would have said that. Muck-raking was regarded as the role of the gutter press, and unworthy of the quality press. While any hack can expose what the powerful are doing wrong, it takes real experience and skill to discern what they are doing right. Upsetting the apple-cart was easy; any young madcap could do that. Much rarer, and much more valuable, was the journalist with a safe pair of hands who accepted his duty to provide support, as well as criticism, for the powers that be, rightly recognizing that an adversarial stance, while the easiest to take, might not always be the right one.

As for leading articles, these too were intended to help rather than hinder. The king's government had to be carried on, and although this did not preclude constructive criticism, or even partisan criticism, it precluded criticism which might endanger the national interest. Hence the conspiracy agreed upon by all the British papers of the time, left-wing as well as right-wing, to conceal from the public, until the very last moment, Edward VIII's scandalous liaison with Wallis Simpson.

In those days, it has to be remembered, Britain was still a great power, with a great empire, the hub of the universe, with the kind of quality newspapers that such an all-important role required. If you want to know what they read like, start taking the *New York Times*, which is the nearest equivalent today. Nobody would read it for pleasure. It is painfully dull, badly written, prolix and boring, full of details, domestic and foreign – unabridged G7 communiqués, for example – which no contemporary British newspaper would any longer dream of printing, for fear of boring readers into cancelling their subscriptions. Nor does this attention to detail extend only to affairs of state; in reporting a city fire, for example, the *New York Times* gives the names, ages and addresses of all the firemen involved, as I was taught to do fifty years ago on the *Glasgow Herald* – a practice, I am rather sorry to say, long since abandoned. *New York Times* readers, like London *Times* readers in the old days, do not feel they are getting their money's worth unless they are bored, rather as patients do not feel medicine is doing them any good unless it tastes nasty.

Thank heavens that it has no longer been the case here in Britain for many years. For with the end of Britain's Great Power responsibilities, even the most educated newspaper readers began to look for gossip rather than for news, for pleasure rather than for business, for speculation rather than for facts – and above all for human interest stories rather than for public interest stories. As the needs of the consumer have slowly changed, so too have the skills required of the producer, which has suited playboy editors, such as myself, well enough; rather better, in the end, than it has suited *hommes sérieux* like Alastair Hetherington. So personally I have nothing to complain about. But what about the quality of journalism itself?

Well, both tabloids and broadsheets have become incomparably more sophisticated, lively and well written, as well as much more adversarial, mischievous and irresponsible, and this has attracted a wholly different kind of recruit. Something rather similar is now beginning to happen to the modernized, motorized police force. Just as in the old days – but no longer – the prospect of spending boring years on the beat put off most graduates from joining the police force, so the almost equally grim prospect of spending years of plodding clerical work at a subs' table put off all but the most desperate graduates from going into Fleet Street. Today, however, the prospect of starting at once on one of the innumerable gossip columns to which contemporary newspapers, broadsheet as much as tabloid, are now so addicted, and of quite soon moving on to investigative reporting, scandal exposure, adversarial leaders and, in no time at all, a signed column with your photograph at the top, has them queuing up for entry. Journalism, instead of being the Cinderella of the professions, has become the most sought-after of all, attracting a quite disproportionate number of the brightest in the land. At my last reckoning I could count more Fellows of All Souls writing for newspapers than sitting on the Bench or in the House of Commons or in the Treasury. True, Grub Street is not yet paved with as much gold as the streets of the City of London, but it is already paved with much more glitter.

In theory such a staggering influx of the very brightest ought to have had the effect of raising standards, and so far as the quality of writing is concerned, that has indeed happened. But what about the reliability of the news, the accuracy of the reporting, and the balance of the comment: have these improved as well? Most certainly not, and now we come, I fear, to the most serious cause of worry. For the journalist as aspiring writer or intellectual, rather than as hack, has little concern with 'mean' facts, as the poet Coleridge called them, if they get in the way of a more 'comprehens- ive' truth that he is trying to make, either in his stories, if he is a reporter, or in his ideas or arguments, if he is a columnist. For the journalist as writer or intellectual fancies himself as an artist, and an artist by definition is someone who has a skill which enables him to improve on nature, as much in words as in paint, clay or music. There is an element of trickery in art – sublime trickery, at best, but trickery nevertheless.

Not surprisingly, therefore, the journalist as writer-intellectual is not content to report a train accident straight – so many dead and injured; so many carriages wrecked, etc. – but must perforce fill out the picture with a lot of speculation and colour, most of which tells us more about the author – what a good writer he is – than about the train crash. No, that is not quite fair. In the journalism of a great writer, like Rudyard Kipling, the reader, as it happens, will learn a great deal about train crashes in general – the essential truth about train crashes; or in Hazlitt's journalism, the essential truth about boxing; or in Hemingway's, the essential truth about bullfighting. But that is not the same as learning all the boring nitty-gritty details of a minor derailment, say, on the 10.20 from Burnley to Accrington. It is precisely that order of nitty-gritty details that the newspaper hack, as against the writer-intellectual, used to be expected to obtain. But not the newspaper writer-intellectual, who feels it *infra dig.* to relate the facts deadpan, and aspires instead, as investigative reporter, to find the facts behind the facts; as feature writer to add a bit of colour to the facts; as columnist to explain the facts; or as leader writer to say what readers should make of the facts. In so far as today's writer-journalist is willing to deal with the facts at all, they have to be exclusives or scoops – i.e. ones which only he is privy to, or ones which he is the first to reveal. Ordinary, humdrum facts, speeches in the House of Commons or communiqués or official statements are of little interest, except as a scaffolding on which the reporter can build a verbal structure of his own designing. When did you last read a speech – unless it is a British minister or an American president confessing a sexual misadventure – reported verbatim or in full? Nowadays reporters are too busy reading between the lines ever to bother with the lines themselves.

Heaven knows, I ought to know about all this, having been one of the earliest offenders. I remember in the 1960s being dispatched by the *Telegraph* – on which most of my journalist life was happily spent – to report on some *coup d'état* in an African capital. Instead of keeping my eyes open in the bus on the way from the airport to the city centre, I had mine buried in some learned tome about the country's history with a view to showing off my new-found knowledge in the next day's paper. As a result, unlike the tabloid reporters on the bus – few, if any, of whom in those days had a degree – I failed to notice the decapitated corpses lying by the roadside. Doubtless my learned dispatch reached hidden depths about the causes of the crisis lacking in those of my tabloid rivals, but in overlooking the corpses it wholly failed to give the readers the essential here-and-now facts which it was a reporter's duty to include.

The *Daily Telegraph* was not pleased. In those days, under Lord Hartwell, it was a paper which had no time for opinionated reporters, or indeed for opinionated leader or feature writers who were more interested in dazzling than informing. Any 'fine writing' was instantly spiked, much to the outrage of the new generation of university-educated would-be columnists, like Colin Welch and myself, who were then seeking to make names for ourselves. Hence the amount we drank. Denied the opportunity to get high on words, we had resource to alcohol. On the *Manchester Guardian*, as it then was, it was quite otherwise. Indulged with masses of space for literary frills, sociological theories and historical analogies, they used up their *bons mots* in print rather than in pubs.

So what is my point? Quite simply that increasingly in the media today, truth is being sacrificed to art (or at least artfulness); reporting to literature. No, this is not a matter of dumbing down; rather its opposite, dumbing up. Newspapers are far more sophisticated, far cleverer, far better written than they ever were before; incomparably more entertaining and readable. A column in *The Times* by Matthew Parris has even deservedly earned a place in the *New Oxford Book of English Prose* – the first column by a hack ever to do so; and it is only a matter of time before a news story in *The Times* wins a place in the next *Oxford Book of English Fiction*.

But therein lies the danger: the picture of the world presented by the media is both much more beautiful and much more ugly, both much more eye-catching and much more dramatic, both much more simple and much more complicated, than in actuality it ever is. For instead of getting the worm's eye – i.e. the reporter's – view, we are getting the artist's view, which is by definition artificial, in a word, unrealistic, owing more to aesthetics than to ethics, more to the corruptions of style than to the virtues of truth.

No longer do we get politics reported straight; we get a columnist's impression of what happened and a sketch writer's impression of what MPs said, which, needless to say, is very much wittier and cleverer than what the MPs actually said. Even wars now get this personalized coverage, which is why we remember the vainglorious names of those who report them – John Simpson, Kate Adie and Robert Fisk, for example – far more readily than we remember the names of the generals who fought them. Every subject is now personalized. It is no longer the House of Commons which a prime minister reports to, but to Sir David Frost; no longer sex we are told about, but so-and-so's sex; and no longer food and drink in general, but so-and-so's food and drink; and most recently of all, no longer cancer but so-and-so's cancer.

Here the name of the journalist John Pilger must be mentioned, since more than any other British journalist he has made it his life's work to champion the cause of the oppressed. Yet whose name do we remember as a result of his lifetime of compassionate campaigning? John Pilger's own. Indeed he has given a new verb – to pilger – to the English language. This is not to suggest that he set out consciously on an ego trip. But that is what this type of personalized journalism is bound to become, particularly in such skilful hands. For try as he does to make the reader feel the suffering of the victims, about which he can only guess, all he really succeeds in communicating are his own sufferings on behalf of the victims, rather as the famous writer Émile Zola in *J'accuse* did in the Dreyfuss affair, turning the limelight away from the wronged captain on to himself. There is something worrying here: the whole of human life, as much on the grand scale as on the trivial – war, politics, religion, sex, culture, food – all reduced to what can be compressed, not into a sonnet, but into, in effect, a column.

As we all know, when the ancient Chinese wished to lay a curse on an enemy, they said, 'May you live in interesting times.' Given today's media, nobody can any longer escape falling victim to that malediction. Just as the painter excludes from his painting any colour extraneous to his personal vision, so does the contemporary journalist-writer-intellectual filter anything uninteresting from his story, leader, column or feature article. This is not out of base reasons of political bias or anything as humdrum as that. It is out of a kind of artistic integrity – a purist desire to produce as grippingly interesting a piece of writing as his word-processor can compose. If the facts are stranger than fiction, they will be included. But if they are dull – i.e. telling things as, for the most part, they really are – out they will go, for aesthetic reasons. Journalism for journalism's sake, that is the new rule, the highest imperative, under cover of which everything can be excused and justified.

In essence what Mr Murdoch has done to and for journalism towards the end of this century is what Mr Harmsworth (later Lord Northcliffe) did to and for journalism towards the beginning of the century. But whereas Mr Harmsworth pioneered a new journalism designed to meet the needs, aspirations and social insecurities of the first generation blessed by universal state primary and secondary education, Mr Murdoch has done the same for the first generation blessed by near-universal state higher education, today's *Sunday Times*, with its sophisticated blend of debunking national institutions and demythologizing national history, being the equivalent of the much more puerile fun and games favoured, a century earlier, by Mr Harmsworth's *Tit Bits*. But if it is true that a society, like a fish, rots from the head downwards, then I fear this second transformation is going to prove more damaging than the first. For while Mr Harmsworth only exploited the credulity, gullibility and social chippiness of the barely literate masses at the bottom of the pile, Mr Murdoch has done the same for the brainy new élites at the top, first the young Thatcherites and now the young Labourites. Unfortunately, dumb these most certainly are not. If only they were.

On the Terraces

LYNNE TRUSS

In the late 1980s, when I was a magazine literary editor, I met at a book awards dinner an important Fleet Street woman who shared with me her plan for a women's newspaper. We were drunk at the time, I admit, but as I concentrated on not sliding off my chair, I said that in principle it sounded dandy. A women's newspaper. Perhaps I sniffed a job.

'What would you put in it?' I asked.

'That's the wrong question,' she said. 'It's what I would leave out.'

'Ah,' I said, pretending to understand, but still mystified. 'Of course. And you would leave out, um – ?'

'I would leave out,' she said, 'the sport.'

At the time this seemed a thrilling, revolutionary concept. Commercial suicide, admittedly; but at the same time a welcome blast of the emperor's new clothes. Wasn't sport an optional, inessential activity, in journalism as in life? Its presence in newspapers was generally unquestioned; but once examined, was indeed odd. Why did every newspaper include a large and well-illustrated section concerned with a subject that was known to leave at least half of its readers utterly unmoved? Unlike home news, foreign news, features, book reviews, columns or obituaries, sports pages dealt with something that simply and self-evidently didn't matter – except to the sad fanatical types I had heard about who devoured *Wisden* in bed and couldn't form relationships with women. Sport had its own constituency, which was both its weakness and its strength. And if women weren't interested, Sport didn't care.

So I have to say I agreed with that Fleet Street executive. If you took sport out of a newspaper, a great many people would not miss it. This is not to say that it was not good stuff, however. Even as an outsider, I knew there were high standards of writing and production involved in sport sections. The reputation of certain 'great' sports writers down the ages was impressive: at random, I knew of Frank Keating, Hugh McIlvanney, Neville Cardus, C. L. R. James. I assumed, also, that when young men aspired to write like Norman Mailer or Ernest Hemingway, they weren't insane. Literary folk often mentioned *sotto voce* that Booker author Timothy Mo *also wrote about boxing* – and then didn't know what to do with so bizarre an item of information except, of course, pass it on.

Personally, however, I sampled newspaper sports writing only once, during the astonishing Wimbledon career of Andre Agassi in 1991, when he burst on to the scene (as far as English viewers were concerned) and reached the quarter finals. As a lifelong Wimbledon watcher, I assumed that with his thrilling service returns, thrilling charisma and (let's face it) thrilling hairy tum, Agassi would be exciting sports writers as much as he was exciting me. So picture my confusion when I turned to the back page and found on Agassi only a grand piece of the 'Time will prove me right' and 'I believe it was de Tocqueville . . .' variety. The writer seemed to assume there was no television audience, which was strange. It was my first exposure to that hilarious sub-genre of sports writing, the Inflated School; and as I chucked it into the bin, I assumed it would be my last.

Since that strange day of disillusionment, however, I have been obliged to think quite a lot about sports journalism, because without warning in the summer of 1996 I became a sports writer. I didn't want to; it just happened. The European Championships were to be held in England (this was news to me), and *The Times*, for whom I'd been a columnist and television critic for five years, asked me to watch the tournament and write about it from the unusual perspective of a non-fan who was a funny writer and was also (I reluctantly suppose) a woman. I remember my initial reaction was that, having once undertaken colonic irrigation for a women's magazine, I ought to give this football tournament a try as well. I expected to be similarly impressed by the experience.

However, I did recognize at once that it was a clever idea. Gimmicky, but clever. I also thought such an experiment would be good for me. Being by nature the neurotic, conscientious type, I was strongly attracted to the idea of writing for once about a subject of which I knew (and cared) nothing at all. It would be liberating. Somewhat cynically, I reasoned that if my ignorance offended anybody, they wouldn't be anyone I knew. What Sport wanted on this occasion was a kind of Trojan horse, they said, taking new readers into the section. They had plenty of chaps who could say that the ball described a parabola and grazed the crossbar in the fifth minute of extra time. I could just go for the drama and witness history into the bargain. A Trojan horse it was, then. Put me on wheels, boys, I said. And open up those gates.

The fact that I at first saw no point in differentiating between Alan Shearer and Teddy Sheringham – and had never heard of either of them anyway – was actually an asset, I was assured. Thus it was that, feeling strangely undaunted, I set out for my first match (England v. Switzerland) with an old friend who knew about football, and on the train to Wembley urgently told him an astonishing secret I had just learned from reading a supplement. 'Did you know that because England is hosting Euro '96, we didn't have to qualify?' Evidently he did know this already, because my old friend silently looked out of the window and shook his head in horror at the doomed enterprise I had embarked on.

True journalism is, of course, about finding things out. But although, in the world of sport, there are many dark dealings to be revealed – about drugs, primarily; and gambling and corruption – coverage of such issues is not the real business of sports pages, and when they arise they will be investigated by a designated News reporter. So the skill and privilege of a sports journalist, it conveniently struck me from the outset, is to be present at an event, be alert to details, and then either describe its immediate effect, or (a luxury which doesn't always pay off) recollect it in tranquillity, with de Tocqueville open on the desk. Uniquely in journalism, its appeal to the reader is entirely in the presentation of the simple fact: 'I was there; I saw it with my own eyes; it happened once and it will never happen again.'

If the case were otherwise, what could be the possible point of reporting in a newspaper (say) England v. Argentina in the 1998 World Cup? At home, 23·78 million people watched this match on television, and I know for a fact they all saw more of it than I did, because from my excellent vantage point in the press box I missed David Beckham's sending-off and had to wait, in high confusion, for a replay on a monitor. But I was there, nevertheless; I saw it (most of it) with my own eyes; England v. Argentina at Saint Étienne happened once on 30 June 1998 and will never happen again. Imagine having a job where just turning up is virtually all that's required. Sports writers who are discovered to be watching their sports on the telly are, I believe, automatically given the sack.

So in time I dropped the television column and began this strange life of attending sports events, initially through the turnstiles and then finally in the press box. My Trojan horse exploits acquired a new dimension at that stage, because I was now infiltrating not just sport, and sports pages, but the sanctum of (male) sports writers – and unsurprisingly, this time the Trojans were having none of it. Women cannot write about football because they don't play it, they often argue – by the same token, of course, theatre critics start each day with a speech from *Hamlet*, while dance critics squat at the barre. Open hostility was rare, but Brian Glanville, a legendary polyglot aesthetician of the game and erstwhile *Times* football colleague, once said in front of witnesses that had he known his spare press ticket was for me, he'd have torn it up.

Luckily, the younger blokes are less aware of the passage in Leviticus concerning women in press boxes, and sit beside me without the same fear of contamination. I've made at least a dozen friends, and things get easier all the time. But I push my luck occasionally. 'If there's anything you don't understand about the match, just ask,' I said once, by way of breaking the ice, and discovered there were certain things you just don't joke about. Still, I must be grateful to sports writing (particularly football) for bringing out in me a previously unsuspected resilience of character. The good opinion of everybody in the world (including misogynist bigots) I find that I no longer care to have. Actually, the only thing that truly annoys me about the male culture of the sports press is that because complaint and co-operation are against the macho spirit, our rooms are often disgusting and under-equipped, and the first chap to find the sandwiches at half-time puts the tray under his overcoat and eats the lot while blocking the view of the telly.

'Why do you put up with this?' I said repeatedly, at first. 'Why is this so uncivilized? Are we not professionals?' But now I just lower my expectations and learn the dodges. At Coventry, there are five chairs in the press room, and you can't get a coffee before half-time. At Tottenham's White Hart Lane the writing room is the size of a bus shelter, and there's no mobile phone signal, so to send copy electronically you have to wander around outside in the rain waving your computer at the night sky. At Southampton, Coventry, Aston Villa, Arsenal and indeed virtually everywhere else in English football, you are crushed together so tightly that you can't move your arms to make a note. At Wimbledon tennis, you get three seats between five people and are forbidden to write in the canteen, yet nobody tells you where the overspill area is, even if you break down and cry. And so on.

But having said all this, the oddest thing about this macho job is that, paradoxically, *it isn't a job for a man.* True, it's a big pressure to file match reports 'on the whistle'. It's even harder, I suspect, to dictate a report of an evening match for the first edition when (inconveniently) the match has only just begun. Tabloid reporters often have to give marks out of ten and pick a 'man of the match' ten minutes into the second half. Cultivating contacts and staying on the right side of powerful managers such as Alex Ferguson must depend to a large extent on the freemasonry of testosterone. But on the other hand, take the debriefing ritual. No poke at all. After every sporting occasion, managers and players must be politely interviewed for their reactions, and week after week it is such a banal process that often I run away early, so as not to hear a level of questioning that ranges from 'How's the leg, Brian?' to 'Still got hopes for the Cup?' and 'You must have been disappointed by the second half.'

Good grief. At the World Cup '98 in France, FIFA operated a sort of zoo called the 'Mixed Zone' in which journalists could form a scrum around players and literally fight to get quotes – despite the fact that the quotes were still along the lines of 'The leg's better thanks' (in Portuguese), 'Yes, we have hopes for the Cup' (in Dutch) and 'The second half was gutting' (in Italian). I saw Brazil's golden boy Ronaldo from a distance of two feet in the Mixed Zone in Marseilles, which was something to tell the grandchildren ('And did you once see Shelley plain?' I thought romantically, gazing at his tiny ruby ear-ring); but unfortunately other people spotted him, too, and in an alarming moment of bombardment started climbing on top of me with tape-recorders held at arm's length and resting notebooks on my head.

At Wimbledon tennis, the press office helpfully provides a transcript service of these press conferences, so that you can read them at leisure and laugh like drains at the whole futile exercise. I remember an interview with the laconic Pete Sampras, which my colleague Julian Muscat read aloud with relish. 'Pete,' ran a typical question from an American magazine journalist, 'do you think that like, being the best in the world kind of like means that you give it your best or like being the best in the world has its own imperatives, like, or do you just think hey, I'm the best in the world?' Sampras: 'No.'

In newspapers, sport has both the luxury and the responsibility of being a world within a world. It has its own reports, columns, letters, features, interviews. The fact that sport matters not at all (yet more than anything) means that intelligent readers will not only accept a wide spectrum of opinion but can be guaranteed to reach the end of a sports section disappointedly shaking it for more, unable to accept it's all gone. Loving sport is intimately tied up with knowing facts about it; with acquiring expertise; with keeping up with league tables and remembering scores from 1967. 'At forty-one, Mark O'Meara is the oldest man in the modern era to win two major tournaments in the same year' might sound like a so-what sort of fact to the uninitiated, but to a large number of people it is fascinating.

Oddly, though, a daily sports newspaper is still not considered a viable proposition in this country. In 1998, *Mirror* Group Newspapers made a half-sincere attempt to relaunch the *Sporting Life*, going so far as to recruit staff before (inevitably) cancelling the operation. Journalists have become so wary of false promises of an all-sport paper that the big names refuse to be connected with it; perhaps this contributed to the collapse of the venture. But I can't believe there is no market for it in Britain, as there is in France for *L'Équipe*, or in Italy for those *Dello Sport* papers that Brian Glanville carries about. And one should not worry that readers of an all-sport newspaper will suddenly stop being interested in the real news; they have stopped doing that already. Though alarmed to admit it, I can attest that people who are truly hooked on sport do lose appetite for other news. At the time of a Northern Ireland summit, I saw a headline 'Adams in Talks', and not only shamefully assumed the Adams concerned was Tony (of Arsenal), but was actually quite disappointed when I realized my mistake.

But as sport has become increasingly a mainstream topic, I would argue that a story about Tony Adams is increasingly likely to find itself on the front page, in any case. If you are not interested in sport, yet read a broadsheet newspaper, I would guess that it's harder than ever to keep it out of your life. When Ruud Gullit was appointed manager of Newcastle United during the 1997–98 season, the story appeared on virtually all front pages. The sacking of Glenn Hoddle was huge. Football is mainstream pop culture, it lends itself to gloriously colourful photographs, and for those who can't stand it, its coverage in respectable papers has to be accepted, I think, as the most acceptable face of dumbing down. The controversial PR appointment by the International Red Cross of glamorous (and brilliant) French footballer David Ginola in place of Diana, Princess of Wales took many people by surprise – footballers are surely not *that* famous? But time alone will tell.

Probably, the sport-free newspaper has never been more urgently required, and my friend from the book awards should get cracking at once. Separatism is sometimes the only answer, and the engulfing of us all by football remains emphatically a gender issue. Various idealisms are in contention, it seems to me. As part of an insidious backlash against 'political correctness', high-profile male columnists are encouraged to demonstrate their common humanity by banging on about football; if the majority of women readers are self-excluded, they are made to feel uncomfortable about it. This is very bad manners, but I don't see what will stop it, especially as I'm as bad as anybody. When asked by a women's magazine in 1998 to write a humorous feature for footie-widows on tactics to survive the World Cup, I had so little sympathy for this joyless assignment that instead I instructed the readers at length to shape up and take an interest. Grasp the World Cup to your bosom, you'll enjoy it, I promised. What's wrong with you people? I railed. And watch out for David Beckham, I tipped. You won't regret it, trust me.

Sport is actually the engine of a newspaper, I now realize. Take it out and the enterprise coasts for a little and then stops. If life were fair to both men and women, this wouldn't be the case, but it isn't, so it is. Readers absorb all other parts of a newspaper by using different bits of their brain; only when they turn to sport (if they do) do their eyes light up and their hands shake. No wonder sports writers sometimes think so highly of themselves. Without being blessed by any other quality than media accreditation, they witness a slice of history every time they leave the house. What was it de Tocqueville said? Damn, I can't remember. But I was there, and I saw it with my own eyes; which as well as being pure sport, is actually pure journalism.

Mr Justice Cocklecarrot and M'learned Friends

RICHARD INGRAMS

'He had heard that the wheels of justice ground fine, but he had not expected those wheels to be so wobbly, so oddly swivelled in every direction but that of the simple truth.' So John Updike writes of his fictional novelist Henry Bech, who in his latest appearance *Bech at Bay* (1999) finds himself involved in a libel action brought by a big-time Hollywood agent.

It is the reaction of almost any author or journalist when confronted by the law. Accustomed to pursuing truth, albeit in the most general terms, he finds himself involved in quite a different ball-game where truth is not strictly speaking an issue. Now the only important question is – can you prove it?

This question of 'simple truth' and its incompatibility with our legal system was brought home to me most memorably in the final libel action in which I played a part, that brought by Robert Maxwell against *Private Eye* in 1986. In the course of a long and from my point of view disastrous cross-examination I was asked by Maxwell's counsel, Richard Hartley, why I held his client in such low esteem. I was about to reply that it might have something to do with the famous conclusion of the 1971 Department of Trade report into Pergamon which decreed that Maxwell was not a fit person to run a public company when Hartley rose to his feet, puffing with indignation. It was quite clear to the judge, he declared, what I was about to say and it was most improper, not to say irrelevant to the issue in hand. To my surprise, the judge, Mr Justice Simon Brown, agreed. So what was far and away the most important fact about Robert Maxwell was the one fact that could not be mentioned in the courtroom.

A good witness will have his answers carefully prepared in advance and will give no hostages to fortune. But perhaps because in the witness-box what you say is 'privileged', I tended to blurt things out. At a later stage in the Maxwell cross-examination Mr Hartley asked me whether I had ever published anything in *Private Eye* which I knew to be untrue. Yes, I replied, the apologies. The judge was not only furious, he failed completely to understand even when I explained that these were usually inserted for reasons of expedience and were drafted by lawyers (indeed I had a rule that the more grovelling the wording of the apology the better, as the more likely it would be considered insincere by the readers).

Given the ways in which the libel laws are weighted against the defendant – the plaintiff has only to sit quietly and wait for his adversary to prove that what he said was either true or fair comment – the temptation to make an out-of-court settlement, to apologize and pay up, is hard to resist. Even so there is a danger here that if the libel lawyers (of whom there is only a small and select number) get the message that you will always pay them to go away, you will soon be bankrupted. Therefore it is necessary from time to time to make a stand and demonstrate that you are prepared to fight.

In my own experience over many years the result was almost always disastrous, not to say extremely expensive. I think the first time I went to court was with Lord Russell of Liverpool, a lawyer who had made a name for himself by writing books about the Second World War with special emphasis on the horrors and atrocities committed by the Germans and Japanese. It was Peter Cook who, prowling around Soho, noticed that Russell's books were on sale in the dirty bookshops and inspired a piece parodying the trial of Eichmann, then proceeding in Israel, in which 'Lord Liver of Cesspool' was accused of corrupting millions with his salacious descriptions of the horrors of war.

When Russell sued, our lawyers advised that we had a very strong case but recommended that we should not call any witnesses as this would allow our counsel to make the all-important final speech to the jury. So we sat in silence while a parade of Russell's admirers (who included Hugh Trevor-Roper) bore witness to his great merits as one of our leading historians. When after three or four days of this evidence our QC finally rose, he began by reading out a *Times Literary Supplement* review of one of Russell's books. 'It might be thought,' the reviewer had written, 'that this book appeals to the readers' most depraved instincts . . .' There was solemn silence in court broken only by David Hirst, QC for Lord Russell: 'Read out the rest!' he cried. Our man reluctantly did so. 'It might be thought that this book appeals to the readers' most deprived instincts, *but it does not*.' Shortly afterwards the jury awarded Russell £5,000 damages – a huge sum in 1967, especially to a small and struggling magazine. The case had one, for me, beneficial effect. I learned that if your lawyer tells you you have a very strong case, you should immediately try to settle.

Another lesson which I learned from hard experience is that journalists are much more litigious people than, for example, politicians who, whatever their faults, are generally thick-skinned and well accustomed to ridicule and contempt as part of their stock-in-trade. Self-important journalists, however, tend to see themselves as lofty figures, above the fray. 'It is utterly impossible,' William Hazlitt wrote, 'to persuade an editor that he is a nobody.' The consequence is that he reacts very angrily when reminded of the fact. I think that in my time I was sued by almost every Fleet Street editor with the exception of the late Sir John Junor, who went out of his way to be on good terms with *Private Eye*. These litigants were not always content with an apology but made the sort of demands which, if the tables had been turned, would have produced a wealth of high-flown humbug about the threat posed to the freedom of the press. The proprietor of the *Spectator*, for instance, agreed to withdraw his writ on condition that *Private Eye* would not publish any more reports concerning the *Spectator* or its business without the approval in writing of the magazine's editor. The *New Statesman*'s lawyers demanded, as part of the settlement, 'no future mention in your columns or in any form or context whatsoever, of either of our clients [Paul Johnson and Sir Jock Campbell] or any director of our company's clients'. The editor of the *Daily Express*, Mr Derek Marks, demanded an undertaking to the effect that we would not publish 'anything in future which is in any way defamatory of the editor or Beaverbrook Newspapers Ltd'.

The editor who was least able to accept that he was a nobody was Mr Harold Evans, in his day a successful editor of the *Sunday Times* famous for his campaign on behalf of the victims of Thalidomide. So sensitive to criticism was he that he even threatened to sue the *Evening News* columnist Lord Arran; who referred to him as 'Dame Harold Evans' – there being an 'imputation of effeminacy', in his view. After a series of libel actions against *Private Eye*, Evans demanded that neither he nor his wife Tina Brown should ever be mentioned in the magazine again.

One of the most bizarre actions was brought in 1971 by Nora Beloff, the political correspondent of the *Observer*. It was at the time that *Private Eye* was busy exposing the activities of the corrupt architect John Poulson and in particular his association with the then Tory Home Secretary, Reginald Maudling. Following a conversation with Maudling's colleague William Whitelaw, Beloff sent a memo to her editor, the Hon. David Astor, suggesting that she should write a long article in defence of Maudling. Astor approved, but in the meantime the Beloff memo was leaked to Paul Foot at *Private Eye*, who gleefully printed it *in toto*. Beloff then sued, not for libel, but for breach of copyright. It turned out to be about the only court case that I won, but mainly, I think, because the judge realized what a precedent it would create if the court decided that any time a newspaper quoted a confidential memo it was liable for a breach-of-copyright action. It is worth noting that Beloff was supported throughout her litigation by David Astor, the most high-minded editor of his day, who still enjoys the reputation of a distinguished liberal journalist.

Not to be outdone, Beloff then brought a libel action against Auberon Waugh, who in his 'HP Sauce' column had stated that she had been to bed with Harold Wilson and every other member of the cabinet – though, he added, 'no impropriety occurred'. Obviously a joke – but, as I quickly learned, in the solemn atmosphere of a courtroom a casual remark intended to raise a titter in the saloon bar can assume weighty significance. Like Lord Russell, Beloff produced a number of her friends to aver that they had taken

Waugh's comment at its face value, and won damages of £3,000. (Waugh had his revenge when in March 1977 Beloff, then fifty-six, married the *Observer*'s sports writer Clifford Makins. 'Even as I write,' he noted in his diary, 'Clifford Makins is exploring the unimaginable delights of her body, never sweeter than when first sampled. If I had been best man, I would have given Clifford the advice I always give bridegrooms on these occasions: take things gently at first, there's no rush. A new bride should be treated like a new car. Keep her steady in the straight, watch out for warning lights on the ignition and lubrication panels, and when you reckon she's run in, give her all you've got.')

A good example of how someone who sues for libel can end up incurring a great deal more ridicule and notoriety than they ever did from the original article. When I wrote my book *Goldenballs* about the long legal battle that *Private Eye* had with Sir James Goldsmith, I prefaced it with a remark of Dr Johnson's to the same effect – 'few attacks either of ridicule or invective make much noise, but by the help of those that they provoke'. Goldsmith was a classic example of a man who wrecked his career by suing for libel. Before he did so, he was a relatively unknown and very successful entrepreneur who had recently made powerful allies of the prime minister, Harold Wilson, and his secretary Marcia Williams. He might have received a peerage from them (as Joe Kagan did); he might have become a powerful press lord as he later tried to do when he made an unsuccessful bid to buy the *Observer* and the Beaverbrook empire. It was only because he made himself conspicuous as a litigant and, therefore, an enemy of the press that he failed in all these objectives and never really managed to shake off the reputation he acquired at the time of a ruthless tyrant unable to tolerate any criticism. (It was interesting to me how similar in many respects he was to Robert Maxwell. For example, both men, one might have thought, would have better things to do with their time than to sit in a courtroom day after day arguing over the rights and wrongs of a *Private Eye* paragraph. On the contrary, Maxwell and Goldsmith seemed to relish the rigmarole of the courtroom, in this respect resembling those Dickensian figures one or two of whom are always to be found at the back of a court scribbling compulsively and following the legal arguments with rapt attention, even though they cannot understand a word that is being said.)

Goldsmith did the press a service of sorts by showing how the law could be used by a ruthless litigant not just to sue but to destroy a publication and put its editor in prison. The law of criminal libel, used by the state so successfully in days gone by to imprison trouble-making journalists, was thought by many to be a dead duck. But Goldsmith successfully brought it to life when he applied to the court to bring a criminal prosecution against me and my colleague Patrick Marnham over an article linking him with the notorious Lucan murder case of 1974. To the surprise of all the lawyers involved, the judge, Mr Justice Wien, gave the go-ahead, and although Goldsmith eventually dropped the action it resulted in Marnham and myself having to stand in the Number 1 Court at the Old Bailey to be acquitted – a distinction not granted to many journalists.

The other powerful ploy which Goldsmith used was to sue distributors, at the same time promising to drop the action if they agreed to stop selling *Private Eye*. When we brought a counter-action on the grounds that this was an abuse of the legal process the court appeared to side with Goldsmith, despite a minority judgment from Lord Denning who sensibly pointed out that it was impossible for a distributor physically to check all copies of a paper before allowing it to go on sale. Goldsmith in fact stopped suing distributors when he realized that it was getting him a lot of bad publicity in the press, but legally speaking there was nothing to stop him proceeding against more and more of them – thus eventually putting the magazine out of business. That remains the case to this day; nor has there been any repeal of the Criminal Libel law.

Yet in other ways things have changed. For example, journalists, I think, have a lot to be grateful for to Mr George Carman, QC. Whenever I went to court it always seemed as if we were on the defensive and expecting to lose. Judges, with the exception of Lord Denning, only very reluctantly sided with *Private Eye*, an organ they regarded with evident distaste. Even our lawyers at times could not conceal their disapproval (I remember, when a cartoon by Willie Rushton of Randolph Churchill as 'The Great Boar of Suffolk' was complained of, our counsel saying with horror, 'You did not tell us that the pig was excreting!'). Carman was the first lawyer in my experience to go on the attack against a plaintiff, even being prepared on occasion to suggest that he or she was only doing it for the money. Perhaps his greatest service to the press was to destroy Mrs Sonia Sutcliffe, wife of the Yorkshire Ripper, if only because she was one of those people who had made a good living out of libel. Her action against *Private Eye*, which ended with her winning £600,000 damages, was a classic instance of the unpredictable lottery-like nature of the libel laws. A small item, published during my editorship, had criticized various newspapers for practising chequebook journalism with the Ripper's relatives following his conviction. It never crossed anyone's mind to think that the article could be construed as defamatory of Mrs Sutcliffe and the others who had been approached with offers. Nor, when she sued, did anyone think that the courts would seriously consider her claim. Yet the case resulted in what were then the highest damages ever awarded in a libel action. Her subsequent demolition by George Carman, when she later sued the *News of the World*, went a long way not only to deter her from further litigation but in helping to force a change in the law whereby defendants can now appeal against the sum of damages awarded by a jury. (Hitherto, the Courts of Appeal could only order a retrial.) More importantly, Carman forced plaintiffs to think twice about going to court by raising the possibility of a very nasty grilling – with accompanying publicity – once he got them into the witness-box. The result has been a definite lull in the number of libel actions.

As for those litigious journalists, the ancient tradition of 'dog don't eat dog' which once meant that only *Private Eye* contained defamatory matter about Fleet Street has long since been abandoned. Nowadays all newspapers are filled with attacks on other newspapers. The result may be boring for the readers, but again, it could help to stem the tide of writs.

Institutionalized Sexism

AMANDA PLATELL

She was freshly arrived in Fleet Street from the provinces. It had been a hard slog to get there. Her new editor had taken an immediate interest in her writing. She was flattered. After two months he invited her to a dinner meeting at the Savoy River Room. The paper's leading woman writer was leaving and she had her eye on the job. The dinner would provide her with the opportunity to convince her editor that a fresh, or freshly made-up, face was right for the paper.

He immediately took control, ordered the wine without consulting her, spoon-fed her bread-and-butter pudding even though she hated it, then dragged her onto the dance floor. During the slow rendition of 'New York, New York', he held her close, too close. Back at their table, he poured the coffee, the tiny diamonds in his wedding ring picking up the candlelight. The *petits fours* were placed in front of her, along with a set of room keys. She made her excuses and left.

It was not the first time, and it would certainly not be the last, that she was propositioned by a male newspaper boss. And she is not alone. Sexism is institutionalized in newspapers. You only have to look around at the number of women and the positions they hold today in national newspapers to illustrate this. Why is it that there have been so few women editors, are so few female executives, except in the traditional 'women' areas like features, fashion, style, health, magazine supplements? Why is it that so many talented young women leave newspapers in their thirties and move into magazines and freelance work? Why is it that in every paper I have ever worked on, women are usually paid less than men for the same or similar jobs? It is institutionalized sexism.

And yet, if it is so endemic, why are there no cases of sexual discrimination or harassment before the courts? I am not aware of a single case brought to an industrial tribunal on the grounds of sexual discrimination in our business. Unfair dismissal, loss of earnings, constructive dismissal, yes, but not the kind of court cases that have appeared in other traditional male bastions like the police and the armed forces. It is one of the more curious aspects of journalism. There's a lot of sexism about, but women tend to deal with it without feeling the need to go to court. The simple truth appears to be that female journalists have developed survival tactics to deal with the beasts of Fleet Street.

One consolation I can offer young women coming into the business is that the sexual attention stops the moment you become a boss. Whereas power is an aphrodisiac in men, it appears to have the opposite effect for women. I can still clearly remember the moment men I worked with stopped making passes at me – it was the day I became deputy editor of *Today*. Desire was turned off like a tap. I've talked to men about it since and they admit, after a few drinks, that power is attractive in a woman, but even stronger is a feeling of intimidation, a belief that power introduces a no-go area around a woman boss. The fear outweighs any possible attraction.

When it comes to sexism in the workplace, most of the women I have worked with have found ways of rejecting the beast without wounding his pride so badly that they can no longer work together. Recently I overheard a conversation in a bar between a group of young female journalists. They were comparing notes on the lines they had used to reject recent advances from male bosses.

'I'd love to, you're so sexy' (loud giggling), 'but I couldn't do that to your wife' (i.e. I just might tell her).

'I adore your mind' (shorthand for 'no one could adore that body': more giggling), 'but my boyfriend works for a rival newspaper.'

'Once would never be enough for me, I'd want you all the time, all to myself' (heavy hint at stalker tendencies and the impossibility of a one-night fling).

'I don't screw the boss.'

The truth is, sexism is so institutionalized in newspapers that it is difficult to know where or how to begin to change it. And, ironically, some of the greatest perpetrators of the inequalities are women – more of which later.

When I started out on my first newspaper, complete with an honours degree in politics and philosophy, my news editor simply laughed when, after almost a year, I asked to be taken off the 'beauty beat'. It was twenty years ago, but things have not changed as much as one would have expected. Of the yearly intake of cadet journalists for the *West Australian* and the Perth *Daily News*, half were men and half women. It was what we now regard as a traditional newspaper operation: presses in the basement of the building, ageing typewriters chained to trolleys where we churned out copy on 'take'-sized pieces of paper which travelled down the length of the editorial floor in a mechanical loop. The reporters were located in the middle of a long floor, the chief sub/night editor reigning supreme at one end of the room, the news editor at the other, their subordinates lined up in a row on either side of them forming a formidable inverted U-shape, sinister cubicles with yellowing glass walls acting as offices for the many executives. The terms open-plan, pods and clusters were unheard of then. If the chief sub or the news editor wanted to bawl you out over a story, your name was bellowed and you had to run the gauntlet and 'take like a man' a very public dressing down. Far more terrifying was being sent down to change a story on the stone. The printers would line the narrow walkway between the hissing and groaning machinery, clanging together anything metal they could lay their hands on, shouting 'hot metal' at the woman reporter.

Within a couple of years the male cadets had secured jobs in politics, news or subbing, the females were flourishing doing animal or human interest stories, the weather, and fashion. At least we could dream of getting a job as a junior court reporter – crimes of passion, family disputes, noisy neighbours – 'girls' work'. Unperturbed (to be honest I was terrified), I approached my news editor again and said I was interested in politics and wanted to cut my teeth on a local government round. He laughed, but not before gathering all the senior reporters around him, all male, to ridicule me first. Almost a year later, after relentless nagging, he gave me

Wanneroo Council to cover: more than an hour's drive out into the bush from the office (most of the roads were then dirt tracks), no mobile phone for security. If you wanted to play with the boys, you had to prove you were as tough as they were.

The meetings usually ended after midnight, I'd get home around two or three and then be back in the office at 6.30 a.m. to transcribe the morning radio news. I was being punished. But someone smiled on me, and Wanneroo turned out to be a corrupt council, providing me with a run of spectacular splashes.

I expected to leave that level of sexism behind when I left Australia – some say the birthplace of the chauvinist – and came to Fleet Street. It proved a false hope. Arriving in London with a backpack,, not a lot of money and a desire to work here for perhaps six months, maybe a year, then go home, I had no contacts and an inferiority complex the size of Australia.

Early one morning I went down to the local newsagent with a pad and pencil and wrote down all the names and addresses of the national newspapers, and several of the big magazines. Back at my digs I proceeded to write to every editor, news editor, features editor and chief sub asking for a job, or shifts. Before leaving Australia I had spent six months on the Sydney *Sun* learning to sub with new technology, as it was then known. I had heard somewhere that it was easier to get a job subbing than writing in London. It was a good time to have arrived, the middle of summer, and there was a lot of casual holiday work going. My first shift was as a features sub on the *Sunday Express*. It was my first bit of luck in this town, but it was not to be my last. Even then, the only copy I seemed to get was 'women's work'.

But when I talk about sexist behaviour in the business today, I'm not simply being politically correct. Whenever men and women work together, especially in fast, stressful environments, there will be flirtations, harmless banter, that offend no one. It may not appear so to the outside world, but journalists are a passionate lot. Often obsessive, compulsive risk-takers, they live on adrenaline and the excitement of the chase of a story. Daily deadlines create an urgency, a tension, that I'd be surprised to find in your average dentist's or accountant's office.

Many of the personalities in a newspaper are larger than life, somehow brighter, more appealing. I would estimate that at any given time about a seventh of the staff of any paper I've worked on were having sex with someone in the office and double that number were contemplating it. Romances happen, affairs happen.

So it is important not to confuse sex between consenting adults, of which there is a great deal in newspapers, with sexism, of which there is also a great deal in newspapers. By recognizing that sexism is institutionalized does not mean I'm a man-hater. Far from it. Many of my greatest friends and allies, and certainly all of my mentors, have been men. Nor does the fact that sexism exists in any way imply that all men are sexist. I have learned more from clever, generous men than I could ever measure.

The institutionalized sexism I'm referring to is not about sex and flirting, it's about pigeonholing women journalists, denying equality of pay and conditions and opportunities, demeaning them and making assumptions about them. It is about a widespread and inherent belief by some men that women can't quite cut it, that newspapers are a man's world, that women are only good for one thing – 'features' – and that ritual humiliation is a way of keeping the girls in their place.

Like the news editor who insisted on calling me up in front of the all-male back bench to debrief him on a story and repeatedly tried to make me sit on his lap to do it. It amused him, anyway. Or my newly appointed (not by me) deputy who, during our first meeting to discuss the job, said: 'If you think I'm taking orders from a fucking woman, you've got another think coming.' Funny how some things stick in your mind. He didn't have to take orders from a 'fucking woman' for long. He lasted two months. Or the editor who gave me a big promotion but refused to give me salary parity with the male executives who were working beneath me on the basis that I was single and didn't need the money. 'You don't have a wife and kids to support,' he argued.

However, the truth is that some of the worst sexists I have encountered have been women. One might have expected solidarity between women to survive when one woman breaks through the male bastions: it seldom does. My belief is that, on the fight up, many women become so damaged, so toughened, that they cease to behave like women. I know how difficult it is to resist that process because I've been subjected to the same pressures myself, and I'm sure that some people I've worked with at times in my career might say I had been affected. I've lost my way at times, been hurt and toughened by the passage, but I've always consciously tried to resist the inherent defeminization. I admit I've had an easier time of it than the female journalists who came before me. They had the toughest journey. But the sad truth is that some women editors treat other women worse than their male counterparts.

Experience has taught me that there are five basic types of women bosses in journalism. The first is what I call the USP Woman, more often than not found in the 'red tops' – the *Sun* and the *Mirror*. Fundamentally, she believes that her uniqueness is more a function of her femaleness than of her journalistic talent. Insecure and terrified of being 'found out', she ensures there are no senior women to detract from her, except in features. She believes her Unique Selling Point is the fact that she's a woman among men, first among unequals, and she's damned if any other woman will be allowed to weaken that position.

The second type is what I affectionately call Biggus Dickus. One gets the impression that this type of woman was so badly shredded on her way through the glass ceiling that she's had to undergo massive emotional surgery afterwards. With big hair and big make-up, she tends towards suits with shoulder pads and is unlikely to be afraid of parading her cleavage. In behavioural terms, she has reconstructed herself as a man. Distinctly mid-market and middle England, she shouts, she struts, she brags, she bullies. It's all about outperforming the male, a savage show of supreme penis power. Her role models are Andrew Neil and Jeremy Paxman, toughness and talent personified.

My third category is the Transsexual. This woman decides at an early stage she will not play the office cleavage game. She favours grey or black trouser suits, white, slightly masculine shirts; she keeps her hair short and wears no make-up. There is something rather beguiling about her, the essential femininity that comes through when a clever woman is forced to conceal her sex – not unlike Viola in *Twelfth Night*. She's usually brighter than the men around her, but considers herself intellectually superior to any woman who wears lipstick. She is not fond of women, prefers the company of men and only feels at home in what she considers the intellectual superiority of the broadsheets.

Fourth is the Free-Market Feminist. She never stops reminding you of her impeccable left-wing credentials and is now slavishly New Labour. She purports to care about women and advancing their cause. The funny thing is, you actually believe her until you take a good look around and see that there is not a single female executive she has appointed – except in features! It's all about spin and perception, not reality. On the way up, the sisterhood is all-important, women supporting each other in the male-dominated world, climbing the ladder two, three, four abreast. As the ladder narrows towards the top, 'one for all and all for one' quickly becomes 'all for me'. The Free-Market Feminist moves from market to market. Principles like the redistribution of wealth are quickly abandoned once she is in power and instead she embraces the free market, with herself as the prize commodity. Her principles are as expedient as her loyalty.

The fifth, the most recent and fast-growing category, is the Third Wave Woman. She is not to be mistaken for the Third Way Woman. There is a lot new but little that is calculating about her. Third Wave Women are the new sisters. They are different from all the above categories because they actually *like* women, and trust them, and feel comfortable around them. They are more likely to wear a Wonderbra than to have considered burning one, yet they embrace many core feminist principles. They believe in basques and basking in each other's success. They network like men and support each other professionally and personally. They are genuinely grateful that ITV's *News at Ten* has been moved as it no longer clashes with *Sex and the City*. The problem is, the Third Wave Women also want a life – a partner, probably a husband and maybe children, and the excitement and appeal of life in the jungle quickly fades. The desire to have a life can prove a severe career handicap, not just for women, but for men as well. Declaring and pursuing the Life option will usually mean you will end up – you guessed it – in features.

A young trainee came up to me recently and asked me if I could give her any advice. I told her what my father, also a journalist and still working part-time at seventy-two, had told me twenty-one years ago. Always dress as though you were going to a state funeral (sometimes you'll be the only one presentable enough to send) and never say 'no' to a job, at least until you're in a position to do so. I added that the other vital ingredients are courage, the ability to act as though you know what you're doing even if you're terrified, and a sense of humour.

The best advice I was ever given was by a gentle and generous Scottish sub late one night. It was near the end of a twelve-hour shift and I was getting the usual ribbing for my accent from the back bench. Normally I could laugh it off, but that night I was tired beyond humour. Frank looked up when I stomped back to my desk, took a long drag on his pipe and said: 'Amanda, don't change anything about you. You've got two things going for you right now – one you're a woman and, two, you're Australian. That gives you the advantage, because everyone will assume you're stupid.'

Death and the Press

JAMES FERGUSSON

Who died in January 1731? The *Gentleman's Magazine* tells us. Sir Peter Verdoen, late Lord Mayor of Dublin; Mr Oliver Savigny, the King's Cutler; Mr William Whorwood, 'Alphabet-keeper, to the Foreign Post-Office'; Mr Morris, the Prince of Wales's coach-maker; another Mr Morris, '*Peruke-maker* in *Pall-mall*, hanged himself, being *Lunatick*'; Viscount Falkland, in France, 'buried at the Church of *St Sulpice* in *Paris*'; Mr Trunket, 'a Perfumer without *Temple-Bar*, well known at *New-Market*'; Mr William Taverner, Proctor, 'at his House in *Doctor's Commons*. He was the son of Mr Jer. Taverner, Face-painter, *remarkably honest in his Business, and Author of the following plays*, viz. The faithful Bride of *Canada*; the Maid the Mistress; the female Advocates, *or*, the Fanatick Stock-jobbers'; and Robert Bristow, aged 105, at Stamford, who 'had lost his Hearing, but had his Sight and other Senses to the last'.

There is something irresistible about lists of deaths. Death confers dignity on a name, however obscure. As war memorials recall autumn after autumn of Remembrance Sundays, their rolls of honour like a litany of falling leaves, so the columns of newspaper death notices put substance to the last mysterious rite of passage. 'Births, Marriages and Deaths' in the daily newspaper are now one of its few unique selling points; they survive as a reason longstanding readers won't change their paper – they stand for a private reality larger than that of front-page stories, of wars and earthquakes, economic booms and changes of government.

Edward Cave, a.k.a. 'Sylvanus Urban', the founder of the *Gentleman's Magazine*, recognized that the anchor of all news is in such local 'domestick' occurrence. In issuing his first monthly number in January 1731, he declared the magazine's purpose as 'to give Monthly a View of all the Pieces of Wit, Humour, or Intelligence, daily offer'd to the Publick in the News-papers, (which of late are so multiply'd, as to render it impossible, unless a man makes it a business, to consult them all) and in the *next* place we shall join therewith some other matters of Use or Amusement that will be communicated to us'.

That first number digests and collects into forty-two pages of text an astonishing volume of information, including, besides foreign bulletins, a poetry section and gardening column, lists of commodity prices, births, marriages, deaths, burials and 'casualties', promotions (civil, military and ecclesiastic) and appointments of sheriffs for the ensuing year. We learn that, of the 1,969 burials between 28 December and 27 January, 992 were male, 977 female, 709 died under the age of two and a further 106 between two and five. The price of coal was 27s. to 28s. 6d. 'per Chaldron', sherry £28–£30 'per T', opium 11s. a pound. This eye for small detail marked the *Gentleman's Magazine* out and makes it as fascinating, and important, an exhibit of historical evidence as it proved, in its time, entertaining and useful to its readers. Later in the century, in 1778, it fell into the hands of John Nichols, who set out in particular to expand the calendar of deaths of 'Eminent Persons', some of whom were simply noted, others more elaborately treated, into a full-blooded obituaries column. In doing so he established a standard of necrology for modern times.

Thus, in a random month in 1791, the year in which Nichols fully took over the editorship, the Deaths column – now entitled 'Obituary of considerable Persons; with Biographical Anecdotes' and running to eight pages of close type – includes Josiah Clark, 92, of Northampton, Massachusetts, one of six long-living sons who between them left 1,158 descendants, 925 still living; Mrs Mary Minchin, widow of 'The Honest Miller', the largest man in Winchester, bequeathing her fortune to the Winchester College cook; Robert Smith, 82, of Lincolnshire, for thirty-eight years a sexton, 'during which time he had buried about 1500 of his fellow-creatures'; Dr Barrow, of Lancaster, in his sixtieth year, who leant too far out of his bedroom to read the time on the town clock; Alexander Gerrard, a barrister attending the York assizes, who fatally mistook his window-curtain for his bed-curtain; and James Heath, 76, 'commonly distinguished by the appellation of "The Wild-one"', and well known, for many years, as one of the most formidable poachers in the kingdom', who never slept in a bed but out in the fields, in all weathers. 'Almost his whole body was covered with hair of a considerable length; and though he never wore his cloaths buttoned in the coldest weather, he never experienced a day's illness in the course of his life.'

Most significant of all, sandwiched in fate's calendar between Mr (Isaac) D'Israeli's mother-in-law and, over his breakfast coffee, Monsieur de Blossette, 'who had written very ingeniously on the ascent, dilation, and diffusion of vapours, as well as on the phaeno-mena of comets, and other subjects worthy a contemplative mind', dies, on 2 March 1791, 'of a gradual decay', the Reverend John Wesley, M.A., 'one of the most extraordinary characters this or any age ever produced'. Some 2,500 words are devoted to the founder of Methodism's passing, judicious, detailed, rather moving, a model of piety but observant of all narrative proprieties. 'Where much good is done, we should not mark every little excess,' opines the anonymous obituarist,

The great point in which his name and mission will be honoured is this: he directed his labours towards those who had no instructor; to the highways, and hedges; to the mines in Cornwall, and the colliers in Kingswood. These unhappy creatures married and buried amongst them-selves, and often committed murders with impunity, before the Methodists sprang up. By the humane and active endeavours of him and his brother Charles, a sense of decency, morals, and religion, was introduced into the lowest class of mankind; the ignorant were instructed; the wretched relieved; and the abandoned reclaimed.

In a single short obituary notice – Monsieur de Blossette or 'The Wild-one' – is condensed the material for a whole biography; in the more extended *éloge*, such as Wesley's, are the distinct outlines of one. The obituary is the first stab at biography – for many subjects the only one; a first, brisk judgement in the heat of news. As such it has importance in the historical record; it is part of that 'newspaper of record' tradition to which newspapers and periodicals such as the *Gentleman's Magazine* aspired, a tradition suddenly defunct in an age when newspapers have lost their self-confidence and the duty to inform defers cravenly to the duty to entertain. It is an especially exacting form of news-gathering. On the one hand, it involves more original labour than a running story; on the other, it is examined by more rigorous standards, from another time. The grieving relative or friend makes an old-fashioned, unforgiving reader.

The British have a genuine talent for the small biography, whether in the crisp digest form of the *Gentleman's Magazine* or in the formalized *Dictionary of National Biography*, perhaps the fastest and most successful such dictionary ever produced. Whereas the *Australian Dictionary of Biography*, say, with a start-date of 1788, still after thirty years lingers halfway through the period 1940–80, the *DNB* covered a much longer period, from the earliest historical times to 1900, in little over half the time. Leslie Stephen was appointed editor in 1882; the first volume appeared in January 1885; the last, under the stewardship of Stephen's assistant and later successor Sidney Lee, in June 1900, followed by three catch-up supplements completed in 1901. The dictionary ran to 27,236 subjects, from monarchs and statesmen to – most usefully in the view of many of its readers – the 'minute names', as Stephen called them, 'the rank and file of the great army'. The officers and *haut cadre*, the general staff and deskmen of Whitehall driving their mahogany battleships, are often spoilt for attention by historians and biographers; the many foot-soldiers who deserve to be remembered perhaps for just one remarkable thing are the very stuff of the *DNB* – those, said Sidney Lee, summing up its achievement, 'whose career presents any feature which justifies its preservation from oblivion'. As it is with the *DNB*, so it is 100 years later with newspaper obituaries, which have enjoyed a great flowering at the end of the twentieth century.

After the Nichols family – enthusiastic obituarists over three generations – relinquished control of the *Gentleman's Magazine* in the 1850s, it was a younger, daily newspaper, *The Times* (founded 1785), that took over the baton. For many years it was the only place to be seen dead in. In its heyday, the newspaper was both an alternative government, the Thunderer delivering its message through its leading articles straight to Downing Street, and a university of the fourth estate, commanding through its various supplements (*The Times Literary Supplement* was first published in 1902, *The Times Educational Supplement* in 1910) a huge battery of specialist expertise.

It is a commonplace among modern newspaper readers that all obituaries are written in advance, that all subjects lucky or worthy enough to be included have first been set down on paper, like Leigh Hunt's Abou Ben Adhem, by a recording angel. If this ever approached being true, it was in the balmy spring of *The Times*'s obituaries, when the days of unattributed journalism were at their apogee, when *The Times Literary Supplement*'s reviews were unsigned and the news-page by-line 'By Our Own Correspondent' made you feel safe as your house. With its retro, newsless front pages (giving pride of place, it must be noted, to its celebrated Births, Marriages and Deaths columns), *The Times* deployed an effortless authority; it was, like the *Gentleman's Magazine* of old, a paper of record, somehow a cut above the rest. When people decried the muck-rakers of journalism, they excluded *The Times*; Room 2, the subs' room that Graham Greene joined in 1926, almost straight down from Oxford, was still a place for gentlemen. The fire burned slowly in the grate; no one was sacked or ever resigned.

As 'top people' read the paper, in the words of its exclusive slogan, so top people organized obituaries of other top people for its obituaries column. *The Times* was an establishment paper in instinct and practice: the Civil Service looked after its own, Oxford and Cambridge Universities appointed special obituaries 'scouts' to organize final aftercare. The inherent problem of commissioning obituaries of subjects in advance is that what many newspapers designate with medical-school humour the 'morgue' will require constant housework; notices go out-of-date for want of new facts or simply fade in the sun – as time passes, all the bases on which they are written shift and they become illegible in a new age. While *The Times* was fat and well provided for, while Room 2 was still populated by gentlemen, all was well; the recording and re-recording angels went about their tasks, the anonymous experts on *The Times Literary Supplement* ran their eyes over old copy, the majestic periods of unsigned journalism (occasionally varied by 'A Friend Writes' or a set of inscrutable initials) bade an imperious, and impressive, *Ave atque vale*. The editor took an active interest – the great Geoffrey Dawson is captured by Lady Cynthia Asquith in her diaries, sitting in his office late at night during the First World War, polishing up his cabinet ministers.

During that golden age of journalistic anonymity, before *The Times* changed ('The days when *The Times* could be satisfied with addressing a small national élite are gone,' announced the last of the Astors' editors, Sir William Haley), before in 1966 it moved its Deaths column off the front page and 'Our Own Correspondent' was allowed the vanity of a personal identity, the paper's obituaries were matchless. Indeed, no other paper even competed. But unsigned journalism is a craft, like any other, and, as the various elements of the paper succumbed to the author byline, so obituaries, with leading articles now the last survivors of the old style, began to suffer. Fewer people could write in that formal mandarin; and the commitment to the 'morgue', so necessary for the column's success, diminished. *Cognoscenti* of antique *Times* obituaries can almost put a date to this moment – a point in any pre-prepared piece when the official narrative stops, like the stair in R. L. Stevenson's house of Shaws, and a later writer or sub-editor plummets willy-nilly to the end.

The *Independent* was not the first British broadsheet to carry signed obituaries – the *Guardian*, for many years after his death, used to carry impeccable signed appreciations by Neville Cardus as occasional pieces on its news pages – but it was the first to establish them; the first to set up a regular daily space for them. The first 'serious' national newspaper to be founded in more than a hundred years, conceived in 1985 and launched in October 1986, it presented itself as a traditional broadsheet with a difference – what its founding editor, Andreas Whittam-Smith, liked to call 'classic with a twist'. Where *The Times* had, in the view of its critics, gone downmarket, the *Independent* would go upmarket; it would seize the high ground but with aplomb. The 'independence' of its title would extend to all areas of the newspaper – to politics, writing, method, layout, photography. It was an inspiring project.

If all aspects of the newspaper were to be rethought, then what about obituaries? If you were going to start an obituaries column from scratch, what would you do? When the question was put to me in May 1986, the answer seemed obvious. There was no point in competing with *The Times* on its own territory – it had been going too long, its bank of advance obituaries was too famously large. The *Independent* should do something different: it should seek a new audience, write a new agenda. There should be transparency. Obituaries should be signed. They should be written not as a journalistic exercise (as miscellaneous politicians would once have been gathered for the 'morgue' by apprentices at a loose end) but by people who knew what they were talking about, peers of the subject or specialists in the field. This would give them historic worth and veracity.

They should be *written*, too, rather than constructed (too often an obituary was nothing more than a *Who's Who* entry with mortar thrown in the cracks); they should answer the big questions (why will this person be remembered, or why does this person deserve to be remembered? what was he or she like?) and not stumble in a morass of chronology (the elements of which would anyway be provided as a free-standing tailpiece). This would make them entertaining: material for the general reader, not just those of a certain age, not just old boys' news.

In the same spirit, they should be boldly illustrated. The best you could hope for in the old days was a simple headshot of the deceased. Why not treat obituaries like any other feature article: if an artist died, why not show one of his or her paintings, if an architect, a building, if an archaeologist a dig, if a politician a dashing action photograph from the archive? A boxer landing a punch, a lion-tamer putting a big cat through its paces, a clarinettist in full blow: such images had traditionally lit up other pages of the paper – why never the obituaries?

Further, who should be eligible for an obituary? When *The Times* had the field to itself, the 'top people', that 'small national élite', knew who they were. They were the establishment. There was a clear system of ranking: civil servants, diplomats, armed forces up to a certain level, peers of whatever level, MPs, Oxbridge but not (generally) 'redbrick' dons, public school headmasters, chairmen of companies (a top 100 perhaps), gentlemen cricketers. Much the same criteria applied as still apply for admission to *Who's Who*: wreathed in secrecy, but neither unpredictable nor intrinsically interesting. Surely a new newspaper could be less parochial, more open-minded, find its own 'minute names', in Leslie Stephen's words, outside the pages of *Kelly's Handbook* and the Diplomatic List?

In the same month, July 1986, as I joined the *Independent* as its obituaries editor, Hugh Montgomery-Massingberd joined the obituaries staff of the *Daily Telegraph*, to become obituaries editor himself five months later. We reckoned that we were the first British obituaries editors ever to have volunteered for the job. (Coming each from odd professional backgrounds, he from *Burke's Peerage*, I from a large general antiquarian bookseller's in Oxford, we could be mocked; but as qualifications for the oddball and ancient historical art of obituary-making they were on a par with any.) If I took my inspiration from the crisp vigour of the *Gentleman's Magazine* and the efficient, surprising and perdurable *DNB*, Massingberd found his in the gloriously anecdotal *Lives* of the seventeenth-century antiquary John Aubrey.

Where the *Independent* sought to do something new, to open up and demystify the obituary, to give it, by attributing authorship, value and plurality of voice, the *Telegraph* under Massingberd (who retired in 1994) set out to subvert the traditional obituary from within. Massingberd's personal enthusiasms for long lineages, powerful actresses and bizarre country-house eccentrics powerfully infected his columns and their (still anonymous) contributors; a sudden vigour, a certain sepulchral hilarity, could be detected amid the *Telegraph*'s previously sedate valedictions. When once a brief parting shot was fired over some gallant major (standard obituary fare always for the *Telegraph*), now scarcely a day would pass without a lengthy encomium of another man who won the war (a 'moustache' in *Telegraph* parlance), complete with fantastic nickname, his citation(s) for valour in full and a few fruity asides. Once upon a time the activities of a deplorable peer would have been so downplayed by *The Times* that only a professional code-breaker with the wind behind him could have descried them; now the *Telegraph* treated them so rumbustiously that the obituary could seem like an elaborate practical joke. The third Lord Moynihan (a low-life brothel-keeper eligible for an obituary only by virtue of title) endured a vintage come-uppance in 1991. 'If there was a guiding principle to Moynihan's life,' the *Telegraph* reported, 'it was to be found on his office wall in Manila, where a brass plaque bore the legend, "Of the 36 ways of avoiding disaster, running away is the best."'

The Massingberd obituary revelled in the subversion of euphemism. For many readers, one of the charms of obituaries had been the deliberate opacity of their language. Devotees of the *Times* and *Telegraph* crosswords rapidly learned the cryptic language of the clues; for the uninitiated, 'obituary-ese' was just as devious and misleading: 'vivacious' meant 'drunk', 'fond of women' implied strings of lovers, and so on. 'He never married' closed an obituary with numbing finality. Did it, or did it not, mean he was a hyperactive homosexual? On the occasions when *The Times*, for example, broke its own rules and declared Robert Helpmann to be 'a proselytizing homosexual', there was outrage. No one was used to such outright language in an obituary; moreover, since it was contentious (Helpmann's friends argued strenuously about the 'proselytizing'), it seemed insulting. As the obituary was unsigned, there was no one to argue with.

With the advent of the signed obituary, taken up formally by the *Guardian* with its 1988 redesign and since adopted to various degrees by papers all the way from Edinburgh to Melbourne, the two schools are often encouraged each to argue its merits. The old school will say that signed obituaries are by their nature flawed, for they represent only one person's knowledge and that person will, by appending his or her signature, be so compromised that nothing will come from his or her pen but gush and tribute; that the obituary will be written with an eye for the family of the subject, not the regular reader or a notional posterity. That is certainly a danger; there is nothing worse than the 'he was marvellous' tribute and no one will ever want to know that 'he will be much missed'. But the other school will argue that, if this happens, it is the fault of the editor, not a collapse of the principle.

The same school will contend that there are few obituaries more worthless than the third-rate unsigned obituary, which is mechanical, possibly stolen or the work of a committee, and in either case unaccountable. Third-rate obituaries are unforgivable; second-rate obituaries, in the nature of newspaper journalism, are better than none; and, I would argue, the best signed obituary beats the best unsigned one, always. It will be the sort readers cut out and file, the sort historians later refer to. Unsigned obituaries, outside Christmas anthologies, are doomed to become items of curiosity only, historical gewgaws.

Who merits an obituary in a national newspaper? The answer is the same as it was in 1731 or 1791. Anyone who is important ('eminent', said the *Gentleman's Magazine*) and anyone who is, in some way, interesting. Both categories offer a wide range of discretion for the obituaries editor; very few subjects choose themselves – even in the days when *The Times* ran without competition, a tiny minority of those covered would have been household names. Besides, different newspapers have different readerships, with very various tastes. It is one of the virtues of the British newspaper market that it can accommodate four broadsheets each now devoting fat space to their obituaries, each publishing between three and five a day, and rarely of the same subjects. One paper may be more devoted to the hunting field, another keener on foreign poets; one partial to old sea battles, another to Aldermaston marchers. Many subjects may never be covered by more than one paper; while the ones that are will, with luck, be covered from a different angle (the *Independent* has a general rule that no contributor should write an obituary of the same subject for another paper – for, if someone is worth writing about, surely more than one person can do it).

Does it matter how late an obituary is published? Probably less to readers than to journalists, who habitually read more than one paper and are by nature passionately competitive. Of course there is a private pleasure in printing '[so-and-so], who died yesterday', but it cannot always happen like that; and there is a tendency, if a newspaper is late already (i.e. scooped by another), not to worry if so-and-so appears later still. In practice, most newspapers like to publish within a week of a death, or within a month, or at worst two months; but one newspaper (the *Telegraph*) gets round this by not offering a date of death at all.

Death. Is the world of obituaries not a very morbid one? Not in Britain. Death is simply the occasion for an obituary; the cue for publishing a small biography. Death itself is rarely mentioned, the cause of death (unless germane to the story) usually not even suggested. Obituaries are documentaries of lives, not deaths. The only necessary observance, not in most cases a severe inhibition, is one of politeness towards the survivors. In the United States, things are conducted differently, and politeness perhaps taken too far. Most newspapers there are still local newspapers – without the curious dislocation 'Fleet Street' enjoys from its readers – and obituaries tend to the deferential and formulaic. Only about causes of death are they less squeamish. In Britain, medical confidences go to the grave; death certificates are not immediately posted and people die 'after a long illness' or 'peacefully in [their] sleep'. In America the full grisly details are cheerfully bruited from the hospital steps the moment the unfortunate has expired. So-and-so died of 'a collapsed pancreas, complicated by ischaemia and severe heart disease'. Does it really help to know?

Even the one American paper with an international reputation for obituaries, *The New York Times*, is blighted by the memory of its former chief obituary writer Alden Whitman, who so thrived on a caricature reputation as 'Mr Bad News' that he gave all obituarists a bad name. Whitman used to potter along, bold as you please, and *interview* his subjects – Harry S. Truman, Sir Anthony Eden, Graham Greene – for their future obituary. After such a visit, Alger Hiss called him, not without reason, 'the angel of death'.

Obituaries, in truth, should have little to do with death. They are celebrations, for the most part, of small lives, lives well lived, the lives not of the great (for with a daily newspaper there are not enough of them to go round) but of people in most ways, except maybe one, much like us. They open windows on aspects of life that are often hardly touched in the regular press: on Monday it might be a bicycle-repair shop owner, on Tuesday a long-jump champion turned hospice founder, on Wednesday an expert on throat cancer or Victorian bibelots, cigarette cards or magic mushrooms. The wide range of obituary coverage across British newspapers is its great glory. Here is rich material both for the reader (who may be bored with the inevitable set agenda of home and foreign news) and for the historian: this is what Raphael Samuel, that ardent devotee of the obituarist's art, called 'the undergrowth of history', thick with evidence, a primary rummage source.

When I am asked which obituaries I have been proudest of publishing in the *Independent*, I think not of the *magna opera* – politicians writing about politicians, one Nobel prizewinning biologist writing about another, that rare obituary of a mathematician that gave one an insight for a moment into the meaning of genius – for all these seem somehow obvious, a mere test of professional efficiency. I think instead of the multitude who might never have had obituaries written about them if the *Independent* – following the torch of the *Gentleman's Magazine* – had not come along. Of all the photographers, monks, bookplate designers, chairmakers, suffragettes, graffiti artists, jazz saxophonists, lexicographers, cartoonists, pulp publishers, puppeteers, mimes, weavers, ferrymen, schoolteachers and master plasterers; of Tom Forster, 91, Britain's oldest working ploughman; Roly Wason, 91, Professor of Archaeology turned Hartlepool bus conductor, who died just as he was mastering the Internet; Dr John Wilkinson, 101, haematologist, inventor and pioneer of the Scouting movement, who in the Second World War trained sealions to defuse bombs; 'Mr Sebastian', 63, body piercer and tattooist, who 'if a piercing site on the body was unfamiliar' would practise repeatedly on himself until he got it right; Winifred ('Winnie the Hat') Wilson, 88, fearless sometime picture dealer to Walter Sickert ('I've still got the best legs in the business'); Eleanor Strugnell ('Granny Struggles'), 106, governess turned missionary among the Mapuche Indians in Chile; Donald MacLean, 66, for twenty-five years director of the Crieff

Highland Gathering and 'the greatest of all the private collectors of the potato'.

MacLean grew 367 varieties, and would sell them by the kilo at most, sometimes only by the tuber. 'When people rang to place an order,' wrote his obituarist Jane Grigson in 1988,

he talked to them for a while first to make sure they were suitable – a character test, as if he were placing children for adoption. He felt that if people learned what quality was in one small sphere of existence, they would then be able to recognize quality in everything else – television, books, politics, social attitudes. Such aims were behind his endless parcelling of tiny orders. Salvation by potato.

And of course he was right.

Watering Holes

ALAN WATKINS

The Fleet Street of forty years ago was perhaps the nearest this country has approached to the classless society. 'Media Studies' had not then been invented as an academic discipline – not that it is of much help today in securing a job on a national newspaper. A few newspapers, notably the *Financial Times*, liked to take on graduates from Oxford or Cambridge; a few others insisted on a spell first in the provinces; most pursued an in-between kind of policy. Graduates were in a minority but were not persecuted on that account. Etonians were largely confined to the racing pages with a small spill over the City pages owing to the then strong connection between the school and the financial markets.

Many inhabitants of the street had either seen military service during the war or done national service after it, which had given them an aversion to authority in most of its duly constituted forms. If the place had an ethos, it was of the sixth form of a somewhat unruly English provincial boys' grammar school. At the same time, however, there was no doubt that many of its admired characters, people whose doings were recalled and sayings recounted – Lord Beaverbrook, James Cameron, Hugh Cudlipp, Trevor Evans, Ian Mackay – were not English at all. The Australians and New Zealanders drew the best cartoons, the Irish had a way with words, the Welsh possessed flair, while the Scots ran things.

The entire ship, anchored beside the Thames between the Law Courts and St Paul's, floated on a sea of alcohol. It may be that the presence of so many Celts and Antipodeans, with their historic affinity with strong drink, contributed to the prevailing atmosphere. Perhaps the explanation lay more in the longstanding connection between writing for newspapers and drinking in pubs, even if the earliest meeting-places in the late seventeenth and early eighteenth centuries sold coffee and chocolate rather than beer and spirits. In most pubs, wine was simply unavailable. Journalists drank beer or (what would now be called 'the drink of choice') Scotch whisky, with gin-and-tonic putting in spasmodic appearances; unless of course they were drinking in El Vino's, of which more later.

Most of all, however, we must remember the change in habits between then and now. Heavy drinking, though not outright drunkenness, was more acceptable both at work and in social life. It would be inconceivable today for a journalist with the known drinking (and, indeed, other) habits of the fifty-year-old Malcolm Muggeridge to become deputy editor of the *Daily Telegraph* or to be seriously considered, as Muggeridge also was, for the editorship of both the *Sunday Times* and the *Daily Mail*.

Every paper had its favourite pub or, rather, the pub its staff tended to frequent, for they would often grumble about it.[1] However, the staff would often divide, sub-editors attending one establishment and, say, the sports desk another. The *Express* pub was the Red Lion, in Poppins Court, an alley just east of the *Express* building on the north side of Fleet Street. Owing to its location, it was known as 'Poppins'. Pubs often had nicknames which could derive from sources other than their addresses. The *Mirror* pub, the White Hart, at the Holborn end of Fetter Lane, was known as the 'Stab in the Back', shortened to 'The Stab', on account of its reputation as the venue for the darkest journalistic office politics. In reality they were no more prevalent at the *Mirror* than anywhere else; though I did once hear a former *Mirror* foreign editor say to a colleague: 'I sent him to Paris because I thought it would finish him off, but I failed.'

Poppins was both short and narrow, a single bar running from end to end. It was warm and cosy and had little shaded lights. The rule then obtaining at RAF flying stations, that spirits should not be drunk at lunchtime, held no sway in Fleet Street. Whisky would

---

1. See generally Peter Corrigan, 'Fleet Street at Closing Time', *Observer*, 27 March 1988.

follow whisky, gin would follow gin. Often no solid sustenance of any description was taken. An *Express* journalist's daughter was once given summer work at the *Mirror* between school and university. Asked what she did all day long, she adumbrated some of her tasks and ended: 'And then I have to get them bacon sandwiches when they come back hungry after lunch.'

The staff of most newspapers in those days, sub-editors and senior 'executives' apart, came and went much as they chose, disciplined only by their deadlines. There was none of this sitting in front of a flickering screen for hours on end, seeing no one, never going out, relying on the telephone not only as a means of communication with the outside world but also as a source of information about it. There was one editor, however, who was exceptional, even eccentric, in trying to impose some kind of office discipline on his staff. That was John Junor at the *Sunday Express*.

Max Aitken, Lord Beaverbrook's son, then employed in a somewhat uncertain capacity in the *Express* building, had the habit of buzzing Junor on the intercom (a feature of every well-appointed editor's office) at one minute past ten every morning. Junor understandably saw no reason why his staff should not suffer similarly in the cause of punctuality. He insisted on office hours from ten to one and three to six, with a generous two hours for lunch. Junor was a bully but an industrious and conscientious bully. He kept these hours himself, departing shortly after six for Fleet Street to catch the number 4 bus to Waterloo.

There were a few journalists for whom he was prepared to break the pattern and leave the office for a drink. Indeed, the real importance of journalists can still be assessed not by their formal titles but by whether the editor is prepared to put work aside and accompany them for a drink. Chief among this small group at the *Sunday Express* was the cartoonist Carl Giles, who lived in Suffolk and came to London every now and then. Junor was realist enough to know that Giles was even more important to the paper than he was. If Giles wanted a drink, a drink he should have. That was Junor's policy. It was as simple as that. Alas, there was no drink in the office because Beaverbrook prohibited it within all his offices. In fact he was critical of the *Mirror*'s laxity in this area, as he was also of its installation of baths in its new premises in Holborn Circus. 'Baths for reporters!' he would say incredulously. 'Whatever will they be thinking of next? We put our money into the foreign service' – which was true up to a point.

So on this occasion Junor took Giles to Poppins at opening time, which was five o'clock. Unhappily two members of the staff had conceived the same idea: Tim Carew and Brian Gardner. The latter was to go on to write *The Big Push*, about the Battle of the Somme, and several other books, notably an anthology of the poets of the Second World War. Carew was also an author, a military historian in a small way of business.

That, indeed, was the reason Junor had hired him in the first place. The editor's reasoning was that, as the paper then specialized in two-page, multi-part serials on sinking ships, battles long ago and deeds of military derring-do generally, it would be cheaper to produce them in-house than to buy books and serialize them. Accordingly Carew, a former regular soldier, was hired at £35 a week – not bad money in those days – to write serials on shot and shell. He was older than Gardner, noisier, for Gardner was quiet, but without Gardner's experience of Fleet Street and its ways.

It was Gardner who took the initiative over the trip to Poppins. Junor was already there with Giles, and scrutinized the two visitors in an unfriendly manner with his prominent and slightly watery blue eyes, but said nothing. The next morning he summoned Gardner and delivered a paternal lecture on the dangers to promising young journalists of falling into dissolute ways. He sent for Carew separately and was fiercer, reprehending him for irresponsible behaviour, in particular for leading a younger colleague to breach the rules about office hours. After some minutes Carew, who held the Military Cross and claimed to have played rugby for the army – the MC was certainly genuine – could stand the homily no longer.

'I've shot better men than you,' he said to the editor.

Shortly afterwards Carew left the paper to devote himself to writing books, as Gardner did also.

Sunday papers tended to have some pubs which they used during the week, others which they used mainly on Saturday nights. In the latter category the *Sunday Times* patronized the Blue Lion in Gray's

Inn Road, the *Observer* (after its move from Tudor Street) the Cockpit in St Andrew's Hill and the *Sunday Express* the Cogers in Salisbury Square. Here it was that I first met Betty Boothroyd, later Madam Speaker, then secretary to the Labour MP Geoffrey de Freitas. We were introduced by her escort for the evening, Llew Gardner, who was different from Brian Gardner, being more dashing in his ways. He was then a *Sunday Express* reporter specializing in by-elections, had been a *Tribune* journalist and was to become a television interviewer.

Another former Tribunite in the pub that evening was Robert Pitman, literary and assistant editor of the *Sunday Express*, who had gone over to the Beaverbrook side so wholeheartedly that even Beaverbrook's friend and admirer Michael Foot was no longer prepared to speak to him; though, oddly perhaps, Foot continued to speak to – and have lunch at the Gay Hussar restaurant with – Robert Edwards, who had enjoyed a similar career and ended up as editor of the *Daily Express* and later of the *People*.[1] Also present was the *Sunday Express*'s news editor, Arthur Brenard, a bully with a beard. Brenard was not a nice man. News editors are often not nice. It tends to go with the job. But Brenard was not a particularly good news editor either, possessing little industry and no flair, deficiencies he was to demonstrate during the Profumo affair of 1963. This evening, however, he made a good joke, all the better for being directed at someone who was in the practical running of the paper his superior. Pitman, though strongly built, was always fussing about his health, maybe with good reason, for he was to die of leukaemia in 1969 at forty-four. On this occasion he abruptly left the company, saying: 'I feel a little queasy.'

As he was going through the door, Brenard said: 'Perhaps it's something he's written.'

In later years Brenard was to suffer a stroke. After great exertions on his and the hospital's part he learnt to speak a few words. So terrorized had he been by Junor that the first and for a time the only word he could utter was: 'E . . . E . . . Editor.'

Around the corner from the Cogers was the Press Club, likewise

1. See Robert Edwards, *Goodbye Fleet Street* (1988), *passim*.

popular on a Saturday. It was to fall on hard times, moving around from place to place like the Savage Club, which in its Salisbury Square period it resembled: battered but comfortable furniture, nineteenth-century prints and cartoons, a proper bar. One Saturday lunchtime a few of us were there with Edward Westropp, the City editor of the *Sunday Express*. An elderly clergyman approached us, rubbing his hands and saying: 'Good afternoon, gentlemen. I trust I find you in excellent health.'

'Be off with you, sir, this instant,' Westropp replied. 'You are a disgrace to your cloth.'

The intrusive clergyman duly retreated. He was, Westropp explained, the Reverend Cyril Armitage, Rector of St Bride's, Wren's Fleet Street church only a few yards away. The rector, Westropp went on, was notorious for joining groups uninvited and accepting drinks he never returned – for cadging. For some reason this is a practice more acceptable in Roman Catholic priests than in clergy-men of the established church. At any rate Westropp was not prepared to encourage it when followed by the Rector of St Bride's.

The other Saturday-night pub was the Falstaff, also on the south side of Fleet Street, along with the Punch, which had a cameo role as the old journalist Denholm Elliott's local in the film *Defence of the Realm*. There was also the Old Bell, a rare Nicholson's pub, just in front of St Bride's, accordingly useful as the place for a fortifying drink before a memorial service at noon. In the silver age of Fleet Street a guaranteed memorial service at St Bride's was the humblest practitioner's solitary perk. The Falstaff had a bar at ground-floor level and another in the basement: in general effect it was curiously like a New York establishment. It was there that Llew Gardner (who would as soon keep a hot potato in his mouth as a witty saying) said to the political correspondent Wilfred Sendall, who was about to re-embark on an account of his adventures on the Continent following the D-Day landings: 'I'm sorry, Wilfred, I haven't got time to cross the Rhine tonight.'

On another Saturday Gardner was having a drink with me, Colin Cross, then a *Sunday Express* feature writer, and Peter Paterson, then the industrial correspondent of the newly-established *Sunday Telegraph*. Cross and I, who had both of us been to Cambridge, were having one of those old college chums' conversations which can quickly become tedious to those unable to participate in them: 'No, no, Cartwright wasn't at Jesus. He was at Christ's.'

Finally Paterson's patience, normally in short supply in any case, ran out. 'I was educated at the university of life myself,' he said.

'Failed, I assume,' said Llew Gardner.

In those days my preferred drink was whisky-and-Schweppes dry ginger. The reason I drank it was that I really did not like the taste of whisky, which, I was later to discover, made me bad-tempered (as it does others too). I was criticized for vulgarity – for the addition of the ginger rather than the consumption of the whisky – by Douglas Clark, the small, clever, irascible inventor of the original 'Crossbencher' style: 'Whose footsteps trip light these autumn mornings? Step forward Hugh Todd Naylor Gaitskell.' Time after time on Saturday evenings, as I was raising my glass for the first or perhaps second time, the telephone behind the bar would ring. The barman would take the call.

'Name of Watkins?'

I acknowledged my identity.

'Call for you.'

'Hello, old man. News desk here. Would you mind coming back to the office to look at a few things in the rivals? Thanks, old man.'

This meant that the early editions of the other Sunday papers had been delivered, having been secured by a process of inexpensive and mutual bribery. They were usually in the office some time after seven. My presence was required to cast an eye over them. James Margach in the *Sunday Times* would be confidently predicting a revolution in the composition of the Conservatives' 1922 Committee; Ian Waller in the *Sunday Telegraph* informing us that the government had a new plan for the railways; and Nora Beloff in the *Observer* providing copious details of some imminent change in the internal organization of the Labour Party's then headquarters, Transport House.

In Clark's enforced absence owing to sudden illness, I was new in the job, only thirty. I assumed the people on the news desk, or some even more exalted authorities, had decided that the stories in the other papers to which they had drawn my attention should, in the argot of the trade, be followed up. Accordingly I made telephone calls, took down notes, wrote a story in longhand (as I still do with an article or a column), then typed it on one of the ancient machines scattered throughout the office. No story produced in these circumstances was ever used, not one. After some weeks of this fruitless industry Junor, freshly returned from his frugal and abstemious supper eaten with a few abject 'excutives' in the Fleet Street Lyons, asked me what I was doing. I told him. He asked who had instructed me to do it. I said it was the news desk. He was greatly amused. Indeed, I had not seen him so amused since he had been informed that the senior photographer had bought a pony for his daughter in emulation of his own purchase of a pony for his daughter Penny.

'We are not remotely interested in all that Nora Beloff stuff,' he said. 'What those chaps are doing,' he went on, gesturing contemptuously towards the news desk, 'is protecting their jobs, in case they miss something. Never write anything for the *Sunday Express* without telling me first.'

In many ways Junor was an excellent editor to work for. However, he rarely put in an appearance on licensed premises, except at the Cheshire Cheese on a Saturday, where he would lunch. This would invariably consist of roast beef, tomato salad, mashed potatoes and (he would insist) a double Beaujolais, after which he would leave his companions – myself, Pitman and Bernard Harris, who composed the leader-writing team – to carry on gossiping, while he returned to his labours in the office. It was at one of these Saturday lunches that Junor, who would then have been in his early forties, delivered himself of the confident observation: 'No one has sex in the mornings' – an early illustration of that usage, 'have sex' for sexual intercourse, which has since become common.

His view was that drinking in Fleet Street 'rots the brain'. By this he did not mean principally that drink had adverse neurophysiological consequences but that journalists endlessly talking to one another in pubs produced no real information of any value. Stories went round and round, becoming more erroneous with every telling. Now lunch: that was different. The best way to obtain information from a politician was to take him out to lunch.[1] Junor was eager

1. See John Junor, *Waiting for a Midnight Tram* (1990).

to pass on his rules for these occasions: always to choose first from the table d'hôte menu, which would almost invariably shame one's guest into doing the same; never to order additional vegetables, certainly not potatoes, which were (it was then universally thought) fattening; above all, to order the house wine. This could be red or white – there was nothing wrong with white wine – but never on any account rosé: 'Only poofs drink rosé.'

His favourite establishment was L'Epicure in Frith Street, which was owned by two Cypriots who wore black coats and striped trousers and did rather good generalized continental food of a kind sadly unfashionable today, with much flourishing of spirit flames. The great men of the *Daily Express*, on the other hand, tended to favour L'Écu de France in Jermyn Street, where Chapman Pincher, ostensibly the science and defence but in reality the spy correspondent, entertained his sources, notably Colonel L. G. ('Sammy') Lohan of the D-Notice Committee. Appropriately enough, the restaurant still maintained, in full working order, the concealed microphones that had been installed during the war at the behest of the security authorities.[1]

Some of these figures, not including Pincher or, of course, Junor, patronized the King and Keys, formally the Kings and Keys but always called the King and Keys, a few yards up the road from the *Express*. Edward Pickering, the editor, Harold Keeble, his associate, and Osbert Lancaster, the pocket cartoonist (and much else besides when he was away from the *Express* building), would have an early evening drink in the 'snug' or private bar at the front of the pub. Lancaster had trained the barman to mix a dry martini, a drink to which he was attached. Lowlier colleagues from the *Express* who ventured into the tiny space were instantly glared away.

The main body of the pub was long and narrow. The landlord was a jovial Irishman who claimed to have fought for the IRA long ago. It was a complete hellhole.[2] Fights were not uncommon. One

---

1. See Chapman Pincher, 'Bugs in the Banquette', *Spectator*, 22 August 1998; *Report of the Committee of Privy Councillors Appointed to Inquire into D-Notice Matters*, Cmnd 3309 (1967); Peter Hedley and Cyril Aynsley, *The D-Notice Affair* (1967).
2. See Michael Wharton, *A Dubious Codicil* (1991), ch. 4.

of its regular customers was a member of the *Telegraph* staff who (away from the pub, admittedly) was given to assaulting his wife, on one occasion, indeed, going so far as to break her jaw. She was a colleague of his on the paper, a reporter, while he was an 'executive'. They could often be seen enjoying a drink together.

Another member of the staff, a senior correspondent in the foreign field, was of polished manners while inside the *Telegraph* building and sober. In this hellish pub he instantly became an insulting drunk. It happened that a new leader writer, Frank Johnson, then a virtual teetotaller, was having a tentative drink. Johnson was later to become editor of the *Spectator* and the most accomplished parliamentary sketch writer of his generation. At this point he was newly arrived from the *Sun* via the *Sunday Express* as a teaboy, local journalism and the *Liverpool Daily Post*.

'Here, you,' this senior colleague cried, 'come over here.'

Johnson duly went, expecting some small compliment on his recent work.

'Why don't you get back to the gutter where you belong?' the senior colleague said to a Johnson who was surprised, shocked even, but whose confidence remained happily unimpaired.

There was another *Telegraph* journalist who had been dreadfully injured in the war and consequently lacked an eye, an arm and other bodily parts.

'If I were you,' the senior colleague said to him in the course of a row, 'I'd go home and cut my throat. Except you couldn't, could you?'

On another occasion he said to Sir (as he then wasn't) Peregrine Worsthorne: 'You're nothing but a tinsel king on a cardboard throne.'

Worsthorne was upset by this. His first, late wife Claude, known as 'Claudie', a Frenchwoman by origin, recounted afterwards: 'Poor Perry, 'ee was so upset 'ee was crying. 'Ee was crying cats and dogs.'

Another frequent visitor to this deplorable establishment was the paper's editor, William Deedes. He had a similar way with the English language. When the young Charles Moore was leaving to edit the *Spectator* (which was not then owned by the *Telegraph* group), Deedes said farewell with the words: 'Good luck, Charles.

Always glad to have you back. Whatever you do, don't burn your boots.'

Another of his maxims was: 'You can't make an omelette without frying eggs.' While of the then Foreign Secretary he observed: 'Say what you like about Peter Carrington, he weighs a lot of ice.'

If the place had an *arbiter elegantiarum*, it was the *Telegraph*'s deputy editor, Colin Welch. Clutching a glass of whisky and swaying alarmingly, he would greet a newcomer he wanted to see with the words: 'Tell me, would you care for an aperitif?'

On any weekly evening in the early 1970s the company might include William Deedes, John O'Sullivan, T. E. ('Peter') Utley, Colin Welch, Michael Wharton ('Peter Simple') and Peregrine Worsthorne. When Frank Johnson joined *The Times* in 1981, I warned him he would not find such a gathering of wit and intelligence as he had enjoyed at the *Telegraph*. So it proved.

But El Vino's in the 1960s and 1970s could certainly rival and usually outperform the lamentable King and Keys. There was a certain overlap of clientele – Welch, Wharton and, a more frequent visitor, Worsthorne. El Vino's (officially El Vino but always called El Vino's) was, still is, on the south side of Fleet Street at the junction with Fetter Lane. It had been established in the late nineteenth century to cater not for barristers from the nearby Temple or even solicitors, who went to their clubs, but for barristers' clerks. The manager in 1960 was Frank Bower, a large, white-haired, rubicund, overheated man who liked to wear ornate waistcoats and display a carnation in his buttonhole. A friend of mine referred to him as 'the florid vintner'. He was not universally popular – in fact he was not popular at all, fairly generally disliked – owing to his habit of expelling people or barring them from the premises completely, often on the flimsiest of pretexts. The other reason for his unpopularity lay in his consciousness of being a Fleet Street 'character'; which, his fancy dress apart, he was not. Bower's family had possessed a financial interest in the establishment but by 1960 control had passed to the Mitchell brothers: Christopher, who ran the bar, and David (later Sir David), who put in more spasmodic appearances and was Conservative Member for Basingstoke and Hampshire North-West from 1964 to 1997.

'This is an extraordinary place,' Paul Johnson once remarked, as if he were paying his first visit, whereas in fact he had been there hundreds of times. 'D'you know, I'm told that one of the waiters here is a Tory MP.'

Johnson, as editor of the *New Statesman*, was one of the emissaries of the higher journalism. The others included Henry Fairlie, formerly of the *Spectator*, Philip Hope-Wallace of the *Guardian*, Anthony Howard and John Raymond, both then of the *New Statesman*, Maurice Richardson and Terence Kilmartin of the *Observer*, and Peregrine Worsthorne of the *Sunday Telegraph*.[1] George Gale was a kind of honorary representative of the higher journalism as well, even though (after a short initial spell on the *Guardian*) he worked for the *Daily Express*. He had read History at Peterhouse, Cambridge, with Worsthorne. Gale, Fairlie, Johnson, Raymond and Worsthorne formed a group which had an existence outside El Vino's, where Gale was never wholly at ease.

Gale's lack of ease had nothing to do with the ambience. He was generously paid, highly intelligent and aggressively disputatious – often, indeed, very rude. But he did not like wine and preferred beer. In El Vino's he compromised by drinking gin. Sometimes, however, he would disappear with a muttered excuse: Gale was a great mutterer and mumbler. After twenty minutes or so he would return. He would have been, I learnt later, to one of the contiguous pubs for a pint or even two pints of beer: for Gale, as I also learnt, was one of those people who were attracted not so much by the alcohol in the beer, or even its taste, as by the sensation brought about by a large quantity of liquid cascading down the throat.

Hope-Wallace, looking like a large Roman senator wearing a pullover and sports coat rather than a toga, presided over a table in the back room, where he talked about operatic singers, French novelists and German poets. He would often be joined by Howard, Johnson, Kilmartin, Raymond, Richardson or Worsthorne. Even before his death at sixty-seven in 1979, following a misconceived visit to a health farm, the management had put up a small brass plaque in his honour just above his usual chair.

1. See Peregrine Worsthorne, *Tricks of Memory* (1993), pp. 149, 153.

'Looks like a coffin plate,' Hope-Wallace said prophetically.

They had spelled his name wrongly: 'Phillip' instead of 'Philip'. Taxed with their error, they replied: 'But we checked with the *Guardian*.'

Fairlie – with Hugh Massingham of the *Observer*, the founder of the modern political column – preferred to do his drinking standing up, at the front of the house, near the entrance from Fleet Street. His companion was usually Derek Marks, the *Daily Express*'s best political correspondent of the post-war period, though later he was far from being its best editor. Here the conversation was louder, jollier, more brutish even, with much ho, ho, hoing, conducted by tall, heavy men with red braces. Fairlie, though above medium height, did not truly belong to this category, as Marks did. So did Michael King, son of Cecil H. King and diplomatic correspondent of the *Daily Mirror* – something of a non-job even in those more enlightened days on the *Mirror* – and so also did Roland ('Roly') Hurman, industrial correspondent of the same paper.

Hurman had a gingerish moustache and dressed in a dark blue, double-breasted, brass-buttoned blazer, a check shirt, a tie which laid claim to some association or other, and cavalry twill trousers. When Marks became editor of the *Express* in 1965, Hurman left the *Mirror* to accompany him, ostensibly in some factitious post or other, in reality as the editor's drinking companion. This was an ancient office in Old Fleet Street comparable to one in a medieval (or, for that matter, a post-medieval) court. The incumbent's duty was to accompany the editor to El Vino's or the pub whenever the editor felt like a drink. Accordingly his work at the paper could not be too important or take up too much of his time and, most of all, he could present no threat to the editor's position.

Roly had spent a long time preparing himself for this sinecure. At the *Mirror* he would arrive at his office from deepest Surrey at half-past eleven or so to find his assistant, Len Jackson, who was older than he was, already hard at work. Hurman would flick through the morning papers, perhaps even make a telephone call. Had Len got the Frank Cousins ban-the-bomb story under control? He had? Good. And what about Bill Carron and the engineers' union? They were always up to something or other. That was being attended to as well? Excellent. Then Roly would look at his watch.

'Bless my soul, it's five to twelve already. I must rush.'

And Roly would stroll down Fetter Lane – the *Mirror*, before its move to Holborn Circus at the north end of the same street, occupied the ramshackle Geraldine House, near the Public Record Office. He would reach El Vino's at midday. At three, when the bar shut, the company would cram themselves into a taxi or even two taxis and make for the Forum restaurant at the top of Chancery Lane. This was owned by a Spaniard and (rather like L'Epicure, referred to above) served continental food with an Italian bias. At half-past four or so the company would disperse. Roly would make the short journey to his office to find Jackson still hard at it. After a few inquiries about progress on Cousins, Carron and other subjects, Roly would look at his watch.

'Good heavens, it's five to five. I must dash.'

And he would amble down to El Vino's again, where he would remain until between seven and eight, when he would take a taxi to Waterloo.

Many journalists, however, gave El Vino's a wide berth, whether because of expense, because of its reputation as a dangerous place to drink in or simply because they did not feel comfortable there. The last two reasons operated with Charles Wintour, editor of the *Evening Standard*, then part of the Beaverbrook organization. Wintour was a chilly but sociable man who preferred smart parties, the company of women and the West End theatre to Fleet Street drinking. Shortly after being made editor of the *Standard*, however, he thought it would be a good idea to put in an appearance in El Vino's for a small glass of chablis (then 2/6d. or 12·5p) just to show he had no side.

This was on a day when Alfred Hinds had escaped from prison once again. Hinds was a professional criminal who specialized not only in burglary but also in escaping from prison and challenging the authorities in the courts, where he represented himself, sometimes with success. In a gentler age, he was accordingly something of a public hero. With his latest escape the *Express* had been beaten by the *Mail*: Lord Beaverbrook was cross. He tried to get in touch with the editor of the *Standard* to remedy matters and was told he was in El Vino's. Beaverbrook was put through on the telephone. After some introductory pleasantries he said: 'Mr Wintour, may I give you a piece of advice?'

Wintour indicated that there was nothing he would like better.

'Mr Wintour, my advice to you is this. You will not find Alfred Hinds in El Vino's public house. Good-day to you, Mr Wintour.'

On the Thursday of the general election in 1970, 18 June, a group of women, chiefly journalists, entered the bar and asked to be served. The house rule, incorrectly reported both at the time and later on, was that women had to be seated in the back room. The incorrect report was that they would not be served unless accompanied by a man. The Irish writer Honor Tracy, much admired (in a journalistic sense) by Hope-Wallace, would often pop in on her own for a restoratif. There were others as well. It was also believed, equally wrongly, that women had to wear a dress or skirt. Not so. At this time, though not later, they could wear pretty well what they liked. Men, on the other hand, had to – as they still have to – wear a coat and a tie. On 18 June 1970 the women were refused service at the bar. They remonstrated. They were asked to leave. They refused. Then they were thrown out with some force.

'That's no way to treat a lady,' Ian Waller of the *Sunday Telegraph* protested to Christopher Mitchell, the manager and part proprietor.

Whereupon Mitchell barred Waller from the premises. Waller was not disposed to accept this treatment without some form of protest. For advice he went to Lord Goodman, the greatest solicitor since Cicero. Goodman pondered the barring of Waller, which was supposed to be permanent, and concluded that an action for defamation would lie. By his conduct, Mitchell had clearly implied that Waller was not a reputable member of society. A letter along these lines was duly composed and dispatched from Messrs Goodman, Derrick. Confronted by this display of legal might, Mitchell retreated, making peace with Waller over coffee at the Kardomah café, Fleet Street.

Meanwhile the Equal Opportunities Commission had taken up the case of the El Vino women. Lord Denning, the Master of the

Rolls, held in the Court of Appeal that the requirement that they should be seated was a well-intentioned courtesy rather than a piece of sexual discrimination. The House of Lords disagreed and overruled Denning, not for the first or last time. Mitchell responded to this defeat by making the rules for women's dress more exigent. In future they could not wear trousers unless as part of a smart trouser suit. They could certainly not wear jeans, as they had previously been allowed to. The artist Karen Usborne once appeared in jeans and was told she would not be served. She retired to the ladies' cloakroom, removed her jeans, put them in her bag and reappeared with her shirt over her stockings. No one objected, and she had her drink.

Twenty years after the invasion and the victory in the courts, one or two women drink regularly at the bar. Otherwise things are much as they were before; except that most of the journalists have gone in the Fleet Street diaspora, and the stricter rules about women's dress are still enforced.

There was much idleness and drunkenness in Old Fleet Street. Its advantage was that it was a news exchange. News about Fleet Street itself was invariably correct. Perhaps it would be more accurate to say that it was a specialist employment exchange. But people left the place to talk to others as well and to look at the outside world as they do not leave their computer terminals today. Journalism was certainly more fun in those days. The papers were better too.

Newspapers and the Internet

ANDREW BROWN

The good news is that newspapers will survive the Internet. People will still read them until someone develops a screen that you can crumple up and put in a pocket, read in the bath, or wrap chips in. Even then, it's hard to see newsprint completely replaced until these flexiscreens become cheap enough to light fires with when you've read them. There really is no better way to display and organize large amounts of static text and pictures than properly printed paper. The bad news, for journalists who don't want to adapt, is that while newspapers will look the same, and probably be sold and read in the same way, they won't be doing the same job. In fact almost everything about them except the paper and the print will change. The news will come from different sources; the advertising will be different; and the reasons people read them will also change.

Much of this has already occurred, invisibly except to those most closely concerned. To take one change already happening. The existence of large, well-published newspapers on the Web, such as the *Washington Post*, threatens the livelihood of foreign correspondents. These are an endangered species anyway, capable of surviving only on broadsheet newspapers. The great dirty secret of foreign correspondence is that most of what you do is to read the local newspapers and rewrite them, with the elegance of hindsight, for London's benefit. It's a wonderful job, which (as the experienced foreign correspondent will tell you) can only be properly performed in agreeable surroundings. If you want to grasp the intricacies of Italian policies, for example, a Roman newspaper can be best appreciated if read at a café table with pretty girls bouncing past and motor scooters dipping and swirling over the cobbles like a flock of starlings.

Actually, this argument is not entirely specious. Immersion in a culture does bring a great deal more than you will get out of a newspaper. But it is difficult to justify this deeper understanding to accountants who run most papers today; and there are not many foreign correspondents who show it in their work. Unless he or she is very conscientious, the foreign correspondent can easily fall into a kind of virtual posting even when he lives in the country he covers: all his contacts are with other journalists, and they all read the same papers and watch the same television. Perhaps the only ways to escape from this ghetto are to marry a native or to have a baby and write about the experience, but neither of these alternatives seems wholly satisfactory.

It will become harder and harder to justify the considerable expense of a foreign bureau when it could be replaced by a fast web connection and the occasional air ticket. I can already sit at my desk in north Essex and read the *San Francisco Chronicle* over the web while listening to fund-raising gospel music on a Berkeley radio station in the same way, and discussing the local television or any other trivia I like with people who live there. Even at peak rate, this will only cost me about £2.40 an hour. At weekends, it's less than 50p. It will be a long time before air fares are that cheap. Of course, this gives me a limited and partial view of Californian society. But that's what I get when I travel in person, too. A properly run conferencing system – what used to be known as a bulletin board, where people can type messages at each other until they have developed a kind of society – has many of the advantages of an old-fashioned club: you get to talk with clever and well-informed people in reasonable privacy. It is cheaper and less geographically limited.

Although a London paper might replace its West Coast corre-spondent with an ISDN line, the trick would not yet work in reverse. There is not enough being broadcast from this country over the web to make up a full picture; and no British paper yet manages to put everything you'd want into its web edition. Americans are better at overcoming the disadvantages of the medium, which are large and strange to anyone coming from a conventional newspaper background. The chief difference is that the designer has no real control over how a page will look to the reader. Visual design and layout on the web are dreadfully inexact: even the latest browsers disagree about how a page should appear, and it will be years before a designer can be confident that a page will be seen as she would like. This sounds as if it abolishes an important journalistic skill. As if to compensate for this inability to display ideas and their connections visually, the web demands a much greater ability to identify and bring out the connections between stories. The arrangement of ideas and supporting material is far more important in electronic newspapers than paper ones. This is a journalistic skill inasmuch as it involves the arrangement and clarification of information in a limited time. But it is an entirely new one, and difficult to learn for British journalists.

A properly told story on the web needs to make sense if read straight through; it also needs to contain links. A web link, one of those blue underlined words on screen, is really no more than a footnote. But it is a footnote that can point at anything: a book, a picture, or even an animation. Click on it and you will be swept away. To arrange this setting for a story needs time, thought and knowledgeable sub-editors, which are all things that the broadsheets in this country have been competing to do *without* for most of the decade. Papers in this country, even when they are hugely profitable, tend to have much less impressive web sites than American ones. They are just much less wholehearted about it, and enthusiasm counts for a great deal in presenting an online paper, as does experience. One of the finest online papers, the *Nando Times*, is also one of the oldest. It serves a small, though prosperous, area of North Carolina. On the web, you would think that it was one of the most important papers on the continent. It's as if the *Yorkshire Post* were to be the most useful and entertaining paper in Britain for foreigners to read.

In fact there are some signs that the British provincial press has grasped the point of web-based publishing more quickly than our metropolitan papers because of its closer link to classified advertising. What you want, when you are looking at such large bodies of data, is a way to organize and reorganize it repeatedly according to the aspects that are interesting. If I want to buy a car, for instance, I will have a price range, perhaps a preference in make or model; and I would like the salesman to be within driving distance of my home. It is most unlikely that the classifieds in a newspaper will be printed in an order which makes it easy for me to sort them in any of the ways that interest me.

By contrast, on a screen it is trivially easy to slice out exactly the advertisements I want. And once I have them on my screen, it should be a matter of a mouse click to get in contact with the advertisers and to find out more about the goods on offer. Sites like this already exist. *Exchange and Mart* on the web is an awful lot easier to use and profit from than it is on paper. One query will find me seventy different second-hand Peugeots for sale within seventy miles of my home. Large sites also make comparison shopping easy. They will find the best prices all over North America for a secondhand book or a new laptop computer. In a couple of years' time, there will be similar sites covering Euroland.

Newspapers with a large base of classified advertising desperately need to ensure that they run the sites that take off, or one of the main reasons for reading them will have been removed. Even *Loot*, the London free paper, has a site full of classified ads. The *Evening Standard*, though, at present has none at all, and I can't help feeling that this is a bad mistake by Associated Newspapers. It is part of my argument that a successful online newspaper is a rather different enterprise from a successful paper one. But it is important, and profitable, to make the reader feel there is a close family resemblance, or that they are the same substance refracted through different media. If they do not follow the links from the paper into the web, they may never find any links from the web back to the habit of newspaper reading.

As a general rule, people care most about those parts of a newspaper that they write, or might write, themselves. This is why only journalists ever notice bylines; sometimes I think that only journalists ever read most of the newspaper. So the things which seem to define the soul of a paper are the letters pages and the obituaries as much as anything. The letters pages certainly translate well into another medium. It is possible for a popular columnist, such as Jon Carroll on the *San Francisco Chronicle*, to maintain a running dialogue with his readers, and for them to keep the conversation up among themselves. They still prefer to read his words on paper, even if they are also available on screen. But discussions between readers on a conferencing system like the Well make the whole experience richer and the readers, probably, more loyal. This is quite different from simply printing e-mail addresses for the writers, as some British newspapers already do. The point is not to put the readers with shared interests in touch with each other. A conferencing system run by a newspaper should become a hundred different letters pages, all self-sustaining, and all drawing readers and participants back each day.

These can seem like ways in which British newspapers could extend themselves into the Internet. But in a sense that is the wrong way to look at the matter, because the shift of a newspaper's essence away from paper has already taken place. Newspapers now exist largely on computer systems, and have done for the last twenty years, since long before anyone thought of publishing them on screen. A paper newspaper is only one way to examine the contents of these systems. it is a printout of a frozen moment in the great stream of copy. Twenty-four hours later, another snapshot is taken; and so on. To read through a run of old newspapers is to find the world portrayed in a stroboscopic rhythm, in which everything jerks between editions. But if the flashes come close enough, as they do when we read a stream of wire services, with reports coming in quicker than they can all be read, then there is a genuine illusion of movement, and of the news constantly changing in front of our eyes. This is still journalism, and produced by journalistic skills. But it is very different from the rhythms of a newspaper. It's more like printed radio.

Yet even 'printed radio' is not the perfect description either, because the web is a more permanent medium. Everything in an electronic newspaper should be archived, and accessible. This means that any story in an electronic newspaper should automatically become three-dimensional: you can trace its emergence and the way in which it changes over time by studying a succession of reports.

This easy access to the past is the one thing that electronic journalism can do which has no precedents in the offline world. Everything else – classified advertising, letters to the editor, and so on – is a development of existing patterns. Three-dimensional journalism is new, and the proof is that people will pay for it. You'd have thought that the news which could be sold for hard cash was the freshest, but this is only true of financial information, where it is a crippling disadvantage to be twenty minutes behind your competition. Otherwise the news for which electronic papers can charge is all old. The big archive sites like Northern Light (www.nlsearch.com) which index and make available the contents of thousands of old newspapers and magazines are a truly wonderful invention. In some ways they are more useful than even the largest libraries.

Research for an article is increasingly something journalists can do at a screen rather than on the telephone or in a library. This brings some loss of depth and perspective. Without prolonged and deep study, no one is going to become the sort of specialist who knows his subject as well as the people he writes about. But the pressure on that sort of journalism is only indirectly technological. It's largely financial and managerial. Most newspapers in Britain are so understaffed that hardly anyone has the time to become an expert in anything. And if you're in a hurry, a screen is a wonderful tool. In the last ten years I have watched e-mail grow from a sort of masonic secret whose possession was almost a guarantee that the owner had something to say, into the vehicle for every sort of imbecility.

Over the same period, the web has grown from a good idea whose point was hard to understand, through the period when it was the definitive resource for any question to do with computers, to the point we have reached today, where it will tell you something useful about anything under the sun. It doesn't have the librarians that a proper library needs – but neither do newspaper libraries nowadays. Certainly, I now have more and better access to newspaper clippings at home than was available to *Independent* journalists during the paper's period of Babylonian captivity in the *Mirror* Group.

One effect of this is that the news is now shaped by the people with the best web sites and the most accessible electronic communications. A university which makes its internal phone directory accessible will be quoted more often than one which does not. Even those bodies which prefer to remain impenetrable in their inner structures, like the Vatican, gain a great deal from putting their documents online. If I want to know what a pope has thought about almost anything, I can download an encyclical on the subject in minutes. The natural result of this is that the Vatican's opinions will be more widely disseminated by hurried journalists. For example, when Pope John Paul II decided to issue an encyclical letter saying that Darwin was right, the Catholic Media office sent me the text in the normal way. But I wanted to know how this changed the previous position. I could have rung them, and found that they didn't know either. Instead, I was able to go direct to the Vatican's site and download the last bull on the subject, published in 1950, in about two minutes.

Technology, though, is not enough to guarantee influence. Commonality of language is important too. The Scandinavian countries are tremendously wired up and have some excellent online newspapers. But I don't see that this will make them more influential in this country, because so few people can read them. It's possible that by bringing American newspapers onto nearly every desktop in the country, the web will do more than even the British Eurosceptic press can do to distance this country culturally from the rest of the continent. But it's more likely that the experiment will simply show that news must always be tailored for a particular community. British journalists will want to read American papers, to see what they can steal; but British readers will still prefer to see the trinkets that these jackdaws bring home arranged in the familiar surroundings of a British newspaper.

Or so newspapers must hope; for one of the natural forms of journalism on the web is the sort of paper that is no more than a frame for other people's content. Again, this is not entirely new. The *International Herald Tribune* is a newspaper (again made possible entirely by computers) which consists wholly of rearranged stories that have been, or could be, published elsewhere. If you look at the most popular sites for news on the web, it is this frame model which they follow rather than that of a traditional newspaper. All the 'portal' sites like Netcenter, MSN and Yahoo!, which are valuable because they deliver readers (or 'eyeballs' in the jargon of the trade) to advertisers, gather other people's news, usually from the wire services, and make it available. In this way, any reader can have access to most of the things that a news desk sees before it makes its selection. This is not hugely attractive: if it were, people would charge for it. But I suspect it may further diminish the number of people who buy a newspaper from a vague desire to know what's going on in the world.

Usually these portals are disappointing compared with properly presented newspaper sites, though they remain far more popular among newcomers to the Internet, who seem to treat them as a kind of television programme. But there are some smaller and more sophisticated versions of this genre which are truly impressive. Arts and Letters Daily (www.aldaily.com), for example, does no more than collect and arrange on one page pointers to the most interesting humanities journalism around the world that day. But the results are wonderful. There's a couple of hours' worth of solid reading available every time I take a look there. Today, for example, there are articles by or about Pontius Pilate, Robert Conquest, Garry Wills, Yehudi Menuhin, Larry McMurtry, and one (from the New York *Observer*) on why celebrity profiles have become so boring. A couple of more specialized technology newsletters do very much the same thing in their fields: and it's easy to imagine that any subject-centred journalism could be done like this in future.

So the disintegration of the traditional functions of journalism has gone even further on the Internet than offline. The reporter and the sub-editor who lays out the page on which the reporter's work appears need never have met each other, and need not even be working for the same organization. But they're both still needed, which may come as a surprise to people who remember that the Internet was meant to level the playing-field, so that ordinary people could make their voices heard. It turns out that it has done no more to spread minority views than Speakers' Corner: yes, these views can be heard, if you are prepared to seek them out, but their audience is tiny and without influence. Having interesting things to say and presenting them vividly are both rare skills, and the combination is rarer still. Its value becomes even more apparent in a world where everyone has nothing to say and the ability to say it at great length.

The outward appearance of newspapers won't change much. But many of the things they now do will be done better on screen. What worries me is that these are among the most worthwhile functions of newspapers, and the ones that readers care about. This evaporation of seriousness to the screen is almost exactly the opposite of what the conventional wisdom supposes is happening: the Internet is currently being sold as an entertainment medium like television, but it is actually best suited as a deliverer of serious factual information out of which the users have to make their own entertainment. This proposition might appear contentious; after all, we know the net is famous for lowering the barrier to entry so that any old nonsense could appear out there. But when print journalism has given us *Bild-Zeitung*, the *Weekly World News*, the *Daily Sport*, and even the *Sunday Times*'s campaign to prove that HIV does not cause Aids, it's difficult to argue that newspapers are intrinsically more reliable than the babbling loons of cyberspace. Of course the worldwide web is full of lunatics and lies; but it's not technology that is responsible for this, but simple human failings like sloppy journalism and ignorance.

Gossip

PETER MCKAY

According to an American wit, anecdotes are merely jokes which have played Carnegie Hall. Likewise the 'diary' is a gossip column pretending to be respectable. It exists, in some form or other – polite, semi-polite, sometimes rude – in all our daily and Sunday newspapers because people like to read about people. In some newspapers (for instance, London's *Evening Standard*) the diary is the most important feature. Elsewhere it is a vital element of the paper's 'furniture'.

The obligatory diary tone is omniscience. The greatest of all modern newspaper diarists, America's Walter Winchell, was advertised with the slogan, 'He sees all. He knows all.' In 1949, Winchell got $702,000 for his radio show alone, paid $3 million in taxes and showed friends bankbooks proving he was worth $7 million. He appeared in films, had one made about him (Burt Lancaster played Winchell in *The Sweet Smell of Success*) and was a confidant of President Franklin Delano Roosevelt. The flyleaf in a recent book by the *Daily Mail*'s Nigel Dempster was Winchellesque in tone: 'For twenty-five years, Dempster's Diary has been a British institution, sending tingles of embarrassment through the heart of Society and frissons of delight among the public at large.'

Diarists have long been the most extravagant show-offs in newspapers. They crow about their scoops, disparage rivals – or 'so-called rivals', as Mr Dempster calls them – and write intimately about the actions and motives of famous people they may never have met. Beneath the surface glitter lies a largely secret world of rows, feuds and favouritism. Having laboured to produce diaries for the *Sunday Express, Daily Express, Evening Standard, Daily Mail, Daily*

Mirror, *News of the World*, *Private Eye* and – for a brief period in the 1970s, under the pseudonym 'Philby' – for the *Socialist Worker*, I have come to believe that what appears is usually less interesting than the process by which information ends up in them.

I once heard a reporter on the old 'William Hickey' column interrogate a duke on the telephone about his domestic life. Was the duchess in residence? No. Had they in fact parted? Er, they were apart at that moment. The duchess's new man friend – might she be with him now? Finally the aristocrat lost his temper, informing his inquisitor that he was a guttersnipe who had no right to pry into private lives and would, by the following morning, be hearing from the ducal solicitors. The Hickey reporter remained unruffled and affable: 'I wouldn't take that tone with me, Your Grace,' he advised. Polite, dogged persistence; a willingness to ask any question, no matter how angry the response is likely to be; retaining always the proper, if servile-sounding, social niceties of 'Your Grace'. That's the diary style.

Where does the information come from? Some disclose inform-ation about themselves without knowing they're doing it. (Aristo-crat to diary reporter: 'Why are you asking all these questions?' Diary reporter: 'This is merely an interview, sir.' Aristocrat: 'I see. Carry on.') Some famous names leak stories about themselves on the understanding that they won't be quoted. This is particularly true of politicians. Others leak stories about rivals as a means of keeping their own misadventures out of the columns. The late Robert Maxwell was once denouncing Nigel Dempster face-to-face on a live TV show when the diarist told the studio audience: 'You might care to ask Mr Maxwell why he rings me with stories from the back of his Rolls if that's how he feels.' A vast number of diary stories come from freelance journalists keeping their ear to the ground, reading local papers or perusing specialist magazines. In the first years of my own career, in the north-east of Scotland, the most juicy stories about lairds, bishops, judges and MPs came from police sources.

My own diary experiences began in 1968 on the old broadsheet *Sunday Express* edited by John Junor. He felt the paper's diary, 'Town Talk', might benefit from the input of a raw 24-year-old

from Banffshire barely able to distinguish between White's Club
and Whiteley's department store. Junor was a journalistic creation
of Lord Beaverbrook and shared the waspish Canadian's passion
for low gossip about exalted personalities. But he had a simple rule,
which he outlined to me after I'd discovered that a household
name show-business personality had a full-time mistress. 'Peter, all
fucking is private. Always remember that. But if your man's
marriage is coming to an end as a result of it, that's a different
matter.'

He insisted that 'Town Talk' got 'quotes' to back up every story,
or at least prove we'd put what we proposed to write to the people
concerned. Even 'I've got absolutely nothing to say to you' was
preferable to nothing. Junor lunched regularly with members of
Harold Wilson's team, even though the *Sunday Express* was a
visceral enemy of what it insisted on calling his 'socialist' government. Sometimes he passed on what he heard to me, always with
the warning, 'You'll have to confirm it yourself.' Sometimes this
involved approaching the minister from whom he'd got the story.
For some reason, they never suspected Junor was our source. I
remember one or two of them telling me: 'Be careful what you write
– I'm a friend of your editor, you know.'

Junor's idea of a perfect diary was a long main story about the
domestic difficulties of a famous couple followed by around six
shorter stories about the personal lives of famous politicians, actors,
singers or television personalities. He also liked us to present at
least two photographs of beautiful young women – usually actresses,
models, or the daughters of aristocrats – who were engaged in some
exciting job or travel plan. 'A beautiful young woman lifts even the
dreariest page, Peter,' he would say. He would gaze longingly at
the pictures I was proposing to use and say: 'She's absolutely
gorgeous. Did you sleep with her last night?'

He took far more interest in the girlie pictures than anything else
in the column. Once I presented shots of the beautiful actress
Alexandra Bastedo and a small story written by my then assistant
Robert Fisk, who went on to build a dazzling career as a foreign
correspondent. Remarking on Miss Bastedo's unusual name, Bob
wrote that her family could trace its Spanish origins back to the

Inquisition. For some reason, this sent Junor into a great rage. He said Bob had made up the detail for want of something more interesting to say about Miss Bastedo. A shaken Bob denied it. The matter was never resolved. Junor said to me: 'I don't trust Bob.'

'Town Talk' replaced the old 'Ephraim Hardcastle' column which had run in the *Sunday Express* since the 1940s. Like 'William Hickey', 'Ephraim Hardcastle' was a team effort with a heavy emphasis on reporting aristocratic misbehaviour on the marital front. Junor said he now wanted 'a proper diary'. The Profumo crisis, the collapse of Harold Macmillan's government and Harold Wilson's new Labour administration persuaded him we should be spreading our net wider and writing about people who were famous because of their jobs or achievements rather than their lineage. Thirty-two years on, 'Ephraim Hardcastle' reappeared in the *Daily Mail*. Its editor, Paul Dacre, is the son of journalist Peter Dacre, who wrote the old Hardcastle column. Paul Dacre asked me to recreate the column, partly as a homage to his father. Now the *Mail* has Dempster and Hardcastle. Readers call them gossip columns, but Nigel and Ephraim see themselves as diarists.

Diarists never call themselves 'gossip columnists' because that's a term of abuse. 'Gossip is a sort of smoke that comes from the dirty tobacco pipes of those who diffuse it,' fumed George Eliot, while E. M. Forster seethed that the practice was 'one of those half-alive things that try to crowd out real life'. Others have said gossips possess 'a keen sense of rumour' and are 'the lifeblood of society', but Roget's *Thesaurus* isn't helpful in suggesting a happier name for this ancient vice: 'spy . . . snoop . . . sleuth . . . fink . . . blabber . . . squealer . . . tell-tale . . . tattler . . .'. So 'diary' it is, although no regular newspaper feature now dares to conform – lest it be considered boring – to the generally accepted meaning of the word: 'a daily record of events or thoughts'.

Diary means a selection of short stories about famous people or institutions, sometimes (as in the *Daily Telegraph*) enlivened by amusing misprints from other journals, or (in the *Guardian*) inanities culled from publicity handouts. Depending on the newspaper, the information offered falls generally into the categories of semi-defamatory, cheeky, intriguing or dull. Diaries are loved or loathed by editors but considered vital, if only as a means of sniping at perceived enemies of the editor.

The *London Evening Standard*'s 'Londoner's Diary' – run by an editor, a deputy and at least four other reporters – aims to be a barbed and sophisticated 'talk' column, its items providing conversational topics for the capital's dinner-tables. Insouciant cheek is the prevailing tone. A former reporter, Malcolm Muggeridge, recalled that, short of a paragraph to fill out the column one day, he added that a certain prominent man was a great music-lover, present at all the great concerts. After this harmless fiction entered the newspaper clipping libraries, no future mention of the man appeared without reference to his love of music. Run for a few months in the 1970s by Max Hastings, who in the 1990s became the paper's editor, 'Londoner's Diary' caused such offence that a senior office lawyer – perhaps in jest – once indicated a steel filing cabinet in his office and said to me: 'Libel writs from Max's diary.'

Long after Harold Wilson retired, a story appeared in 'Londoner's Diary' suggesting he may have lost his memory after being anaesthetized during delicate surgery in London. When the first edition appeared, the paper's then deputy editor, Roy Wright, who hadn't previously seen the story, appeared red-faced in the diary department, crying, 'This is outrageous. Writing about a former prime minister's losing his memory is disgracefully intrusive – we'll be hauled over the coals by the Press Council.' Mr Wright was hardly mollified to be told by the then diary editor, 'I shouldn't worry, Roy, he'll probably have forgotten all about it by tomorrow.'

The office lawyer (every word is read by a rota of legal professionals, some, alas, less expert in knowing what is permissible than experienced diary journalists) once put down a column I had written and, sighing deeply, said, 'Practically every word you have written about Mr X is defamatory and, if so minded, he could attract a substantial figure by way of damages from a sympathetic jury.' He didn't argue that the story was untrue, or unfair. Simply that in the casino of a libel action, the chances were that we would lose. So, should I cut from it that which was defamatory, or spike it altogether? Time was short – it always is in newspapers – but I could live with either decision. That would not be necessary, he replied. He was merely giving me his legal insight into the content of most diary columns. It was 'an acceptable editorial risk' and he was inclined to let it go.

Broadsheet diarists, mindful that their readers may recoil from items which seem to be gossip without a redeeming public interest dimension, prefer to write about personalities who have been elected to office or are known for the public positions they hold. The difficulty here is that anything truly interesting about famous public men and women, ranging from the conflicts they face in their jobs to domestic setbacks in their lives, is likely to be selected for the news pages. This means they can either write items anticipating newsworthy events likely to befall the characters in question, or provide deeper background on stories which are breaking or have broken. Diaries in the broadsheets are in general far more acidic than they used to be and far less a notice-board of events deemed too boring for the news or sports pages.

The Times's approach to diary columns – an innovation in the Thunderer as recent as the 1970s – has always been tentative. 'PHS', their first excursion into (for them) this highly questionable area, was written by an experienced news journalist, Michael Leapman, whose hobby was gardening. He amused and instructed readers by detailing his attempts to grow vegetables in a South London allotment, as well as making droll remarks about the passing scene. I recall him pondering the mystery of a man he'd seen leaving South Kensington Underground station with a cabbage tied to his head. In the late 1990s, written by an editor with a small team of helpers, it is noticeably more barbed and gossipy, although the language remains orotund in the old-fashioned diary style.

The *Daily Telegraph*'s 'Peterborough' diary – named after Peterborough Court, a tiny thoroughfare next to the paper's former Fleet Street offices – strives to reproduce what its authors imagine to be the topics of conversation at London clubs. For many years an ideal item would have concerned the matchless collection of shooting-sticks possessed by an eminent army officer, or the chance meeting with a famous artist which led a brigadier's wife to exhibit a collection of her watercolours. From the 1980s, 'Peterborough''s content has included items about pop singers and other show-business alumni, but the ancient, urbane tone – contriving to suggest that the diarist is being commendably open-minded by writing about such marginal figures – has remained constant. Even in the 1990s, Peterborough still attracted the services of young journalists able effortlessly, it seemed, to emulate the dry 'live and let live' circumlocutions of an Oxbridge common-room.

The *Financial Times*'s diary – signed by 'Observer' – refines this style for the City personalities it discusses. City diaries as a sub-species rarely break stories which are followed up elsewhere, but the best of them – the *FT*'s and the *Daily Telegraph*'s are both good – often contain read-between-the-lines smoke signals about major business people and their organizations.

The *Guardian* diary's approach under Matthew Norman, who writes columns elsewhere about general subjects, television and sport, is mocking and sardonic. While most other diaries tend to avoid mentioning well-known journalists, the *Guardian* has made this a speciality. The tone and preferred content of the present diary was created in the early 1980s by Alan Rusbridger, who later became the paper's editor. The technique involves establishing a troupe of strolling players, characters whom the diarist considers absurd. John Major's brother, Terry Major-Ball, is a *Guardian* favourite. So is the film director and newspaper columnist Michael Winner.

The *Independent*'s diary, 'Pandora', began in 1998 and was written by a former editor of the Mohammed-Al-Fayed-revived *Punch*, Paul Spike. It conforms to the prevailing broadsheet style in that most stories seem to be written with an air of amused disdain. There's more interest in recycling stories which have already appeared in New York gossip columns, but it is an attractively presented feature of a paper which, despite heavy investment by Irish tycoon Tony O'Reilly, still seems starved of editorial resources.

The doyen of newspaper diarists is Nigel Dempster of the *Daily Mail*, whose column – in reality, a page – began in 1974. His page in the *Mail on Sunday* started in 1987. He employs a deputy, three reporters and a sub-editor and in general writes about people with titles, self-made tycoons, show-business stars, members of the Royal

Family, politicians and racing types. After leaving Sherborne school, Nigel enjoyed a varied career before becoming a tipster for the *Daily Express*'s 'William Hickey' in the early 1960s. The comedian Frankie Howerd said a handsome, well-dressed young man arrived on his Kensington doorstep one day offering, without obligation, to demonstrate a new type of vacuum cleaner. Nigel flung a bag of wood shavings over Mr Howerd's fine carpets and plugged in the machine. 'It didn't work and he was very distraught, but we didn't make a fuss because he was a nice young man with very good manners,' Mr Howerd later recalled.

Having established himself as a successful Hickey informant, Nigel was soon employed full-time and became the column's 'lead machine' – the reporter who produced most of the main stories, which in the 1960s were usually about society love affairs, engagements, marriages and divorces. He possessed stupendous energy, a network of contacts among the upper-middle-classes and aristocracy, an encyclopedic memory for names, faces, fortunes and the secrets of the nation's most prominent families. He tore around London in a souped-up Mini-Cooper, got himself invited to the best parties, prowled the top restaurants and nightclubs, remembered everything usable he was told and typed it up at furious speed before racing off to find more gossip.

Sometimes readers of Mr Dempster's *Daily Mail* column, with its confidential asides about the rich and famous, presume the author is conceited, but the truth is otherwise. He's far more interesting than the average name he writes about but too modest to (as he sees it) burden readers with details of his own life. In person, he's outspoken, disputatious, scandalously indiscreet and very good company. By comparison, his diary persona is rather prim. He has a headmasterly habit of signalling jokes with exclamation marks!

Trained on 'William Hickey' in the old *Daily Express*, he has flourished while his old mentor has twice been killed off. The first time was in the 1980s when 'William Hickey' was replaced by a column under the byline of his editor at the time, Ross Benson. Dempster arranged a 'funeral' in which he was pictured dancing on the coffin of his 'so-called rival' outside St Bride's Church off

Fleet Street. Revived in the 1990s, poor Hickey was again killed off in 1998 and replaced by a column written by his latest editor, the genial Irishman John McEntee.

Newspapers without diaries are like fish and chips without salt and vinegar, but editors are subject to periodic fits of revulsion and uncertainty over their resident gossips. A stinging diary pricking the pomposity of the rich and powerful – or, less admirably, intruding into their private lives with scant public interest justification – exposes editors and proprietors to complaints from friends and acquaintances and the paper to regular, costly libel and defamation complaints. The late Jimmy Goldsmith deluged editors and proprietors with complaints and to a degree succeeded in muzzling newspaper diarists. But they simply took their Goldsmith stories to *Private Eye*, provoking Jimmy to rage about the 'symbiotic' relationship between Fleet Street and the scandal magazine.

The most devastating attack on diarists this century was made by the journalist Penelope Gilliatt, who died in 1993. In a 1961 article for Jocelyn Stevens's magazine *Queen* entitled 'The Friendless Ones', she savaged the methods of 'William Hickey' and the *Daily Mail*'s 'Paul Tanfield' to such effect that the second Viscount Rothermere disbanded the latter. Her animus was provoked by diary reports of her romance with playwright John Osborne, for whom she left her first husband. Mr Osborne was himself a great hater of newspaper diarists. His 1959 musical *The World of Paul Slickey* was a thinly veiled assault on 'William Hickey'.

America's greatest diarist, Walter Winchell, was ruined partly by a massive six-part series about him in 1940 written by the playwright St Clair McKelway for the *New Yorker*. McKelway wrote that of 239 separate items in five Winchell columns, 108 were 'unverifiable', and of the remainder, 41.2 percent were completely inaccurate. McKelway wrote: 'When statesmen, novelists, artists, composers, professional men, book publishers and entertainers go beyond mere tolerance of gossip-writers, and actually co-operate with them, as they do every day, they suffer inevitably from a loss of human dignity, as does the girl who shows Winchell how she can wiggle a muscle in her chest. This is a social evil.'

Perhaps so, but Winchell was a towering figure in the United

States journalistic landscape. He was briefed personally by President Roosevelt and in the 1930s was the first American journalist to warn readers about a rising German politician, Adolf Hitler. Winchell summoned our then ambassador to Washington, the Marquis of Lothian, to his table at the 21 Club and asked what Britain proposed to do about Hitler. Lord Lothian replied: 'We're going to fatten the tiger, Mr Winchell.' To which Winchell replied: 'I've seen big tigers and small tigers. I never saw a fat one.'

Winchell became a great force – and a lesson to all modern diarists – because he had a point of view. Critics said he praised to the heavens shows he'd never seen, and condemned books he'd never read, but his mixture of disclosure and opinion was lapped up by millions of readers in over a thousand papers. Some diarists fashion what they believe is a pleasing personality and think that will hold readers, but we should no more attach ourselves to gossip columnists without views than to acquaintances who never say what they think or feel about anything.

The Art of the Interview

LYNN BARBER

People often talk as though the newspaper interview is a new invention, a terrible symptom of our 'celebrity-obsessed' culture. In fact interviews have been a staple of the press for at least a hundred years – and have always been seen as a deplorable parvenu. Even in the 1860s, the *Chicago Tribune* was complaining that: 'A portion of the daily newspapers in New York are bringing the profession of journalism into contempt so far as they can, by a kind of toadyism or flunkeyism, which they call interviewing.' The usual complaint is that interviews are 'trivial' but, oddly enough, this complaint is never labelled at the sports pages.

At their best, interviews are informative and entertaining; at their worst they are no more boring than, say, political leaders or football reports. Editors love them because they are a cheap way of getting glamorous names into the paper and hopefully attracting readers who wouldn't normally buy it. Readers rarely admit to liking interviews but – judging by the facility with which they reel off complaints about them – must read them pretty attentively. Interviews are the despised little sisters of journalism – just as novels once were of literature – and are here to stay.

The earliest interviews tended to be of the 'Tell me, Famous Person, what brings you to London?' variety – as indeed the earliest television interviews were. Deferential and unsceptical in tone, they were designed to elicit information but not evaluate it – basically the journalist gave the famous person a platform on which to say the same things he or she might have said in a speech or article. Such interviews still have their place in the press but mainly on the political news pages. The 'celebrity' interview (I hate that word, but we seem to be stuck with it) got going in the early twentieth century when women interviewers appeared. They were still deferential but they noticed things, and they attempted to answer not only the question 'What did Famous Person say?' but also, and more importantly, 'What was Famous Person like to meet?' In fact the 'Celebrity at home' format was so well established by the turn of the century that Sarah Bernhardt complained to the *Strand Magazine* in 1905 that she was worn out with answering the same questions over and over, and she would have no secrets left for her memoirs.

The best interview ever, I think, was Lillian Ross's profile of Hemingway, 'How do you like it now, gentlemen?', published originally in the *New Yorker* in 1950, and reprinted for many years in her book *Reporting* (now, alas, out of print). It covers two days Hemingway spent in New York in the spring of 1950 and describes his various meetings and conversations, and a hilarious visit to a gunshop. The style is light, reporterial, fly-on-the-wall, though very carefully crafted to present a rounded portrait of the man. What is interesting is that despite Ross's studiedly non-judgemental style, it produced a storm of outrage when it was published. Many readers of the *New Yorker* said they were 'devastated' by its cruelty, others congratulated Ross on exposing Hemingway as a fraud. But in fact, as Lillian Ross explained in *Reporting*, she intended it as an affectionate portrait of Hemingway – and moreover Hemingway saw it as that. She sent him the article before publication; he asked for one deletion, which she made; they remained friends for the rest of his life.

When I started in journalism in the late sixties, the best interviews were to be found in American magazines, especially *Playboy*, *Esquire*, the *New Yorker* and later, *Rolling Stone* and Andy Warhol's *Interview*. Interviews in Britain were fairly sparse and almost unknown in broadsheet newspapers. But since then the bandwagon has rolled and now there is hardly a magazine or newspaper *without* a regular celebrity interview. As a consequence, marketing departments have become far more sophisticated in handling this free publicity bonanza, and it is very rare nowadays to get an interview with a star without the intervention of a PR. And whereas when I started in the sixties, PRs were generally a fairly dozy lot of clapped-out hacks, nowadays they are alarmingly professional.

PRs are usually employed, not by the stars themselves, but by the film company or record label or publisher or whatever that is putting out the star's product. Their job is to get as much publicity as they can at the right time – i.e. just before the launch of their product. Ideally, they would like every magazine, newspaper, television and radio channel in the territory to carry interviews in the week of the launch. Editors, on the other hand, don't want to be running the same interview at the same time as their rivals, so there is much jockeying for position, trying to get an 'exclusive' interview or, failing that, a 'first' interview – and often much lying and betrayal on both sides when PRs promise an exclusive and then give it to everyone, or when editors promise not to run the interview till August, then run it in July. I always think this has more to do with gratifying editors' egos than satisfying readers, but anyway it goes on, and it's a hard-fought battle. There is often a similar battle about photographs – stars invariably want to supply their own, whereas editors want to send their own photographers – and various minor skirmishes about where the interview will be conducted and how long it will last (I refuse to do any that last less than an hour, but PRs commonly expect magazines to publish a 3,000-word cover story on the basis of a twenty-minute interview, which is a complete no-win situation for the journalist – and, I would say, for the reader). Finally, when all these negotiations have been concluded the PR will say, almost as an afterthought, 'Oh and by the way, he won't answer any personal questions.'

Beginner journalists always say, 'Why do you put up with it?' They believe that stars should give interviews to anyone who wants them, whenever they want them. But of course it doesn't work like that. Stars are in a sellers' market, with an ever-increasing number of magazines and television programmes vying for the use of their names. And because stars usually hate giving interviews and will only devote limited time to them, the PRs – rightly, if they are doing their jobs – splinter this time into ever smaller nuggets so they can spread the publicity over as many outlets as possible. But when you get to the situation – which is quite common nowadays

– that film companies will fly journalists to Los Angeles to spend just *ten minutes* with a star, or to attend a one-hour 'round table' press conference with a dozen other journalists, I think it is time for editors to put their feet down and say, 'This is not providing a service to our readers.'

But, interestingly, the star shortage has forced editors to give writers their heads. To fill the gap between the three interesting sentences the star has uttered and the 3,000-word article needed to provide a selling magazine cover story, writers are encouraged to indulge in whatever diversions they can invent along the way. Old Fleet Street hands sneer at such efforts as self-indulgent, and obviously they *can* be, but they can also be tremendously good fun. And again, this supposedly new post-modern development of the picaresque interview actually has very long antecedents. Rudyard Kipling's 1889 interview with Mark Twain starts with a good ten paragraphs about the difficulty of finding Mark Twain's house, complete with the statutory cab-driver who doesn't know the way.

Martin Amis claimed in the introduction to his *Visiting Mrs Nabokov and other Excursions* that: 'The star interview is dead, as a form. The great post-modern celebrities are part of their publicity machines, and that is all you are ever going to get to write about: their publicity machines.' Oh pooh – this is mere whingeing. Stars have *always* been part of their publicity machines – probably even more so in the golden age of Hollywood when they actually had their biographies invented for them by studio press officers – and the whole job of the star interviewer is to try and separate the kernel of a real person from the shell of their image. This is not 'post-modern' – it's been going on for at least fifty years, probably a hundred. But what has changed, and I think improved, in the past decade or so is that readers are now more aware of the nature of the transaction. In the past, especially with the Hollywood columnists of the forties and fifties, there was a sort of collusion between journalists and stars or studios, to the detriment of readers: nowadays, I hope, journalists are more firmly on the readers' side.

There has been much discussion recently about the ethics of interviews, largely prompted by Janet Malcolm's book, *The Journalist and the Murderer*. She presents the interview as a betrayal – as if two people have met and had a friendly private conversation, and then one has gone out and published the other's secrets to the world. But that isn't how interviews work. Famous people aren't green – they know that this nice friendly woman coming to see them is not a long-sought soulmate or a kindly psychotherapist but a journalist intending to write a piece for publication. And the journalist, in turn, knows that she is only there by virtue of her job, as a delegate for the readers. This doesn't mean that interviewer and interviewee can't subsequently become friends – it has even happened to me a couple of times – but the friendship develops *subsequently*, not at the time when every minute really belongs to the readers.

I think problems sometimes arise with inexperienced journalists, who often find it hard to be sufficiently detached in interviews. They are flattered that a famous person is apparently confiding in them (even telling them things off the record!); they respond to the famous one's kindness with genuine enthusiasm; they find themselves agreeing fervently with everything the famous one says. And then they go back to the office, out of the famous one's orbit, and listen to the tape and decide they don't like the famous one after all, and, because they are rather annoyed with themselves for being 'taken in', write a particularly bitchy piece. I always tell beginner journalists: Look, all you have to do is be punctual, be polite, and ask questions. You don't have to express agreement or disagreement; you don't have to forge a friendship; you *only* have to ask questions, and that way you don't commit yourself to anything. And, by the way, *don't* let them tell you anything off the record, because it will make your life difficult when you come to write the piece.

There are as many techniques of interviewing as there are interviewers, and any 'good' technique is one that results in a good piece, so it is impossible to generalize. I belong to the minimal question school – ideally, I want the subject to do all the talking, with only occasional interruptions from me. But other interviewers – usually men – want the interview to be more like a conversation or even a debate, which is effective for eliciting opinions, not so good for illuminating character. It can produce an awful lot of hot air. Another technique I am wary of is the 'sisterly confession' school of interviewers who talk about their own disastrous childhoods, love lives, drink problems, etc. in the hope that the interviewee will occasionally chip in and say, 'Oh, me too!' Marlon Brando complained after being interviewed by Truman Capote, 'The little bastard spent half the night telling me all his problems. I figured the least I could do was tell him a few of mine.'

Another approach which *can* be brilliant but only in the hands of a master is when it is the interviewer who does all the talking. The best example is Norman Mailer's 1976 interview with Jimmy Carter just before he became president, in which Mailer lectures Carter for an hour on religion, Kierkegaard, the sexual revolution, until finally, 'Mailer ground down into silence, furious with himself for scattering prodigious questions like buckshot. He looked across at Carter. He was realizing all over again that the only insanity still left in his head was this insane expectation he had of men in public places. Carter nodded sadly. He looked a little concerned. He had every right to be.'

But to go back to the Janet Malcolm problem, about the ethics of interviews. Her difficulties all arose because she misquoted someone, or she'd 'doctored' quotes to the point where they actually meant the opposite of what was said. Thus one absolutely elementary precaution in interviews, it seems to me, is to use tape-recorders. Even if the journalist prefers taking notes – as some journalists do – they can still have a tape-recorder on the table. Nowadays most editors insist on it, as libel insurance, and I think they are right to do so. I wish interviewees would also use tape-recorders to safeguard themselves from being misquoted. Tony Benn and Michael Winner routinely do this in Britain, and Warren Beatty in the States, but it should become standard practice. Also it is a useful answer to people who ask for 'copy approval' – meaning they want to check the article before publication – to say, 'Well no, it's against our principles, but by all means tape-record the interview so that if there is any dispute about what you said, you have your own record.' Of course a few magazines – notably *Hello!* – do allow copy approval, but I think it is betraying the readers.

How accurate should quotations be? In my view, *entirely*

accurate, dud grammar and all. Part of the joy of interviews is to reproduce different modes of speech, different turns of phrase, new words, new jargons, new extravagances of psychobabble. Sometimes words are so new that you can't be sure how to spell them – I am still a bit unsure about 'Puh-leeze' and 'Duh' though they crop up in almost any interview with Hollywood actresses. I am sometimes told off for using too many quotes, but surely it is mad to interview someone and then not quote them? And I like the quotes to be exact, not some gentrified paraphrase. The only way in which I will tidy a quote is to cut out excessive repetition of stock phrases like 'Do you know what I mean?'. People who say 'Do you know what I mean?' tend to say it in every single sentence and it is just too painful to read over and over again; nevertheless, I would always keep enough of them in to convey their frequent presence, and their irritation.

Obviously you don't quote everything someone says, or even a large proportion of it, and this I think is where the real ethics question arises. The journalist has *all* the power when it comes to writing the piece: she chooses which quotes to use and which to omit, which to highlight and which to minimize. I use a lot of quotes compared with most interviewers, but they probably still only amount to at most two pages out of a twenty- or thirty-page transcript. So obviously with this degree of selection, one has almost limitless opportunities for 'slanting' the interview, favourably or unfavourably. All I can say is I don't aim to do that and I hope I don't, but it would be a hard one to argue in a court of law. Again, the only real safeguard – for both parties – is the tape-recorder.

The worst interview abuse is the quote taken out of context, of which the most notorious example was Maureen Orth's line from Mrs Thatcher in *Vanity Fair* – 'Home is where you come to when you have nothing better to do.' It sounded terrible. But Mrs Thatcher's office immediately objected that she was talking about her grown-up children, and imagining herself telling *them*, 'Home is where you come when you haven't anything better to do. We are always there.' Everyone who listened to the tape said it was ambiguous. But, given that it *was* ambiguous, it was clearly wrong to present an isolated sentence so damagingly out of context.

I don't think there is any effective way of policing the fairness of interviewers, although editors (and certainly fellow journalists) usually know which ones are trustworthy and which aren't. I used to work alongside an interviewer who got complaints about practically every piece she wrote, and one day I looked at her notebook and saw that she had, at most, three sentences of quotes from which she was inventing whole paragraphs. Such journalists usually get rumbled eventually, but it's hard luck on their victims along the way. One elementary precaution would be for a fact-checker or sub-editor to listen to the tape of every interview.

Many or even most student journalists are keen to do interviews until they try it, and then they aren't. They often find it un-cool to ask questions; they find it uncomfortable and humiliating to be taking all this interest in someone else without getting any reciprocal interest back; often they are rather resentful of the idea of 'stars' anyway. I think it's particularly difficult for young men to be good interviewers because they just aren't socially attuned to the idea of taking a polite interest the way girls are. Girls, on the other hand, find it difficult to ask provocative or challenging questions; they tend to want to agree with whoever they are interviewing, to find their similarities, and to minimize friction. Perhaps these gender differences are already *passé* – I hope so – but I still think many student interviewers set off thinking an interview will be an ego trip and come back feeling really unhinged.

Interviewing is *not* an ego trip. Writing up the interview can be, but that actual hour of sitting in a room with a famous person who is almost invariably making rude remarks about the press, claiming that 'You can't believe anything you read in the cuttings', often telling you in a vaguely threatening manner that they are friends with your editor or proprietor, saying that they can only talk about 'the work' and expecting you to collude with them in trying to sell their film or play or whatever to your readers – whom they obviously regard as suckers – often entails a lot of biting one's tongue and self-suppression. I do it readily because if they behave badly I know I will have more fun writing it up afterwards – I'm sometimes thinking to myself, 'Oh *please* make me hate you more!' – but I think it comes as a shock to beginner interviewers to discover just how contemptuous many famous people (especially actors) are of the press and, by implication, of the public.

The absolute hell side of interviewing, for me, is the hotel-room circus where a Hollywood star has flown into London for a day to talk non-stop about their latest film. Often they have to get up at five to do breakfast television, and will have done twenty radio interviews, four television and ten print interviews by the time you see them. They are dazed with talking, hoarse with talking, often literally mad with talking – they gabble half the plot of the film and half an anecdote, they repeat whole paragraphs, they can never remember the question and they jump like startled deer if you ask a question they have never encountered before. But because they are big names, you somehow have to make the interview work, which in practice means making them seem more interesting than they are. This is where I get very twitchy and resentful about my job: why *can't* I just say that I interviewed Robert Redford in his hotel room but he didn't say anything memorable or interesting? But it's no good – readers still want to know what he said even if you warn them it's deadly dull.

Against this, the joy of interviewing interesting people is almost infinite. I remember, particularly, a lunch with Rudolf Nureyev under a vine trellis on an island in Lake Como – his strange accent, his enormous vocabulary and knowledge of books, his physical fragility (I didn't know it, but he was soon to die of Aids), his nostalgia for his early days in London, his pain in talking about his childhood in Ufa, his astonishing knowledge of plumbing and the problems of installing a desalination plant on his island off Naples (I remember thinking even at the time, My God, this is *Nureyev* teaching me the difference between a reservoir and a cistern and a holding tank), the extraordinary breadth of his enthusiasm and interest. I also remember Roald Dahl – again, shortly before he died – taking me to his little shed in the garden where he wrote and showing me his sacred objects – like a Joseph Beuys – the writing board, the legal pad, the rug for his legs, the array of old hip joints from all his previous hip replacements, the ball of silver paper from all the chocolate bars he had eaten. Actually I can think of dozens such interviews where, even while I worried about my next question and whether the tape would run out, I was aware that I was experiencing a golden privilege.

And what does the reader get out of it? Well, first, one hopes, entertainment and information, and a useful reminder amid the grandiose global concerns of newspapers that individuals are important too. When people say interviews are trivial, I think how *can* they be trivial, when they're about childhood and parenthood and emotions and relationships? Surely these are more important than sports results or twenty ways with light fittings? I love the way that interviews can, as it were, spring serious subjects onto the unsuspecting reader. If I interviewed 'a transvestite' it would be used on the health page and my daughters wouldn't dream of reading it; if I interview Eddie Izzard it is billed on the front of the newspaper and they are fighting over who reads it first. I don't want to sound too goody-good about this because obviously it's not the prime purpose of interviews – I don't think, 'Oh I must interview Mo Mowlam because she suffered a brain tumour,' but I do think, if I interview Mo Mowlam, it is quite *useful* to talk about her brain tumour as well as the problems of Northern Ireland. And it is cheering for readers with similar problems to find a successful person discussing them rather than one of those gloomy case-history characters called 'Brian, an electrician'. But obviously people who think private lives are trivial will find interviews trivial, and should go back to reading the sports pages. Modern newspapers are big and baggy enough to accommodate us all.

On Media Dons

NIALL FERGUSON

> *Atque inter silvas Academi quaerere verum.*
> And seek the truth in the groves of Academe.
>
> Horace, *Epistles*, II

In Robert Harris's novel *Archangel*, the character of Christopher 'Fluke' Kelso personifies the disgraceful yet romantic status of the 'media don'.[1]

Numerous details reveal that the character is closely if not exactly based on Norman Stone – formerly Professor of Modern History at Oxford and now Professor at Bilkent University in Turkey. This immortalization in a best-selling work of fiction probably qualifies Professor Stone as the pre-eminent media don of our day. The author of one of the most brilliant British history books of the post-war period (*The Eastern Front, 1914–1917*), he is now better known to the public for his journalism in newspapers like the *Sunday Times*. But it can only be a matter of time before another novelist finds a niche for Dr David Starkey, an expert on the high politics of the court of Henry VIII, but known to millions as 'the rudest man in Britain' thanks to his performances on the BBC radio programme *The Moral Maze* and his own Talk Radio show. Dr John Casey, Fellow of Gonville and Caius College, Cambridge, must be another candidate for somebody's *roman à clef* – not so

---

1. Robert Harris, *Archangel* (London, 1997). By 'media don' I mean strictly people with full-time academic posts who also write in the press or broadcast on television or radio. Excluded, despite their undoubted scholarly credentials, are writers who prefer or can afford to work outside the formal institutions of higher education.

much for his mastery of English literature, but for his ability, at the drop of a cheque from Associated Newspapers, to write a thousand words on almost any subject under the sun. And what of Professor John Vincent, who enjoyed a heady period of notoriety when he combined the duties of Professor of History at Bristol University with those of political columnist for the *Sun*? No reader of his pugnacious tabloid pieces could possibly have guessed that this was the same man who has devoted years of scholarship to editing the diaries of the fifteenth Earl of Derby. Nor can many readers of Roger Scruton's journalism in the *Salisbury Review* and elsewhere have realized that he was the most remarkable polymath of his generation: philosopher, novelist, composer and, most recently, fox-hunter.

I write as a member of this fraternity – though one who for many years sought to conceal the extent of his journalistic activity from his academic peers and seniors. When, as a hungry graduate student, I wrote a column for the short-lived *Sunday Today*, I refused to have a byline photograph, appearing in silhouette and using the pseudonym 'Alec Campbell'. The same Alec Campbell was sub-sequently – while I was researching my D.Phil. in Hamburg – the *Daily Telegraph*'s West German correspondent. On returning to England, my *Doppelgänger* then spent two or three days writing leaders for the *Telegraph* – an ideal arrangement from my paranoid point of view, as leaders are anonymous. But Alec Campbell also appeared frequently in the pages of the *Daily Mail*, churning out 'why-oh-why' leader page articles (as in 'Why, oh why, is the country going to the dogs?') and book reviews. As a junior research fellow in Cambridge, I also wrote a self-indulgent column for *Punch* in the 1980s under the improbable name 'F. F. Gillespie'.

Later, under pressure from editors to become something more like a real person, I became 'Campbell Ferguson' – but my *Daily Mail* byline photograph featured a pair of thick-rimmed spectacles which I did not in those days require. In short, I led a double life. I spent half my time in London, pontificating on everything from superpower disarmament to Scottish nationalism, half in Oxford, cudgelling my brains into understanding the German hyperinflation of 1923.

This secretiveness struck my friends in the media as sheer paranoia. But just because I was paranoid didn't mean my university colleagues weren't out to get me – or would not have been if they had known I was moonlighting in Fleet Street.

My camouflage was in fact surprisingly effective, aided and abetted, of course, by the fact that few academics read the *Daily Mail*. But there is a profound contradiction between being secretive and publishing articles every week in national newspapers, even if they are pseudonymous. Moreover, the two worlds of newspapers and universities are not so completely separate that the flow of information from one to the other can be strictly policed. One drab, drizzling day I was mortified to hear that while dining at All Souls – and doubtless encouraged by the very good quality of the guest-night claret – a senior executive at the *Mail* had let slip not only that I was writing for her paper but also (far worse) that I was being paid roughly three times an All Souls Fellow's stipend for doing so.

I can well recall thinking, on being told this, that my academic career was over. I would now be discredited, a word which then loomed as large in my imagination as 'excommunicated' does in the mind of a trainee priest. I faced a choice, which was put to me starkly over lunch (a brace of pheasant apiece) by the then editor of the *Daily Telegraph*.

His proposal was that I should bin my thesis, abandon academic life and become a full-time journalist. It was a generous and flattering offer, and I thank my stars that I said no. I had just been offered a research fellowship in Cambridge. It paid about a quarter of what was being offered to me to go full-time at the *Telegraph*. But the thought of at last having a fellowship – which signified to my mind a decent set of college rooms, dining rights and above all some academic *status* – was too much. Instead, I resolved to end my double life by (gradually) 'coming out' as a media don. The aliases went. The byline photographs became more or less recognizable. I even began to 'do' radio and television – a big step out of the closet, as you simply cannot appear on the box without somebody noticing.

The effect was and is rather curious. Many academics, I have come to realize, are fascinated by the media. They would dearly love to be asked to write by a newspaper, or to appear on television (hence the old story about the unworldly don asked to appear on television for a modest fee, who replies enclosing a cheque for the sum mentioned). But the fact that only a handful ever receive such invitations creates a tension, not to say ill-feeling. This does not express itself as overt jealousy, but as frosty disapproval or, worse, as light-hearted banter intended to convey that one is no longer taken seriously. There is a strong predisposition to believe that the media dons achieve their modest celebrity, not by being good at writing for a general audience, not by assiduously cultivating editors, but by renouncing their intellectual integrity. And the more they appear to lead glamorous existences – not only making some money but moving in media and political circles – the more certain their colleagues become that the media dons are nothing more than highbrow call-girls.

But if they – I should say 'we' – are prostitutes, then the brothel has a distinguished history. For it is a great myth that the media don is a modern invention.

In the eighteenth century, the gap between the fledgling press and the ancient universities, concerned as they were primarily with theology, was fairly wide. But by the mid nineteenth century, even the most ecclesiastically-minded academics could discern the benefit of being able to address 'the public' (meaning in the first instance the political and social élite) through the press.

Writing in *The Times* under the name 'Catholicus' in 1841, John Henry Newman, then a Fellow of Oriel, published a series of seven scathing attacks on the secularism of Sir Robert Peel's government.[1] Also an Oriel Fellow before his marriage obliged him to accept a college living, the Reverend Thomas Mozley was one of the nineteenth-century *Times*'s most prolific leader writers. (It was he who observed: 'To write a leading article may take only from two hours to two hours and a half, but then all the rest of your time you are a crouching tiger, waiting, waiting, to make your spring.')[2]

---

1. *The History of The Times*, vol. I (London, 1935), p. 406.
2. *The History of The Times*, vol. II (London, 1939), p. 126. A man less like a tiger in aspect would be difficult to imagine.

Later academic leader writers included G. C. Brodrick, a scholar
and later Warden of Merton College, Oxford; and L. H. Courtney
– though he had left his fellowship at St John's, Cambridge, by the
time he joined *The Times* and later went into politics. So learned
was Courtney, originally a mathematician, that he was referred to
by the editor John Thadeus Delane as 'a library in breeches'.[1] Nor
was the direction of the traffic always from academe to Fleet Street.
In 1848 *The Times* journalist George Webbe Dascent narrowly
missed being made Regius Professor of Modern History at Oxford;
five years later he was successful in securing the chair of English
Literature at King's College, London.[2] Relations between the universities and the influential quarterlies, now sadly extinct, were
closer still.

In the first half of the nineteenth century, it was natural that
academics, who were then a species of clergy, should write mainly on
religious subjects. But with the reforms of Oxford and Cambridge,
which ended the obligation on college Fellows to remain unmarried
and did away with Anglican exclusiveness, this began to change.
A new kind of 'public moralist' emerged, engaging in debate across
a wide range of political and social issues.

It is nevertheless important to remember that many of the most
famous writers of the Victorian era – think of Thomas Carlyle or
John Stuart Mill – were not university professors. Even Matthew
Arnold's professorship of Poetry at Oxford was a mere ornament
to his well-established literary career (like Mill, he relied on a civil
service post for his daily bread, while Carlyle lived by tutoring,
writing and lecturing). Though he used his fellowship at Trinity,
Cambridge, as a kind of launching-pad for his career, Thomas
Babington Macaulay was always more than a media don: his entry
into politics owed much more to his articles in the *Edinburgh
Review* than to any academic achievements, and he never occupied
a university chair. At the same time, newspapers had much less
of what is now called 'comment' than they have today, and the
regular column was as yet unknown: the bulk of journalism was

1. *ibid.*, p. 451.
2. *ibid.*, p. 121.

written by full-time correspondents, rarely men with university educations.

It was above all the development of modern history as a new academic discipline which brought the worlds of university and press into close communication. So long as the subject was dominated by English constitutional history, with its emphasis on the medieval period, the gap still remained. But with the development of diplomatic history in the early twentieth century, it narrowed swiftly.

In this, the First World War acted as a catalyst, galvanizing academics too old to fight into writing about the very recent past for a mass audience. Oxford historians led by H. W. C. Davies and Ernest Barker wrote *Why We Are At War: Great Britain's Case* – also sometimes called *The Red Book* – which the University Press managed to publish as early as 14 September 1914 (barely two weeks after the manuscript was delivered, a record for that publisher).[1] In the same vein, the Oxford Professor of Greek, Gilbert Murray, churned out *How Can War Ever Be Right?* and the apologetic *Foreign Policy of Sir Edward Grey 1906–15*. This was only the first shot in a four-year bombardment of upmarket propaganda by academics, eager to elucidate for a wider public the mystery of Britain's obligation to uphold, even at the cost of three-quarters of a million lives, the neutrality of Belgium.

After the war, as disenchantment set in, John Maynard Keynes launched his journalistic career by sneering at the fruits of victory in his hugely influential and misleading pamphlet *The Economic Consequences of the Peace* (1919). The volume of Keynes's subsequent newspaper writing on the subject of German reparations up until 1923 is remarkable; it certainly cannot have left him with time for much serious reflection on economics (witness the journalistic quality of his *Tract on Monetary Reform*, compared with the *Treatise of Money*, his first serious theoretical work, which did not appear until 1930). He wrote for the *Nation and Athenaeum*, of which he actually became proprietor in 1923, for the *Sunday Times*, for the *New Republic* – for anyone, it seems, who would

1. Niall Ferguson, *The Pity of War* (London, 1998), ch. 8.

print him. He even covered the Genoa Conference in 1922 as special correspondent for the *Manchester Guardian*.[1] Between 1920 and 1923 he wrote no less than ninety-four newspaper articles in all. Having been consistently proved wrong by events in Germany, he turned his attention to Britain, waging a rather more plausible campaign against the return to the gold standard, once again in the form of pamphlets and articles. *The Economic Consequences of Mr Churchill* started life as a series of articles for Beaverbrook's *Evening Standard*.[2]

G. M. Trevelyan was another Cambridge media don of the same generation (though he held no academic post between 1903 and 1927, when he accepted the Regius chair of Modern History at Cambridge). When not writing books, he wrote occasional pieces for the *Spectator*, the *Nation* and *The Times*. A fine example of shameless hackery was his lead article for its commemorative edition to mark George V's Silver Jubilee in 1935, which eulogized the monarchy as 'a bulwark of freedom in evil days' and praised 'the adaptability of our flexible constitution to meet sudden extreme dangers'. He capped this in a piece following the coronation of George VI which declared, in language worthy of the most craven of court correspondents: 'English democracy is in love with the Crown . . . the Crown is the one symbol that all classes and parties can without reservation accept.'[3]

It is impossible to imagine any such sentiments emanating from the Marxist media dons who came of age in the thirties. The London-based economic historian R. H. Tawney was one; the Oxford Fabian and guild socialist G. D. H. Cole another; a third, the diplomatic historian E. H. Carr, who started and finished his career at Trinity, Cambridge. Of all of them, Carr was the most directly involved in journalism, to the extent of going full-time for

1. Most of the articles can be found in *The Collected Writings of John Maynard Keynes*, vols. XVI, XVII and XVIII, ed. Elizabeth Johnson (London, 1971, 1977, 1978).
2. Robert Skidelsky, *John Maynard Keynes*, vol. II: *The Economist as Saviour, 1920–1937* (London, 1992), pp. 4f., 27f.
3. David Cannadine, *G. M. Trevelyan: A Life in History* (London, 1992), pp. 17, 69, 122f.

a period. In 1938 he was recruited from Aberystwyth University by Geoffrey Dawson, then editor of *The Times*, to bolster the newspaper's pro-appeasement line. Later, as assistant editor between 1941 and 1946, Carr deftly resurrected the discredited policy, recasting the Soviet Union as the power to be appeased. He also turned *The Times* into a champion of the nascent welfare state: his was the famous leader on 5 January 1945 which linked 'the great twin scourges . . . of war . . . and of unemployment', without apparently noticing that nothing combated the latter better than the former.

Like Carr, the greatest media don of all was a man of the left and a Russophile, though no appeaser. This was A. J. P. Taylor. In the course of a supremely prolific career, Taylor managed to write:

23 books
13 pamphlets
45 essays
459 newspaper articles
4,500 book reviews

– to say nothing of 450 radio and television broadcasts, including the famous ITV lectures which made his a household name.[1] Most of this was done between 1938 and 1962 while he was a Fellow and Tutor at Magdalen College.

Principally a diplomatic historian, with an uncanny ability to construct a readable narrative on the basis of the most turgid diplomatic correspondence, Taylor was an inveterate troublemaker, whose attachment to a line of argument grew in more or less direct proportion to the number of people it annoyed. He was a Communist in his youth but evolved into a quirky kind of Radical, whose populist suspicion of 'the establishment' was balanced by a very English libertarianism. The man was a paradox in tweed. He advocated friendliness towards Stalin, yet venerated Churchill as 'the saviour of his country'. He opposed British entry into the European Economic Community, yet favoured British withdrawal from Ulster. He rejoiced at the miners' victory in 1972, yet lamented the effects of the Heath–Wilson inflation on his savings.

All this made for good copy. But Taylor's real appeal to editors

1. Adam Sisman, *A. J. P. Taylor: A Biography* (London, 1994).

was that he could produce his copy at phenomenal speed. He was gifted with a prodigious fluency of expression. The sound of Taylor typing a piece recalled a Maxim gun strafing the enemy line. Lectures were prepared in his head and delivered at breakneck speed without notes or hesitations. When he performed this trick on television in front of audiences of several million, a new species was born: the telly don.

Perhaps the crucial respect in which Taylor differed from previous media dons was this willingness to broadcast to – and write for – the masses. When he began a column for the downmarket *Sunday Pictorial* in 1951, the editor of the *New Statesman*, Kingsley Martin, pleaded with him to consider the effect on his academic reputation. Taylor replied:

> I ask myself: ought I to be content with teaching ten or fifteen under-graduates at Magdalen, or even with writing for the fairly limited readers of the *New Statesman* and the *Manchester Guardian*? If [the *Sunday Pictorial*] gives me the chance of addressing five million people, ought I to take fright . . . ?
>
> As for my academic reputation . . . it has done me more harm to write for the *New Statesman* that the *Sunday Pic*, simply because academic people read the one and not the other.[1]

'You only do it for the money,' lamented Martin. 'No,' replied Taylor, 'I do it because I'm good at it.'

Of course, Taylor was being disingenuous. He did it because he was good at it *and* for the money. Indeed, there is a necessary if not sufficient explanation for the advent of the media don, and that is the meagreness of academic salaries. Repeatedly in the twentieth century, dons have asserted their right to be paid as well as senior civil servants. Never have they achieved this, and it now pays better for a young man to join the police. After tax, a don's salary will barely pay for a nanny. On the other hand, though cash-poor, academics are time-rich: the traditional calendar at Oxford and

1. *ibid.*, p. 203.

Cambridge comprises three eight-week terms, and during those terms the average teaching Fellow gives tutorials for between eight and fourteen hours a week, and lectures at most once a week. Examinations and administration can devour much of the remainder, but the fact remains that dons have more free time – or rather, more time for 'research', a word which truly covers a multitude of sins – than civil servants. They also retain the option to compress their teaching, or to do it, as Maurice Cowling used to do at Peterhouse, after dinner.

So they need the money and they have the time. Journalism offers the perfect complement: it pays substantially better than teaching, and it can also be done at odd times. Keynes made between £1,500 and £4,000 a year from journalism in the early 1920s.[1] Kathy Burk has calculated that Taylor made on average £7,000 a year from his media work.[2] In 1997 prices, that amounts to a peak of £77,280 a year for Keynes and £52,920 a year for Taylor. These figures should be compared with a recent survey of ten writers of fiction, four of whom named sums of up to £70,000 as the 'suggested annual income of writers'.[3]

It is not difficult to see how Keynes found time for hack work. Although he had only one term off from teaching in Cambridge between 1919 and 1937, his teaching load was light: just eight lectures a year, and several hours of supervisions for King's College undergraduates, which he used to do on Friday or Saturday evenings. Taylor too was a beneficiary of a faculty special lectureship in his later Oxford years, which substantially reduced the number of tutorials he had to give.

It would be wrong, however, to see money as the media dons' sole motivation. Writing for newspapers widens an academic's social circle (and journalists are generally a great deal more amusing to dine with than other dons). More importantly, it is an indirect route into the corridors of power; or at least lets one look in through the corridor windows. The more trouble-making sort of media don

1. Skidelsky, *Keynes*, vol. II, p. 27.
2. Kathleen Burk, 'The Millionaire History Man', *Spectator*, 22 February 1997.
3. Alain de Botton, 'The Cost of Letters', *W Magazine* (1998), p. 16.

prefers to remain outside the political tent. But Keynes worked at the Treasury before and after going in for journalism, and was always more comfortable among the mandarins than among the hacks.

This raises an important, if somewhat pompous, question. Are those academics who write for newspapers, whatever their private reasons for doing so – and no matter how mercenary those may be – simultaneously performing a public duty? Not, perhaps, when waxing indignant on some triviality ('Why, oh why, must young people listen to personal stereos on trains?'). But when Roger Scruton, Timothy Garton Ash, Norman Stone or Mark Almond wrote – as in the 1980s they very frequently did – on the subject of Communism in Eastern Europe, they assuredly were not prostituting their intellects. On the contrary, their journalism did much to make intelligible to the wider public the revolutions of 1989–90: events which conspicuously baffled the professional Kremlinologists in the universities.

And this, after all, is one important reason why (to turn to the other side of the equation) editors have for so long been willing to give column inches to dons. Admittedly, it was a belief cherished by the late Sir David English that almost any view could be lent credibility if, at the end of the piece, the author was stated in italics to be a Fellow of an Oxford or Cambridge college, as well as a 'top' historian. But the currency of academic journalism would long ago have been debased if there were never any substance to the media dons' output. The collapse of Communism in 1989–90 was a case in point; as was the disintegration of Yugoslavia. When history is being made, newspapers and their readers need expert historical knowledge which few journalists possess; they need it fast; and they need it intelligible.

I well remember the arguments which went on in the *Telegraph* leader conference on the day sterling left the Exchange Rate Mechanism in September 1992. Senior executives who shall remain nameless insisted that Norman Lamont's strategy of raising interest rates to punitive heights would work. I had been reading some dense economic history on the events of 1931, when sterling left the gold standard, and insisted the game was up. That day I earned my corn, part of which I duly spent that night on a performance of Verdi's very apposite *The Force of Destiny*.

Such justifications, however, cut little ice back in the universities. This raises an interesting question: when and why did media dons become objects of disapproval? Keynes's journalism does not seem to have done his reputation much serious harm. But the same cannot be said for A. J. P. Taylor at Oxford – as foreseen by Kingsley Martin, who had warned him about the effect of tabloid journalism on his career. In 1952 Taylor was passed over for the chair of Modern History. Four years later, according to Taylor's autobiography, Sir Lewis Namier considered recommending him to Harold Macmillan for the Regius professorship. 'Of course,' Namier remarked, 'you must give up all this nonsense of appearing on television and writing for the *Sunday Express*.' Taylor petulantly retorted: 'What I do in my spare time is no concern of yours or of anyone else.' The chair went to Hugh Trevor-Roper, who – by a rich irony – was subsequently exposed to public humiliation when he lent his authority to the bogus *Hitler Diaries* published in . . . the *Sunday Times*.

When his faculty special lectureship was not renewed in 1962, Taylor left Oxford. His last post was as honorary director of Beaverbrook Library, a sinecure created for him by the press baron whose papers he had helped to fill and whose biography, in a strange act of homage, he wasted time writing.

The loss of Taylor was (to use a journalistic phrase) a public relations disaster for Oxford, which appeared to have dropped its best-known historian for the sin of addressing a popular audience. When I arrived at Taylor's old college, Magdalen, in the 1980s – having applied precisely because Taylor had once taught there – I was amazed to find him still unrevered. His old enemy in the college, the medievalist K. B. McFarlane, was far more fondly remembered, though he had published just one book in his entire career. 'Journalistic' was the supreme insult in the lexicon of his successor, Karl Leyser. I can well remember how he tortured me at our Schools Dinner (after our Final examinations, but before the results) by expressing his opinion of Paul Johnson – another Magdalen man who had come to personify in his mind all the unspeakable baseness of the word 'journalistic'. 'He got a second,' Karl gleefully told me. 'I alvays said zat he had a *second-class* mind.' How I prayed for a First that night.

It is significant that Karl Leyser had been born in Germany. For in many ways the belief that academics should confine their attention exclusively to academic research originated in Germany too. It came to the English universities between the wars, with the arrival and ascent of (to name but two) Geoffrey Elton and Lewis Namier; it was encouraged by Germanophiles like Herbert Butterfield. Germanization meant that doctorates became the *sine qua non* of election to fellowships. Scholarship came to be measured out in footnotes. In time, prose intelligible to the lay reader gave way to jargon beyond his ken.

Yet all this was and is absurd. Apart from anything else, the Germans have never really practised a strict separation of *Wissenschaft* and *Publizistik*. To be sure, anyone wanting an academic job is obliged to serve an apprenticeship so long and so demoralizing that the risk of writing for the press is out of the question. By the time the coveted professorship has been obtained, the urge to be a hack has long gone, if it was ever there; and in any case the pay is so much better than in Britain, why bother? Yet without academic contributors, a weekly like *Die Zeit* would never have been able to stoke up the 'historians' quarrel' about the Holocaust in the 1980s. And as for the rest of Europe, the idea that academics should not write for newspapers would be regarded as absurd in Italy or France. In Italy it is thought far more absurd for a professor to waste his time teaching students.

Even in American universities, which adopted even more of the conventions of German academic life than Britain, it is permitted to write the occasional piece opposite the editorials. Indeed, the *New York Times* would not be able to sustain its exalted standard of unreadability on the 'op-ed' page without enlisting academics, the only kind of people capable of writing pieces like 'A New Role for the UN in Central Africa?' or 'The Next Phase of Health Care Reform'.

*

More important than academic Germanization in making British media dons unpopular has been the political polarization of university life. It was no coincidence that today's best-known media dons came to the fore in the early 1980s, following the election of Margaret Thatcher as prime minister. From Stone to Starkey to Scruton, they were united by a readiness to defend Thatcherism in print. The demand for such pieces was almost insatiable, given the strong backing the Conservatives were then receiving from newspaper proprietors – not to mention the persistent unpopularity of the government, which seemed to necessitate cheerleading comment. But the antipathy towards Thatcherism in the universities, among both staff and students, was as intense as enthusiasm in Fleet Street. This meant that those of us who put pen to paper in the government's defence risked ostracization in the workplace.

The hatred of John Vincent knew no bounds in Bristol when he began to write his column for the *Sun* in the 1980s. Norman Stone encountered similar reactions in Oxford. Only in Peterhouse, Cambridge, was it safe to be an academic Thatcherite (though this was perhaps the only respect in which Peterhouse could be described as safe). In Oxford, to contribute to anything to the right of the *London Review of Books* was to incur the permanent loathing of that faction of the Modern History faculty which sipped its coffee and plotted in the King's Arms of a Saturday morning.

It would be a gross exaggeration to say that the media dons of the 1980s have been persecuted for their publicly stated beliefs. But it is certainly a strange coincidence that so many of them have since left the British university system. J. C. D. Clark has left Oxford for Kansas; Norman Stone is now in Ankara; Roger Scruton has given up teaching altogether. One case is particularly sad: that of Professor John Gray, once Oxford's most articulate defender of neo-liberal economic policy, who felt obliged in the early 1990s – under mysterious circumstances – to recant. Today he inveighs against the evils of unregulated capitalism in, of all places, the London School of Economics and the *Guardian*.

The academics who supported the Thatcher governments will probably always be hated, not least by those in Oxford who conspired to deny her the honorary degree which was her due. Still, there are signs of a new spirit of tolerance, particularly in the higher echelons of university administration.

The universities are slowly coming to recognize that they need the media dons. They attract students who, in the increasingly competitive higher education, even Oxford and Cambridge cannot expect to drop into their laps. They make universities visible to the ordinary taxpayer, who continues to pay for a substantial part of the cost of British higher education. They may even attract benefactors, who are more often to be met at the dinner parties of press barons than of those of faculty board chairpersons.

Two signs of the changing times are the fact that there is now a chair in Language and Communications named after Rupert Murdoch in Oxford, while the eminent Darwinian biologist Richard Dawkins glories in the title of 'Professor for the Public Understanding of Science'. If that is not a licence to be a media don, I don't know what is.

What a shortlist they will have when they find the money for a similar chair in History: the 'Fluke' Kelso chair, perhaps.

Female 'Firemen'

ANN LESLIE

Isn't it a great disadvantage being a woman when working and travelling in mad, bad and dangerous corners of the world? The doughty adventurer Dame Freya Stark thought not: indeed in 1934 she wrote, in *The Valley of the Assassins*, that the great advantage of 'being a woman is that one can always pretend to be more stupid than one is, and no one is surprised'. (By 'no one', she meant men.)

The madder and badder the country, the more true that is. I am a female 'fireman', the jargon name given to those foreign correspondents who are not permanently based abroad, but who spend their lives flying in and out of the world's trouble-spots. I have worked in around seventy countries so far – covering wars, famines, civil and social collapse – and have on the whole found that, contrary to expectation, my gender has proved to be no disadvantage at all. Most mad, bad countries tend to be extremely macho societies: it is therefore bred into young Ivan, Mohammed, Li, Yusuf, Juan, Dragan and the rest that women are destined – often by 'God's will' – to be inferior to men.

As such, these foolish females are – again by 'God's will' – prone to hysteria and confusion, have poorly wired brains which simply cannot grasp the importance of regulations, are genetically incapable of filling in forms properly and are, most embarrassingly, prone to bursting into tears over *the slightest thing*. Even the most stunted, scrofulous and crotch-scratching example of local manhood believes, in his heart of hearts, that he is – compared to a mere woman – a Master of the Universe. The woman who conforms to his bird-brain stereotype is therefore no threat to him at all.

Thus the ability, when appropriate, to play the bird-brain has proved, for me at least, to be an essential component in the female fireman's armoury – despite the fact that, in reality, one veers rather more to the role of P. G. Wodehouse's formidably fierce Aunt Agatha, who wore broken bottles next to the skin.

The fact is that Ivan, Mohammed, Li and the rest do not like powerful, know-it-all women: such terrifying creatures make them doubt their own masculinity – and this, in some parts of the world, is a dangerous doubt to implant in what passes for the mind of a man with a gun. But your job is not to educate them in gender-equality politics: your job is to get them to help, not hinder, you.

Which brings us to the importance of the handbag in the female fireman's repertoire. When some axe-faced bureaucrat, immigration official or security goon points out (correctly) that I do not have the proper papers, I heave my handbag on to the desk and insist: 'Oh, but I *do*! It's just that I can't *find* them!' I then, like some truffle-hunting pig, begin searching through the bag, fishing out bits of old make-up, broken car keys, letters from my daughter, eyebrow pencil, airline socks, some very small teddy-bears for a godchild, false eyelashes, broken Kit-Kats, parking tickets, a Tina Turner CD, spare tights, dead batteries, empty pill bottles and an ancient recipe for Irish stew. As the pile of handbag detritus builds up on the apparatchik's desk, it begins to resemble a miniature version of the grotesque Smoky Mountain, the huge refuse dump outside Manila in the Philippines.

After a while, the blocking official begins to get exasperated: he does not want to see all this rubbish piling up on his desk, and he does not want to listen any more to the twitterings of this silly woman. Besides, he is by now convinced that failure to produce the right papers is not sinister, but merely proof that I'm terminally disorganized and batty – in short, 'a typical woman'. Rather than endure any more of this Smoky Mountain stuff, he'll often, with patronizing weariness, wave me through.

But bird-brain behaviour has sometimes to be alternated – or combined – with what I describe (having been born in India) as Daughter-of-the-Raj imperiousness. When in that mode, a female fireman has to behave as if she has an inalienable right to be wherever she chooses to be, and therefore simply cannot understand why anyone should question it.

I needed to employ this mode to get into the kings and presidents area at the funeral of Emperor Hirohito of Japan. Security was tight, not only because of the presence of so many world leaders, but because of bomb threats by Japanese left-wing groups, and the international press were corralled by the deeply conservative Imperial Household Agency into a freezing tent about half a mile away in a muddy field.

'Where's your pass?' I was asked by various security officers as I marched towards the VIP tent. 'Oh, don't be so *silly*,' I'd say firmly but with, hopefully, a certain Grand Duchess charm, as I swept on by. I ended up standing in the same row as the then President George Bush. I'd once interviewed him aboard Air Force One and I realized, as he kept peering at me, that he was thinking: 'Have I met this woman before?' Perhaps just in case I was the queen of some minor European country whom it would be crass to offend, Bush kept giving me slow, slightly puzzled, lopsided smiles of 'recognition'. Needless to say, had I had an AK47 stashed under my voluminous fur coat, I could have wiped out most of the world's leaders in a couple of minutes flat.

But harmless bird-brain, rather than undaunted Daughter-of-the-Raj, works better in the long run. Indeed, so effective is the former that I have found that assorted thugs round the world will become oddly protective. 'Please, dear lady, you are our guest! We honour and respect women in our culture!' they'll tell you with extravagant chivalry. (This is, obviously, not the moment to remind them that you know for a fact that rape, bride-burning and genital mutilation are rather more endemic than chivalry and respect in what they call 'our culture'.)

They become especially protective if you show them pictures of your husband, your child, your household pets; if you chirrup on about how you cook sheep in your country, and how the way that they cook sheep in their country is so much more delicious, and how you are so looking forward to cooking sheep, in their manner, for your family, and how you truly believe that making clothes for the family is indeed one of the highest callings a woman can aspire to, but alas, such are the cruelties of life for women in the West that one is obliged to work in a job like journalism.

But the *coup de grâce* is, almost invariably, to ask to see pictures of their own families. Hand-grenades are put away, Kalashnikovs discarded, and out of their stained uniforms come tumbling dog-eared snaps of 'my eldest son, I am so proud, he is only eight years old, but he will be a very brave fighter, and this is my daughter – yes, you are right, she is very beautiful – and this is my mother'. (Often their eyes become seriously moist at this point and their moustaches somewhat tear-soaked. Killers are notoriously senti-mental about their mums.)

Is this manipulative behaviour immoral? Perhaps it is. But it usually gets results. Moreover, one needs to find out why these men behave as they do, what motivates them, what they consider to be important in their lives. By getting your interviewees – especially if they are bafflingly violent men – to relax, to trust you and to tell you their grievances and the story of their lives, you'll often gain an insight into why, however reprehensibly, apparently ordinary men (and sometimes women) feel driven to systematically murder their neighbours. To understand all is not, in my view, to forgive all, but without some understanding you cannot hope to grasp the com-plexities that often underlie such apparently irrational behaviour.

The more dangerous the interviewee, the more important it is that you 'waste' time at the beginning by chatting about everything *except* what you really want to know. ('Was it you who ordered the murder of those women and children in Port-au-Prince?') If your first substantive question threatens your hopefully by now 'beautiful friendship', do not pursue it. Start twittering again about babies and sheep recipes as if you hadn't really realized that you'd asked the question at all. My mantra in potentially difficult or dangerous interviews and negotiations is always 'one step forward, two steps back'.

Your first substantive question is in the form of 'inoculation'. By the time your second substantive question comes they've had warning, and the shock to their system on discovering that you are not perhaps their new best friend – whose prime concern is for their mother's arthritis – is therefore not so severe. You must keep your most difficult, or potentially enraging, questions to the end – having of course worked out the location of the nearest exit.

In Bosnia I once came across an idealistic American radio reporter who evidently didn't understand the 'inoculation' principle. In a local bar in the Bosnian Serb 'capital' of Pale, a murderous band of paramilitaries, so-called Chetniks, were carousing, wildly drunk, their beards sodden with booze, their death's-head regalia clotted with vomit. They began singing a song which I recognized (whose lyrics roughly translated as 'Death to the Muslims! Let us rape their women, destroy their children, burn their homes, for the Holy Cause of Greater Serbia').

The American reporter, pushy and naïve, noisily demanded, in her 'public's-right-to-know' way, that she tape-record them and that they defend their views to her. But the Chetniks were obviously not in the vein for a reasoned discussion of local geopolitics. She, a child of the US Constitution's First Amendment, persisted. One of the enraged Chetniks then tore the tape out of her recorder and slowly began eating it; his gold teeth were tangled with black tape, broken bits of cassette plastic littered his beard. He then wrapped his arm, complete with knife attached, round her throat, threatening to slit it like a farmyard pig's.

Luckily for her, one of his friends restrained him, and the reporter fled, terrified. Later I suggested to her that she should have 'made friends' with the Chetniks first before trying to question them and record their drunken maunderings. 'But you can't make friends with psychopathic killers! It's *immoral*!' she insisted. I disagreed: 'You must *especially* make friends with psychopathic killers – on the whole, nice people don't try to cut your throat.'

The 'inoculation' principle can, of course, take time. In Cuba, for example, I was trying to get the first interview with Fidel Castro's daughter Alina, a deeply unhappy woman who eventually defected to Miami. Her apartment was guarded by secret police; I was followed everywhere. However, thanks to a Cuban expert in London, I'd been given the name of a local contact who might be able to get me into the apartment. But, not surprisingly, the contact didn't know whether he could trust me. Trust-building therefore meant hours of talking about everything *but* Fidel Castro's daughter. Yes, I had seen the great Cuban film *Memories of Under-development*, yes, I knew all about *Santeria*, the local version of voodoo, yes, I had read some of the great Cuban poets.

To establish trust you must always, wherever possible, research your subject, read the poetry, see the films. Cheerful ignorance of a culture never opens doors, and those who don't actually do the research, but try to blag their way through, are very soon – and rightly – caught out. The Cuban trust-building exercise eventually worked, and I got the interview with Alina.

I usually work on my own abroad, without a photographer. I'm sometimes asked whether I'm not afraid of being raped. No, not especially. Frankly, along with novelist Fay Weldon, I do not believe that rape is a 'fate worse than death'. You can, albeit with difficulty, get over rape, but you can't get over death. Admittedly, in thirty-seven years of journalism I have never been raped: the only time I came close to it was in the Gulf States at the start of the oil boom in the mid-seventies, and the man concerned, wielding a knife at the time, happened to be a highly educated, charming Yemeni, with an extensive knowledge of Shakespeare. Could have happened in Sloane Square.

But two female foreign correspondent friends have been raped while working in dangerous parts of the world and (surprise) they tell me, with many a wry shrug, that, given the choice, they *definitely* prefer rape to death. Indeed, to assume that forcible and unpleasant penetration by some oafish, murderous, illiterate and often drunken gunman is actually worse than departing this life for ever is, in effect, to accord the penis an importance as a weapon of war which it does not deserve.

I was reminded of this when interviewing rape victims in the former Yugoslavia's conflict. All the women were, of course, traumatized; all those whom I interviewed were, at least nominally, Muslims. But the Westernized Muslim women seemed to me better able to endure what had happened to them than those who were more traditional. The latter were full of the shame *they* had brought on their menfolk, and believed that, for the 'crime' of being raped, they deserved to be rejected by their families.

*

When I began my career in journalism, after coming down from Oxford in the sixties, I was desperate not to be confined to the 'girlie' ghetto of frocks, gossip and knit-your-own-royals. As a feminist I believed that I should not only be as tough as any man, but make sure that every man knew it. If you couldn't prove that you had 'bigger balls than the men' (as one tough woman reporter put it to me), then you deserved the girlie ghetto.

The role model suggested to me was another woman reporter who wore combat fatigues, swore like a trooper, and shouted 'Kill, kill!' much of the time – and she was only covering the Pennines. Because of her, I learned such essential techniques as how to remove the diaphragms of public phones so that your rivals couldn't use them; how to remove the distributor-head in their car engines (to this day the only part of a car engine I can recognize); and how to let down tyres so that you could get a head start on your rivals in any car chase. And this was *still* only the Pennines.

So, hey, I had 'balls'. But nothing prepared me for my first big foreign trip in the sixties to Mexico, where I was to follow the drugs trail north from the poppy fields in the mountains and on into southern California. Before acquiring permission to enter two of the most notorious and lawless drug-producing Mexican states, I was informed by the martial-law police that I had to carry a gun at all times, and be trained to use it. I demurred: Mexicans, especially the kind I'd be dealing with – the drug-running *traficantes* – are born with guns in their teeth. By the time I'd got the gun out of my handbag, either I would have been riddled with bullets or, more likely, would have shot my own toes off.

My protests were to no avail: training was insisted upon. At the firing-range, the police marksmen struck me as a very rum lot: not only did they smell of tequila, but most of them seemed to have little bits of their anatomy missing – an ear here, a finger there, a nostril there ... How did these mutilations occur? Such 'flesh-wounds of honour', they told me, strutting with pride, were the result of fiercely fought battles with the *traficantes*. Later, one of them admitted to me that they'd shot off bits of themselves by accident, when drunk.

Best to get rid of the gun, I thought, and aim for the totally harmless look. A month later, in a remote area of Durango province, I was looking for a particular heroin-poppy field. As I trudged up the hill, a band of moustachioed *traficantes* leapt into view from behind the cactuses, aiming their ancient Lee-Enfield rifles at me. They suddenly stopped in astonishment: nobody, absolutely nobody, had ever come trudging up their gun-bristled hill wearing white gloves, a white-and-yellow Horrocks frock (in those distant days, the epitome of the bourgeois Celia Johnson memsahib style), and carrying a white handbag. Naturally these brave peasant sons of Zapata laughed like drains. I was obviously so mad that I was not worth wasting bullets on. Not only that, but I became a kind of exotic trophy to be shown off to the rest of their mustachioed Lee-Enfield-draped chums. Never had any trouble from the *traficantes* after that.

I do not believe in journalists carrying guns – it suggests you are a combatant – and that first experience of 'gun culture' convinced me I was right. I'm also very uneasy about wearing a helmet or a flak-jacket (though nitpickers like insurance companies and husbands tend to insist on it). This is because you are often in a place where the local population cannot afford to acquire a helmet or flak-jacket, and are being shelled and shot at every day. It is almost insulting to them to interview them about the horrors they've endured, and are enduring, while you yourself are kitted out with as much protective armour as a warrior on the field of Agincourt.

One of the few *disadvantages* of being a woman is that, in certain parts of the world, you're constrained by local dress codes, which can prove rather inconvenient workwise.

Before going out to Saudi Arabia for the build-up to the Gulf War, I had to have a training session at RAF Brize Norton in how to put on a Nuclear Biological and Chemical protection suit and how, by observing the colour changes in the tabs on my NBC suit, I would know which particular gas Iraq's Saddam Hussein had released – and thus which antidote to jab into my thigh. The first problem came with definitions of 'colour': being a woman – who, via fashion mags, knows all about subtle differences in colour tone – I tended to argue. 'You call this purple? I'd call it *puce*! Look, this isn't *green*, it's more *jade*!'

I decided to wear at Brize Norton what I would be wearing in Saudi: one of my 'Widow Twankey' outfits. I had worked in Saudi before and had, as a result of harassment by the *Muttawah*, the religious police, acquired a set of flowing, all-enveloping garments (the 'Widow Twankeys') in order to avoid exciting the *Muttawah*'s persecutionary juices. But getting into an NBC suit while wearing a Widow Twankey is not a speedy matter. My instructor despaired of me: '*Once again*, Ms Leslie. You were dead fifteen minutes ago.' Needless to say, after arriving in Dhahran, and despite the Scud missile warnings, I never wore the hot, cumbersome NBC suit. I figured that wearing it would kill me with heat exhaustion long before one of Saddam's little canisters could get to me.

What a foreign correspondent working in a strange land needs above all is a good local 'fixer', and good fixers are expensive. The fixer is far more than a mere interpreter: he or she is someone with contacts, someone who knows (sometimes in the biblical sense) the man or woman in charge of special passes, or has access to the bloke who can 'borrow' an official car to get you through military checkpoints, or who is a cousin of the woman who is sleeping with the police chief, and who therefore might help you out. Ideally, a fixer should also have a sense of humour, otherwise – in times of privation and danger – the strain can get to both of you. A spot of gallows humour, especially from someone who knows the madness of his own country well, is a great releaser of tension.

Once, in the coup-ridden Congo, I stood on the river bank and pointed to a huge clump of water-weed floating by. 'What exactly is that stuff?' I asked. My Congolese fixer thought for a moment, then threw his head back and laughed uproariously: 'Probably the last Minister of Education!'

Being a woman journalist does not give you an advantage in acquiring the fixer in the first place: contacts and hard currency, in cash, are always what count. Former spies or secret policemen are particularly useful as fixers not least because, understandably, they tend to know all the relevant addresses and phone numbers. One of my favourite fixers in Soviet Russia was a KGB man who, in a flurry of publicity, was expelled from London by Mrs Thatcher for 'activities incompatible with . . .'.

Hanging on to your fixer, once acquired, despite the vast amounts of money being offered by rival organizations, does I think require certain (perhaps stereotypical) 'female skills'. The women correspondents I know tend to find it easier than men to empathize instantly with the private and emotional lives of the person who's working for them, and can thus build up a bond of loyalty.

When working in Communist East Berlin, I had found a wonderful East German who, beautiful and fluent in English, had once been married to an American pop star who defected to the East for ideological reasons: probably the only person (other than spies and terrorists) who'd made the journey in that direction. (He was then used by Kruschev, Ulbricht and Honecker to promote a new 'Soviet' form of pop to rival the 'decadent' Beatles.)

I was already working with her in East Berlin when the Berlin Wall came down, heralding the end of the Cold War. In the early hours she and I, both with tears flooding down our cheeks, drove through Checkpoint Charlie in her battered East German Wartburg; our car was one of the first to cross freely into the West. We were greeted by thousands of West Berliners shouting their welcomes and showering us with champagne. Later in that deeply moving, exhausting, exhilarating November week, the city became the magnet for the biggest international press and TV contingent I've ever seen, and all were desperate for a fixer − preferably mine. But she and I had been through so much together, and had shared so much of our personal lives with each other, that she stayed loyal.

But often a good fixer does not even speak passable English. The world is full of Arthur Daleys, duckers and divers, men who've got little scams going, thanks to their second-cousin-twice-removed in the Politburo, the benefits of which − for a price (and a lot of exchanging of family photos) − they will make available to you.

One of the best of this breed I found in a remote region in north-east China, close to the border with North Korea: the nearest big city was Vladivostok, in the far east of Russia. I wanted to investigate the hidden famine of North Korea. My Arthur Daley only spoke Mandarin and Korean; but no matter: the minute I saw him I felt that he was my man. After long experience you acquire an instinctive ability to recognize who is the right Arthur Daley for you, even when you're in one of the wildest and most remote parts of the world. It's a bit like falling in love at first sight: you know you are 'destined' for each other – at least for the next couple of weeks!

It was thanks largely to him that I was able to get into even more remote regions where North Korean refugees, fleeing from the famine which may have killed up to 3 million people, were hiding in Chinese-Korean peasant dug-outs. If caught by the Chinese authorities they'd be arrested, shackled, and sent back to a likely death in their own country across the Tumen River border.

Often a fixer can rescue you from your own journalistic failure. A few years ago, I was trying to get into what was then known as Zaire. It was at the time of the second *pillage*, the name given to the bouts of destruction and pillaging of the capital Kinshasa, which occurred because the army had taken offence at being paid, yet again, in utterly worthless 5-million-*zaire* banknotes (inflation at that time being roughly 7,000 per cent).

Their staggeringly corrupt paymaster, 'President for Life' Mobutu, the dictator in the leopard-skin hat (who liked to be known as the 'Red Hot Chilli Pepper'), was not in his looted capital; his presidential palace there, twice the size of Buckingham Palace, had long been deserted. He preferred to spend his time in his Pink Palace on the Côte d'Azur, or in the 'Versailles in the Jungle' which he had created for himself in his remote home town of Gbadolite.

This mad Versailles (since looted by his equally appalling vanquishers) had fountains which were computer controlled, and he'd built himself an international airport so that he, his wife, his mistresses and his entourage could jump on to a chartered Concorde whenever it took their fancy to do a bit of Parisian shopping. (When his wife flew to France in a private jet, a giant Hercules transport plane was also dispatched to carry back ten tons' worth of her purchases.) When one Washington banker, to whom Mobutu had turned for yet another 'development loan', coldly suggested that he might try using his own looted wealth to help his people, he had replied dismissively: 'Oh, I couldn't do that. My people could never repay me.'

I had been refused a Zairean visa and was stranded on the wrong side of the border river in Brazzaville in the Congo, the former

French colony. Even the legendary, self-styled 'Congo One', a vast and fearsome Congolese woman renowned for fixing more or less anything, let me down. 'With the second *pillage*, even I am afraid to cross the river *à ce moment*!'

Then I met Mr Massamba. He did not speak English, I did not understand the local language, he did not understand my O-level French – but he had a document enabling him to cross the Congo River at will. He could not actually get me into Kinshasa, but . . .

Thanks to the *pillage*, the already barely functioning Kinshasa phone system had collapsed and tropical storms had disabled the satellite phones. But I suspected that mobiles might still be operating and, since I could see Kinshasa from my Brazzaville hotel, the signal should work. (At that time Brazzaville mobiles were unavailable.) I suggested to Mr Massamba that he might cross the river and, let's say, 'acquire' a Kinshasa mobile (plus some vital mobile phone numbers) for me. This he duly did; I did not ask him how. (One of the many unwritten rules of fixerdom is that, so long as one does not suspect murder, one does not ask too many questions.) Despite failing to get into Zaire, I still – thanks to Mr Massamba – got the story by dint of standing on the banks of the Congo River and interviewing those on the other side.

The fixer's role in foreign corresponding is almost never acknowledged publicly: after all, lone gun-slinger 'star' correspondents like to pretend that they did it all themselves. But all correspondents know how vital a fixer can be and, if they're sensible, will never exploit them. I do not hold with the American Republican theory that 'a man who cheats on his wife will cheat on the country'; but I do believe that a foreign correspondent who, in any way, cheats on his fixer may well cheat on his readers. I still do not forgive a correspondent I met in China who, literally, cheated on his Chinese fixer – her name translated as Comrade Bright Lily – and I was not at all surprised to discover that he had cheated on his readers, and the truth, as well.

In every hot spot there is always one hotel where the international media congregate: this is not mere herd instinct, a chance to drink in the bar with your mates. The press hotel becomes a clearing-house for news and rumour, it's the crowded haunt where the local 'spooks' – Sigurimi, Mossad, CIA, Stasi, Shik, KGB, FSB, PSB, Ton-ton Macoutes, MI6 agents – hang out in the bar (they're grilling us, while we grill them). Moreover, it's the place to which brave but frightened local people will often try to come if they want their stories to be heard, hoping that the presence of the international press will protect them.

In Albania, when virtual civil war was raging, a group of dissident Tirana journalists fled into the press hotel seeking protection from the murderous pro-government Shik gunmen: we hid them in our bedrooms and bathrooms until we thought they were fairly safe.

Old Indochina, Middle East, Balkan, African or Central American hands – they all have fond, and sometimes less fond, memories of the press hotels they have known.

Famous examples include the Al Rashid in Baghdad, the Holiday Inn in Sarajevo, the Hyatt in Belgrade, the St Georges and Commodore in Beirut, the 'Intercon' in Amman, Meikles in Zimbabwe, the ill-named Grand in Priština the American Colony in Jerusalem. 'Remember the Camino Real in San Salvador?' an old Central American hand mused to me recently. 'Remember the time when you arrived late at night from Tegucigalpa, and your room phone kept ringing and there was nothing but clicks at the other end, and you thought it was the lousy Salvadorean phone system? The next morning I broke it to you that it was the usual "welcome" from the death squads to any newly arrived foreign correspondent, warning you not to write "slanders" about them.' He laughed: 'The clicks were their usual clicking on and off of the safety catch on a gun!'

In poor, insane, beautiful little Haiti the press hotel was always the Olofsson, immortalized in Graham Greene's *The Comedians*. Everyone came to swap tales on the filigreed verandah of the gently decaying wooden building. Murderers, saintly missionaries, journalists, Ton-ton Macoutes and – especially – the Olofsson 'star', the model for Greene's police informer Petit Pierre, Monsieur Aubelin Jolicoeur (Mr Prettyheart). A wildly camp father of six, Mr Prettyheart would nightly prance across the Olofsson verandah wearing his white suit and swinging his silver-topped cane, a foulard scarf tied Noël-Coward-style round his black neck.

There were safer, more efficient hotels, but none so expressive of Haiti. Night after gun-punctured night I would lie in my bed in the ghostly gingerbread mansion, gazing on a portrait of the black Emperor Jean-Jacques Dessalines in his Napoleonic tricorne hat – and listen, as Greene must have done, to the distant staccato sounds of the poor killing the poor in the interests of the rich.

The famous foreign correspondent Nicholas Tomalin, killed on the Syrian Golan Heights in 1973, once said that all you needed to be a good journalist was 'a plausible manner, rat-like cunning and a little literary ability'. Most of us like to believe that it's our 'rat-like cunning' which gets us our better stories. But in my case it's quite often just chance – as when I got a bizarre interview with Gorbachev and his wife Raisa during a superpower summit on a Russian ship moored off the storm-lashed coast of Malta. (I'd originally set off in a determined search for a cup of coffee, and somehow both the American Secret Service and the KGB failed to nab me before I ended up in Gorbachev's private suite.)

And again it was a chance event that turned a boringly formal interview in Delhi with the fearsome prime minister Indira Gandhi into something rather different.

Mrs Gandhi had dictatorial tendencies (shortly after our meeting she suspended democracy and imposed the Emergency) and she did not like journalists, particularly Western ones, a couple of whom she expelled. She was not terribly keen on other women either, whom she largely regarded as a bunch of snivelling wimps. But, through a London contact who had been a great friend of her adored late father, Jawaharlal Nehru, I had finally secured an interview with the subcontinent's Iron Lady.

Nervous about the encounter, I had prepared the interview meticulously, ordered a curry from my luxury hotel's room service, and retired to bed early. In the small hours of the morning I woke, convinced that I was dying. Thanks to the poisonous curry supper, I was vomiting and bleeding from more orifices than I thought existed. When later I staggered in to the prime minister's office, and began gasping out my questions, I kept having to say, 'I'm so sorry, Prime Minister, but could I borrow your bathroom?'

My appalling state suddenly softened the Iron Lady and she became solicitous and grandmotherly, like the *ayahs* I knew from my Indian childhood. She laid me on her couch, sang Brahms's Lullaby to me and recited her favourite poetry (she knew by heart Walter Turner's poem 'Romance': 'Chimborazo, Cotopaxi, they had stolen my soul away!'). She talked at length about her loves and fears, for herself, her two sons, and for India, and at one point seemed close to tears. Despite her public air of high-handed arrogance, privately at that moment she seemed to sense an oncoming doom. (And doom, of course, came: her favourite son Sanjay was later killed in a flying accident, she herself was assassinated by her own bodyguard, and her son Rajiv died at the hand of a Tamil Tiger.) No 'rat-like cunning' got me that revealing interview: just amoebic dysentery.

The only time where rat-like cunning truly came into play was when I was trying to get into Gorazde in Bosnia, then under siege by the Serbs. The latter were refusing permission to the world's journalists to visit the front line. But I knew about a famous Serb Orthodox church on the front line which had been desecrated by Gorazde's Muslims. I talked endlessly about the church to the Bosnian Serb military men, said how I longed to see it, how tragic it was that such a great example of Serb culture had been destroyed, but yes, of course, it was far too dangerous to go there now. I insisted I had absolutely no desire to go anywhere near the mortars and the sniper bullets, that I had my family to think of, and besides I was *much* too scared. No male war correspondent could convincingly play this tune, no male journalist would be able to convince the soldiers that all he really wanted to see was some half-wrecked old church. But 'women are like that', aren't they, into churches and art ... Eventually the Serbs were almost insisting that I visit the church: 'You have shown an informed interest in our culture and history, you do not assume that the Serb people are all savages!' And so I got to the Gorazde front line, and was the only journalist there.

But the fact that there are more women like myself working as foreign correspondents has caused some dismay. According to some critics there has been a 'feminization' of foreign news reporting. As one old news-agency reporter put it to me: 'Too much of the "dying baby" syndrome in foreign reporting today!' According to him, the 'I' word is too prevalent: one must tell the 'objective' truth. But what is the 'objective' truth? And where do you get it? From the congenital liars at the Ministry of Information? From the equally congenital liars at the 'rebel' HQ? You may be the person 'on the spot', but in a war zone you often cannot tell what is going on over the next hill, let alone kid yourself that you are in magisterial command of the whole picture.

But while you can, and should, always say to readers 'this is what I have seen', you cannot leave it at that: if you do there's a tendency to indulge in the 'pornography of grief'. It's vital that you still try to put what you *have* seen into as broad a context as possible, based on your background knowledge of the wider issues.

Do readers these days care about obscure and baffling conflicts in 'faraway countries of which we know nothing'? And even if people are interested they can get their information from the television coverage – so why bother with newspapers? I believe that readers who've had their interest awakened by television do want to know more about the situation than often simplistically emotive pictures can provide.

But I would say that, wouldn't I? That's because I have the immense privilege of being one of those whose job it is to write that 'first rough draft of history' – the privilege of being there on the midnight streets of Berlin when the Wall began to fall; in a humid Moscow when the coup against Gorbachev collapsed; outside the prison gate in the sunny, windswept winelands of South Africa when Nelson Mandela walked out to freedom after twenty-seven years.

Historians in the future may decide that that 'first rough draft of history' was not 'right'; but it must remain one of their sources. After all, it was, however fallibly, written by someone who was there.

Breakfast at Claridge's:
Getting the Sack

STEPHEN FAY

Sir Peregrine Worsthorne was taken to breakfast at Claridge's to
receive his professional death sentence from Andrew Knight. David
Montgomery also chose Claridge's to inform Richard Stott that he
was no longer editor of the *Mirror*, although he did not waste time
over a meal. Montgomery did the deed in the lobby. At least
Worsthorne had the comfort of two perfectly poached eggs on
buttered toast.

Worsthorne's mournful experience at Claridge's led him to specu-
late about the circumstances of being sacked. He had continued to
enjoy his poached eggs on toast – a dish of which, it turns out, he
is 'inordinately and insatiably' fond – despite Knight's grim news
that, since the daily and Sunday papers were to be merged, he would
no longer be editor of the *Sunday Telegraph*. 'One is not on one's
guard at breakfast,' he wrote in the *Spectator*.

He thought the manner in which a person is sacked was important.
It wouldn't do to be sacked over a ham sandwich in a pub. Dinner
at the Gavroche might be acceptable, and Worsthorne seemed to
find it tolerable that Viscount Astor sacked Donald Tyerman from
the editorship of *The Times* over spinach soup in his Carlton House
Terrace residence. (Apparently, Astor more usually preferred to
sack journalists in the lavatory, so he would not have to look them
in the eye.) Journalists on the *Observer* knew the end was nigh
when another Astor, David, invited them to lunch at the Waldorf.
They needed no reminding of the rule Philip Hope-Wallace learned
at his father's knee: 'Never work for a liberal employer, dear boy,
they'll sack you on Christmas Eve.'

Worsthorne's preoccupation with cuisine and environment in the matter of being sacked is significant because he does not question the principle or the justice of the sacking itself, merely the proprieties. In this unquiet trade, sacking is taken for granted. Journalism is unlike the law, where strict disciplinary codes have to be invoked before anyone can be expelled, or teaching, where the unions reject the very concept of members getting the boot. In journalism, the boot is a way of life, and getting the sack is part of the collective psyche of the trade. Despite the cries of outrage that accompany most sackings, a high proportion of journalists have shared the experience at some time or another, and are remarkably sanguine about it. It happened to my father, and it has happened to me twice. Anyone who hasn't been fired knows colleagues who have. Every journalist has a favourite sacking story.

The first lesson about getting the sack is that status and hierarchy offer no protection. I suppose there have been three great editors since the end of the Second World War, and two of them were fired. Hugh Cudlipp was dismissed from the *Sunday Pictorial* in 1948; Harold Evans fell foul of Rupert Murdoch in 1981. Only David English died with his original boots still on. Proprietors who do not own 50 per cent of the shares are no less vulnerable. When Cecil King was fired by the *Mirror* board, he phoned the BBC and ITN himself to spread the news. David Montgomery did not have to bother when fired from the *Mirror* board. The broadcasters already knew.

The next thing to grasp is that, like trade, sacking comes in a cyclical pattern: a reign of terror is followed by a period of relative calm, which is only the prelude to another period of dread. In the years after the war, Lord Beaverbrook set the standard for capricious behaviour. My first memory of Fleet Street is of my father coming home and telling us that that man who lived down the street had been fired that morning. A friend of Beaverbrook's had taken exception to a paragraph our neighbour had written for *In London Last Night*, the *Standard*'s gossip column. But the job market was more fluid then (the saying was: 'He'd cross the Street for ten bob'). Most journalists Beaverbrook fired soon got work elsewhere.

These were alarming years at the Mirror group too, though the atmosphere grew calmer when Cudlipp returned in 1952. True, he did sack the editor of his women's page while dancing with her at a Christmas party; and the story is told of Cudlipp first that, when he fired the *Sunday Mirror*'s astrologer, his victim said, 'I wasn't expecting this' – to which Cudlipp replied: 'That's why you're fired.' The same exchange was later attributed to Kelvin MacKenzie, which suggests that it is a story that attaches itself to legendary editors, who must be seen to be witty as well as original and incisive.

Cablese – used when the Post Office charged by the word – was still common then, leading to classic exchanges that are repeated so often that no one knows where they originated. This one is between the foreign news desk and an idle foreign correspondent:

'Why un-news?'

'Un-news good news.'

'Un-news unjob.'

'Upstuff job arsewards.'

The next stage in the cycle lasted from the sixties to the late eighties. Sacking went out of fashion. This happened because the National Union of Journalists grew much stronger, and proprietors like Roy Thomson had no opinions about the work of individual journalists. These were the last, golden years of over-manning, which was as transparent in editorial departments as in the composing or machine rooms. The late Peter Jenkins, then of the *Guardian*, used to say that you could afford to fire half the staff of the *Sunday Times*, and, since the quality of the work was uniformly high, it wouldn't matter which half.

The union intimidated managements, though some, like that of the *Telegraph*, were not hard to frighten. In the four decades of Michael Berry's benevolent management, the only case anyone can now recall of a sacking was of a lady reporter who was so drunk after lunch that it took two strong men to shoehorn her into her desk. Her subsequent sacking by the hated managing editor, Peter Eastwood, was regarded as truly shocking and quite unforgivable.

The sack came back in the nineties. The NUJ had imploded;

instead of making propaganda, proprietors have become obsessed with making profits, and they know that the quickest way to please the shareholders is to sack a lot of journalists. Editors have been appointed who have brought the word back into everyday usage. David Montgomery was so enthusiastic about sacking large numbers of journalists at the *Mirror* and the *Independent* that even Lord Hollick, the proprietor of the Express group, thought he was too cruel. Richard Stott was forced out of the *Mirror* because he 'couldn't control the Lefties in features'. (Montgomery had called Stott to Claridge's to discuss 'a matter of national importance'. After he had been fired, Stott asked him why he had lied about the purpose of their meeting. Montgomery replied that that was just 'tap dancing'.)

One of the qualities that makes a modern editor is a ruthless streak. Andrew Neil set the standard at the *Sunday Times* by expeditiously clearing out Evans's old team, and then turning the new staff over so fast that it made you dizzy just to hear the news – though the news was usually imparted to the victim by an underling. (People about to go were 'entering the departure lounge'.) Max Hastings and Dominic Lawson – who sacked Worsthorne for a second and then a third time, without the benefit of poached eggs – have shown that history is dead at the *Telegraph*. Rosie Boycott, starting slowly at the *Independent* and getting into her stride at the *Express*, has shown that a woman can do it as ruthlessly as a man.

But enough of the sweep of history. It is time for some case studies.

Lord Beaverbrook claimed that he did not interfere with his editors. That was a lie. Various editors tell convincing stories of futile attempts to turn aside the wrath of the Lord. Charles Wintour, for example, tried to salvage the job of a political writer, but Beaverbrook was implacable: 'Small head, big feet, won't do,' he declared. Bob Edwards did his best to protect Peter Forster when he was the *Express*'s chief book columnist, but could do so no longer after Forster went on to write a piece about Scrooge, a character Beaverbrook despised. Believing that it was Edwards who was responsible for his fate, Forster wrote a television column in the *Spectator* which began: 'Consider the clown Edwards.' In it,

Forster wrote: 'He is an all-purpose clown; no work is too dirty for him; he can jump through any number of hoops; as the bogus head of an incomprehensible organization, his ability to mismanage is classic and incomparable.'

Forster then claimed that the Edwards referred to was Jimmy Edwards, the great comedian. But no one in Fleet Street thought so. Nor did my learned friends, and Bob Edwards extracted an apology and a sum in damages from the *Spectator*. Edwards says that his action was inspired by the sense of injustice he felt because, although he had been the messenger, it was Beaverbrook who really fired Forster. But surely that is what editors of the *Daily Express* were for.

Beaverbrook did not tell even the architect of the *Express*'s post-war success, Arthur Christiansen, to his face that the game was up. Christiansen returned to the office after recovering from a heart attack to discover Sir Edward Pickering sitting in his editorial chair. Later Christiansen said that Beaverbrook had seen him to the lift and said: 'I'm sorry to see you going down.' Beaverbrook's best biographers, Anne Chisholm and Michael Davie, say this does not sound like Beaverbrook, but the perfunctory dismissal of his main man at the time sounds exactly like him.

Beaverbrook stories are good currency in journalism. Most are told fondly. Since his Foundation paid for me to go to university in New Brunswick, I can be fond myself, but the truth is that Beaverbrook was at best a fearful humbug, and at worst a dreadful shit. (Though Clement Attlee might have gone over the top when he said of Beaverbrook, 'He was the only evil man I ever met.') Take the example of his treatment of an *Express* correspondent in Washington DC. While this man's secretary was on holiday, he hired his wife to take her place. On learning of this, Beaverbrook fired him. Wintour reports that all attempts to have the poor man reinstated were rebuffed: 'He wouldn't listen. Beaverbrook said that we couldn't have nepotism on the *Express*.' His son Max had already replaced him formally as chairman of the company – which would do as a dictionary definition of nepotism.

Beaverbrook never thought Max was up to the job, but the son inherited the father's ability to sack journalists. Max Aitken sacked

Bob Edwards twice. At the *Express* today, the case of James Hughes-Onslow, who was sacked by Rosie Boycott, shows that journalists can turn on their tormentor with a ferocity that Beaverbrook never experienced. Posing as a potential purchaser of Boycott's house, Hughes-Onslow infiltrated the bathroom and left a packet of fish fingers behind a wooden casing, where it lay, undiscovered, until the house smelled of rotting fish. His revenge was a dish that was best not eaten at all.

The notorious sackings of Hugh Cudlipp and Harold Evans are recorded in their autobiographies, and each tells a cautionary tale in inimitable style. Cudlipp was fired in 1948 by the editor of the *Daily Mirror* who became the company chairman, Harry Guy Bartholomew (better known as Bart), for having failed to print in the *Sunday Pictorial* a dispatch from Cecil King, who was touring Nigeria on management business and had seen a riot in Enugu in which many died. As with many sackings, the offence of which Cudlipp stood accused was merely a pretext. Bart had survived as long as he had by always undermining his rivals, 'When he said to me in 1937, "I'll tell you this, you'll not get any help from me – no help at all," he meant what he said,' reported Cudlipp in *Walking on the Water*.

Bart toyed with Cudlipp for a while ('Christmas was coming and there were few things that appealed to him more than a pre-Christmas firing-squad'). Then he delivered the *coup de grâce* – 'with all the subtlety accorded to a tenth-rate sub-editor who turns up late on the first morning of a month's trial'. Cudlipp joined the *Express*; Beaverbrook's welcoming cable said: 'I have sought your companionship for long.' It didn't last long though. When King became chairman of the *Mirror* in 1952, Cudlipp returned forthwith.

The lesson from Harold Evans's description of being fired by Rupert Murdoch in *Good Times, Bad Times* is in a commentary in square brackets interpolated in a statement made by Murdoch to ITN:

'It is true that I asked Mr Harold Evans for his resignation. This was done on Tuesday 9th March [accurate so far] with the unanimous approval of the independent directors. [With their knowledge, yes. With their approval, no. "Unanimous" and "approval" are carefully chosen to suggest a board resolution, which he did not have. Robens called it "sloppy"; there are other terms.]

'Mr Evans agreed to give his resignation [untrue] but has been negotiating terms for his departure. These have now been agreed [the terms, yes, but not the departure].

'At no point has there been any difference, stated or otherwise, between Mr Evans and myself about the policy of the paper [lie: "Stated or otherwise" attempts to give it an air of precision and honesty].'

The only serious omission from Evans's account is not his fault, since he did not know how Charles Douglas-Home – whose reputation was one of the most inflated of all – manipulated an organization called 'Journalists of *The Times*' (Jott for short) to create a false impression that a majority of the journalists was opposed to Evans. I realized this shortly after having fallen for this story myself. But there were just enough old *Times* hands left on the paper to enable Murdoch to use their opposition to attack Evans.

Evans had not understood the difference between *The Times* and the *Sunday Times*. When he was editing the *Sunday Times*, his colleagues knew his weaknesses, but regarded his strengths as more important. They stood round him in a circle, looking out, and defending him from attack. At *The Times*, a circle of executives faced inwards, and stabbed him. Years went by before he shook off the bitterness he felt.

Mike Randall, whom Evans asked to join him at the *Sunday Times*, was more philosophical. Randall, a lean man, had succeeded William Hardcastle, a fuller figure, as editor of the *Daily Mail*. When a friend remarked to Lord Rothermere that he had changed editors, he came up with one of the finest examples of proprietorial cynicism: 'I tried a short, fat one, and that didn't work. So now I'm having a long, thin one,' he said. The long, thin one was determined to take the *Mail* upmarket. 'I knew eventually I would be fired. I couldn't beat the odds, but I wanted to have a bash,' said Randall, who was sacked soon after the *Mail* was declared Newspaper of the Year.

That Rothermere was Esmond, the 2nd Viscount. His son Vere, who turned Associated Newspapers into a formidably successful newspaper group, was not addicted to sacking staff. Disenchanted employees did say that the *Mail* had an alternative method: 'People they wanted to get rid of would be driven mad by the news desk,' says a veteran of that desk. Of course, when Max Hastings became editor of the *Evening Standard* he did not follow the general rule, and sacked journalists with the same energy he had shown at the *Daily Telegraph*. Alexander Chancellor, to whom it had happened on the *Telegraph*, says: 'I think it's an itch with Max, like someone having to drink blood once in a while, or they die.'

Chancellor is the most talented magazine editor of his generation, although that did not prevent Dominic Lawson from relieving him of the editorship of the *Sunday Telegraph* magazine. Having been given the bad tidings, Chancellor strolled out of Lawson's office on to the editorial floor to spread the news. Within minutes, Lawson ran out of his office and thrust an envelope into Chancellor's hand. It was a note and it read: 'I was awe-struck by your courage and dignity during our conversation. I admire you more than ever.' Chancellor found the note faintly insulting – 'the inference was that if you did not break down in tears, you were courageous'.

He was rather more surprised, however, to discover that Lawson had been offended to learn that his personal and intimate sentiment had been shared with other members of the staff. Perhaps Lawson thought it would be interpreted as a sign of weakness that would undermine his authority. Chancellor took it as evidence that some editors are reluctant to accept the consequences of their actions. I used to think that editors who get used to firing people are those who don't care whether they are liked or not. Not so. Some – no names, no pack drill, but they know who they are – are anxious to show the management how ruthless they are, while letting colleagues think that they are on their side. But you can't run with the hare and hunt with the hounds.

The *Guardian* is the sort of liberal newspaper that Philip Hope-Wallace's father warned him against – although he became its dramatic critic, and he was never fired on Christmas Eve. Until the acquisition of the *Observer*, editors who worked for the company were secure enough. There have been only four *Guardian* editors since 1945. The *Observer*, on the other hand, has had four since 1991. The most reputable of those *Guardian* editors was A. P. Wadsworth. The whole Fay family genuflected at the mention of his name, and I would not dream of throwing out the printed copy of his lecture to the Manchester Statistical Society on *Newspaper Circulation, 1800–1954* which he sent to my father shortly before he became London editor in 1955. But Wadsworth was not as nice as he looked, for his liberal credentials were not altogether pure. In 1948 he conducted a purge of three journalists he believed were members of the Communist Party. The exercise in British McCarthyism involved sacking Geoffrey Goodman, now the distinguished editor of the *British Journalism Review*, and a Commander of the British Empire.

Nothing was said at the time. Indeed, I don't believe anything has been said about it until now. The *Guardian* has a way of sacking people by sleight of hand, so that spectators don't see. In some cases, even the victim is unaware of it, as in the case of a hapless television critic called Mary McManus, who worked in the Manchester office. The editor had been looking for a pretext to sack her, and one finally appeared in 1957 when ITV's first transmissions were to be seen only in London. Mary McManus was informed that since television would be reviewed from London in future, there seemed to be no future for her.

'Well,' she sighed, 'I'll just have to go to London.' And so she did. But that did not deter the *Guardian*. On her arrival in London, she found there was no desk for her in the London office. After using various surfaces, like the wall or her lap, to write on, she eventually got the message. (Mary McManus's successor was Bernard Levin.) In my father's case, the *Guardian* invented a cock-and-bull story about his stepping aside gracefully to save the jobs of two reporters during a financial crisis. I'm still not sure whose blushes this was supposed to spare.

The sacking of Reg Mounce is uncommonly well documented. We know the text of the office memorandum he received from the editor. Marked 'Private and Confidential', it read: 'After giving the matter considerable thought, I have come to the conclusion that you would be wise to begin looking round with a view to making other arrangements. I do not feel that this office can give sufficient scope to your talents. Three months' notice is customary with us, as you know, but if you were particularly anxious to leave sooner I believe you would find us reasonably accommodating.'

We know of the overbearing Mounce's reaction. He phoned one of the people he went drinking with each midday and shouted: 'This crap's from you, is it?' Reg, a picture editor, did not believe the editor could possibly have sacked him, and, instead of organizing his farewell party, he set out to find the perpetrator of what he took to be a hoax. Reg Mounce is still in place at the end of Michael Frayn's *Towards the End of the Morning*, the best novel about journalism since *Scoop*.

I had thought the newspaper in Frayn's novel was based on the *Daily Telegraph*, but when I checked, he said his inspiration was the *Guardian*, where he worked in the fifties. Frayn reports that he got the idea of Reg Mounce's refusal to accept the sack from a heroic story he tells about the celebrated author and journalist Richard West. According to Frayn, West is sent to cover a sheepdog trial, which he covers from the point of view of the sheep. The editor is not amused. West is sacked; a letter is in his cubby-hole in the reporters' room.

West takes the letter to the news editor, a Scot named Cockburn. 'What's this?' he asks.

'It looks like the sack,' says Cockburn.

'What shall I do?' West asks.

'Put it back in the envelope, and put the envelope back in your cubby-hole. Pretend you never got it.'

This is the kind of story that is almost too good to check, but, like a cobbler to his last, I spoke to West. He denies it, dammit. There is, however, more than a germ of truth in it. West was told to look for another job after a three-month trial on the *Guardian*. Since the only job on offer was doing PR for the North-West Gas Board, West stayed on – for so long that the *Guardian* relented and gave him a staff job.

Like so many stories about sacking, this is turned into a joke. To an outsider, one of the mysteries of modern journalism must be how little outrage is expressed at so much blood on the floor. The explanation often involves economics. At the *Independent* the constant exodus is principally the result of its losses. The *Daily Mail* does not fire people, because it is a confident, profitable operation and there is no reason to. The *Express* fires substantial numbers of journalists because Rosie Boycott is desperately trying to reinvent the paper to reverse its falling circulation.

Some sackings are a matter of timing. Peter Stothard justified his night of the long knives at *The Times* by saying that, if it was to be done, it was better done shortly after his arrival, when it would cause less surprise. The commotion died down quickly, and many of the victims were soon saying that it was the best thing that had happened to them. There's a vital clue: in the nineties, most journalists who get the sack also get a pay-off. Redundancy is a common euphemism for sacking, but it carries with it the expectation of a substantial sum of money. No doubt there are still personal tragedies, but on the two occasions when I have been fired, I cried all the way to the bank.

This tells us something unpalatable about journalism. It cannot be a profession, because members of a profession set standards and expel people only when they are not met. It can't be a vocation because that involves belief, and people do not give it up. It is not even a craft, because members of a craft try to protect their colleagues, by going on strike if unbearably provoked. The fatalism of journalists shows that journalism today is more like show business than anything else.

Why Tabloids Are Better

CAROL SARLER

Let us spare the poor man's blushes, and refer to him here simply as a very senior back-bench executive from the *Sunday People*. He is one of those deliciously ink-in-the-veins types; he has worked in Fleet Street since . . . well, since he actually worked in Fleet Street, and he gives great gossip. Which is how we came to be swapping tales over a recent lunch, when one of mine involved mention of the editor of the *Observer*. It stopped him short; my friend had never heard of him.

A week later I was supping a glass with the back-bencher's direct counterpart from the *Observer*. In the interests of pure research, I asked if he could name the editor of the *Sunday People*. He could not.

Only nine national newspapers appear on the British streets each Sunday, yet this is the extent of the distance, inside the industry, between two of them – a distance that is mirrored, it must be said, in the daily market as well, and a distance that is all about the deep suspicion and dislike between the broadsheet and the tabloid journalists.

Until 1993, I shall confess, I was right in there: suspecting and disliking along with the best of them. For years, I had been a run-of-the-mill broadsheet bunny, skipping around on the freelance treadmill that would take in 6,000 words for the *Sunday Times*, or a profile for the *Guardian*, perhaps a couple of interviews for the *Independent* and a 'comment' here or there for the *Observer* – all muddled in, naturally, with the days when there was no work at all and you just *knew* you were going to starve to death. Then the call came. Bridget Rowe, at that time editor of the *Sunday People*, wanted to know: would I be interested in writing a weekly column?

A red-top? Me? The only thing more extraordinary than the invitation was what had provoked it: I had come to Miss Rowe's attention because she had read my 8,000-word, rather harrowing investigation into homeless youth, published in the *Independent on Sunday*. She deduced that I could write her short and snappies . . . from this? It made no sense to me at the time – but at the time I did not know, and Miss Rowe did, that the similarities between any one piece of contemporary journalism and any other are greater than the differences.

Her faith was my spur (oh, all right: her faith *and* her capacious purse) and today I am one of the tiniest handful in the industry – count the others; you won't reach five – who write tabloid and broadsheet, on a regular basis. I love the two, I love the mix. But I am saddened by the stand-off between my two little worlds, and disappointed by the naked snobbery ladled upon the tabloids by the broadsheets. I was recently asked, on a radio programme, what was the difference between writing for the two. I said, briefly, that the broadsheets had so much to learn from the tabloids. The look on the interviewer's face mirrored that on those of my erudite broadsheet friends, who still – damn them – stare aghast and ask, 'Darling, why do you do it?' This is why.

To walk through the tabloid door, after fifteen years on 'the other side', is like being allowed to stay up late with the grown-ups. There is an absolute professionalism that is at once terrifying and exhilarating. All broadsheets have one or two bright sparks upon whose slender shoulders the product rests; tabloids are staffed by entire teams of bright sparks whose conversation – whose informed conversation – makes their company a joy.

Just for a start, tabloid journalists read the newspapers. Not just their own and those of their direct competition, but they read all the broadsheets as well; a compliment not returned. Neil Wallis is 'my' fourth *Sunday People* editor, and not one of them has yet, as far as I can tell, arrived at work without having read every one of the dailies first. In working terms, this means that I have never called in with a reference to a story, no matter how tiny, that my editor has not read before me. (That's if they don't call first: 'Look!' Mr Wallis will yell, at an unconscionably early hour, 'page twenty-four of the *Guardian*! Just what you were talking about!')

Compare and contrast with the broadsheet section editor who boasts that she only ever reads the *Daily Telegraph* because nothing else is 'necessary'. Or with her colleague, of even higher title, to whom I suggested an idea based on a story that had run all week on front pages. She had no idea what I was talking about and excused it with an airy, 'I haven't seen the papers yet this week.' It was Friday at the time. They do not even read their own papers. A *Sunday Times* senior editor queried a reference I recently made to a minor celebrity on the basis that she had never heard of the woman. There had been a profile of this celebrity in the *Sunday Times* only ten days earlier.

The production process on a tabloid is a thing of beauty to watch. Let me take my own page in the *Sunday People*, which will carry eight items of opinion ranging (I like to think) from sad to angry to witty, as appropriate. Each will have its own headline, there will be at least two pictures, a half-tone here or there and changes of typeface to pretty it along. Think, by way of comparison, of a 'comment' page in, say, *The Times*. Think how much more complicated to do mine; yet do it they do, in far shorter time than *The Times* and with many fewer errors. I still wince at the memory of *The Times* sub who once altered a quote so that my important source was left saying the opposite of what he had actually said – and after this wholesale transformation she had the gall to leave it in quote marks. She rebuffed my subsequent complaint with the robust defence that 'I thought I'd got the gist of what he was saying.' It was a long time ago. She is still employed there.

The tabloid picture desks are better operators, too. Where a broadsheet picture desk will pester the writer, often in a hostile tone because we make them work for a living – 'Where on earth do you expect me to get pictures?' – a tabloid picture desk just . . . somehow . . . just gets them.

The professionalism extends beyond the editorial team to their colleagues; to the legal departments, for good instance. I used to have little respect for newspaper lawyers, having met only the broadsheet version. One of the top beagles at Wapping once told me, in the presence of an editor who, significantly, did not argue with him, that I was risking the credibility of a story by describing its subject as 'a neat little woman, in her spick-and-span council house'. Why? Because, came his assured opinion, that was a contradiction in terms and 'everyone knows that people who live in council houses are slobs'. (He is still there, too.) But at Mirror Group the lawyers have become friends. They want your piece to work and they want to help. These days I frequently call them, in advance of submitting copy, to work with them on the best way of speaking out without paying out – boy, have I learned a lot about 'not ascribing motive'. And their equanimity is especially generous, given that the huge bucks paid out in tabloid libel cases put the lawyers' jobs directly on the line.

Of course, the payback for the pleasure of working in such surroundings is the commensurately increased expectation upon you, the writer. There is so much to learn, so quickly. There are no built-in false deadlines so you do not file late. Ever. If you are ill, there is sympathy – but they still need the copy. If you do not know a correct spelling you find it; yes, that should be taken for granted, but it still amazes me how many writers will submit broadsheet copy with 'subs please check' beside an awkward name. Because you are writing to shorter lengths, you lose the luxury of an on-the-one-hand and an on-the-other – which, as we all know, is a marvellous escape clause. If you have room for only one discrete fact or only one set of figures, they had better be right. Also because you are writing to shorter lengths, your first reaction is that you cannot possibly get anything said. But you can, yes you can.

A couple of recent examples: you will recall the fuss, in the summer of 1998, when it was revealed that Peruvians eat guinea-pigs; a fuss that sent hapless hacks to the wilderness to sample the scant flesh of the small beasts and to report back in orchestrated disgust. Had I, that week, been asked to write a broadsheet comment to 1,000 words I could easily have done so. I could have pointed to the inherent xenophobia of the public reaction; reminded readers that diet is essentially linked to culture, to history, to geography, to availability; chucked in, for good measure, a spot of religion and diet taboos – seafood for Jews, cows for Hindus – and rounded it all off with a cautionary reminder about one man's meat being another man's poison. In fact, for the *Sunday People* I wrote fewer than thirty words:

Much cross-cultural outrage this week at the discovery that Peruvians eat guinea-pigs. 'How could they?' came the cry. 'They're so *SWEET*.'
Yes. And lambs aren't?

All right, not a pinnacle of literature. But I venture that, essentially, the same point was made. By the same token, in January 1999 I felt 'written out' on the subject of Ireland; I had done all the essays that I had in me, yet here it was, back in the news, needing to be addressed once more. I found precisely thirty-six words, as follows:

Mo Mowlam has sternly warned that the IRA absolutely *MUST* surrender its weapons. She is, of course, right.
But the trouble with Dr Mo's warnings is that they never answer the obvious rebuttal:
Or else what?

Aside from the economy of space, the bonus for the writer is that in learning how – when necessary – to condense one's thoughts thus, the pen is all the sharper when writing longer pieces elsewhere. There are other invaluable lessons from the tabloid world that carry over into anything we write, anywhere else. Top of the list is what we learn from the readers; it is with unease that I must admit to not having previously known enough about those with whom I share the green and pleasant land.

To write for the *Observer* is to guarantee a most enjoyable dinner on the day of publication. All the assembled chums will have read the piece; some will congratulate and even those in disagreement will refer with respect to the fact of it being published at all. Indeed, to write for the *Observer* may even be an extension of a dinner party – quite often the thoughtful Sunday morning offering will have had its genesis in the roaring debate that took place over the raspberry coulis the previous Wednesday. And nothing wrong with that: we all need to eat.

But to write for the *Sunday People* is to write in the certain knowledge that none of the chums will admit to having read it (admit is the crucial word, more of which later). So no feedback there, then. Instead, there is the mailbag: hordes of letters from hordes of strangers that, between them, add up to an eye-opening explanation of the world around us. I know why people voted as they did; I know why, too, so many today express their bitter disappointment with the result. I understand the depth of feeling on homosexuality, capital punishment and gun abolition (anti/pro/anti); I know that nothing I write, ever, will greatly change that feeling – though I write it, anyway – and I have learned well that the tabloids do not have a fraction of the power over public opinion that some would allocate to us.

But there! That is the nub of the snobbish industry opposition to tabloids, is it not? – that broadsheets are there to stimulate those capable of debate and of making up their own minds . . . while tabloids are there to exploit and to manipulate Common Man, the built-in assumption being that he is somehow less capable. There is a breathtaking, arrogant irony here. For it is always the left-of-centre liberal, who most concerns himself with the enfranchisement and civil rights of Common Man, who is also least happy with Common Man's free vote on reading material. What is really going on, of course, is that his expression of contempt for the reading material is actually an expression of his underlying contempt for the reader himself. I recall once accepting a lift home from a member of Demos. Upon enquiring what I did for a living, he let out the predictable snort: 'Ha. Well. You wouldn't expect me to read the *Sunday People*, would you?' Yes, actually; if you are part of a left-wing think tank, I do think you should read a Labour-supporting newspaper read by millions. But it was such a common reaction: élitist pride, rather than proper shame, in refusing to acknowledge the newspapers chosen by most other people.

Which brings me to the last lesson learned when you start to work within the tabloid market: you also start to read it, really read it, and in the process to understand why the overwhelming majority of all potential readers make the choice that they do. I always did at least some tabloid reading, so I am not as guilty as our Demos man. But I literally could not do my job today if I did not read all of them, every day. Indeed, on rushed days I only read the tabloids – and that is an acid test. Because on such days I do not find myself lacking an iota of news or information. Everything is in there, in a form designed for the reader rather than for the ego of the writer, and anybody who even dreams that the writers 'write down' is missing something important: at their peril dare they try. Tabloid readers are not a fraction as stupid as some would like to believe, and generally more demanding than most. Which is why there is no political news, in, say, *The Times* that holds a candle to the concise, accurate, informed reporting of Trevor Kavanagh in the *Sun* or Paul Routledge in the *Daily Mirror*. There is no foreign story in, say, the *Guardian* that is as compelling as a spread – any spread – by Ann Leslie in the *Daily Mail*. And there is no sports page, anywhere (or so cab-drivers regularly inform me), that beats the legendary coverage in the *Sunday People*.

I have of late had reason to test this further. I have been spending an increasing amount of time in the US from where, thanks to technological advance, I can continue to write my page for the *Sunday People*. My time is spent in a remote area, far from news vendors, but I can now read all the British national newspapers (except, because of some daft Neolithic flounce of its own, the *Daily Mail*) on the Internet. The difference between reading them that way and reading them as nature intended is that the Internet version is more or less text only – which, with copy thus unadorned, serves to make you really see what it is that you are getting. I call up the *Mirror* and the *Sun* first, printing out as I go anything I might care to use when writing at the end of the week; then I add *The Times*, the *Guardian* and the *Telegraph*. And when you're left with just a pile of sheets of paper with stories on them, you notice that all the actual *news* was printed out from the first two papers – everything selected subsequently was amplification, most usually in the form of opinion. Perfectly enjoyable, don't misunderstand me. But quite, quite unnecessary to quench a need to know.

There is, in fact, a very good reason for the breadth of coverage in the tabloids which is not remotely mirrored the other way around (when Dame Iris Murdoch died, her death made a *leader* in the *Sun*; do we really think that, when the time comes, the same tribute will be paid to, say, Danielle Steel in *The Times*?). The reason is that the tabloids have a great many more ABC1 readers to worry about than do the broadsheets – oh yes, they do. The broadsheets like, as well they might, to talk in percentages. So, for instance, the *Independent on Sunday* will boast that 79 percent of its readers are ABC1. But cut to the chase and deal with actual figures and the truth is that it is read by 624,000 of this much sought-after group – while the *Sunday People*, slaving five floors above them in the Canary Wharf monolith, is read by more than double in the same category (1,338,000, latest National Readership Survey, which takes me back to my point about my middle-class social circle not admitting to reading it; in their sneaky, secretive, under-the-bedcovers, hypocritical way, of course at least some of them read it).

Similarly, the *Sun* also has twice the ABC1 readership figure of its stable-mate *The Times* – and I very much suspect that it makes little difference to Rupert Murdoch where those readers are; he would be equally miserable to lose them from either camp. So if it takes a nod from the editor of the *Sun* in the direction of Iris Murdoch to keep the posh guys happy (all 2,974,000 of them), then nod he will. Meanwhile, the *Mail on Sunday* now has a greater reach into the ABC1 class than any other publication in the country – a title stolen from, curiously, the *Radio Times*.

And this is why, I suppose, I am so impressed by my new friends in this tabloid business: because they need to reach a bigger and therefore broader audience, their knowledge needs, correspondingly, to be bigger and broader too. Their natural instincts, formed by their education and their training, may be less *Finnegans Wake* than Finnigan, Judy – but they can do both if they must; rarely, if ever, can you say that of their broadsheet equivalents. A final word on the subject of these journalists and, especially, of the editors among them: I have yet to find any serious cynicism. There are issues upon which I would disagree with them, but almost without exception they themselves do believe in what they say and what they publish. Rarely do you sense an attitude of, well, yes, it's nonsense – but it will 'do' for 'them out there'. This, most certainly, is the province of the broadsheet editor.

So, you may well be asking, what is this? A hymn to tabloid journalism? A glorying, a revelling in who they are and what they do? A defence of technique and tactic, regardless of who gets hurt? Well, no. Of course not; even if, when provoked, I have been known to make some kind of a fist of such a defence. Once, on Radio 4's *Moral Maze*, I was attacked by Edward Pearce for what he called tabloid 'hypocrisy'. As I suggested to him at the time – and heck, did he get cross about it – the real hypocrisy is to be found among the papers for which he was writing, the papers who pick up on a salacious story and reprint it for the baser edification of their readers, together with the invitation to enjoy on the one hand and condemn on the other. 'Look what that dreadful *Mirror* said!' is much the line. Oh, tut-tut-alonga *Telegraph*.

But, when unprovoked by Mr Pearce, I must be truthful and say that there are many things that have – and do – gravely upset me upon their publication in a tabloid newspaper. And just because I am not personally responsible for them is not an excuse; I take their shilling, I have blood on my hands. Some are just plain silly. Although today such stories would not be included in the *Sunday People*, different editors do things different ways. I was with friends one midnight in 1994 as the first editions hit the bookstalls – and there it was, 'our' splash: 'I Was Raped By Aliens!' Never mind, consoled one friend; at least it didn't say 'Elvis Is Alive!'

The following year, during party conference season, I arrived in Blackpool on the day after that Sunday's splash . . . which was (I know you can see this coming): 'Elvis Is Alive!' I telephoned the editor back at base camp, and told him that it was all right for him, hidden behind his desk, but I was out here surrounded by other journalists who were teasing without mercy. What do I say to them, I demanded of him, next time they ask me about Elvis being alive?

The reply was gruff. 'Tell them to prove he isn't.'

Other instances, however, are not such harmless fun. As I write today, I have in front of me a tabloid page that makes my teeth hurt. The story is (probably) legitimate enough: Texan model Jerry Hall has a twin sister desperately ill with cancer and has flown her to Britain in what sounds like a last-ditch effort to save her life. But the picture . . . oh, the picture. It is a snatched snap of the woman looking like a monster from a children's book: stooped, crippled, steroid-bloated – and made the worst by its juxtaposition with another picture of the beauty she was before she became ill. In God's name, why? She is not a public figure. She did not bring her illness upon herself. She serves as neither warning nor lesson to anyone. I promise you, my bewilderment is as great as yours, who do not take the shilling. And my shame the greater, because I do.

I also have an unimportant but personal peeve about the occasional two-faced leap to the higher moral ground when it suits a tabloid editor to make it. Do you remember all the fuss about James Hewitt and the letters he had, written to him by the late Diana, Princess of Wales? 'He should not be allowed to keep them, the cad, the bounder!' went the pompous and outraged editorials. Why not? 'Because he might Make Them Public!' they howled . . . each and every one of them prepared to make the letters public on his behalf if they only believed they could afford them.

But that is a tiny matter compared with this, the central question here: why even might Miss Hall's sister's photograph be published and why even might there be bidding for Diana's letters? Because, my friends, they sell newspapers. That is to say, in this country they sell newspapers; it is a peculiarly British trait within the English-speaking world. It does not apply in the US, where the 'kiss-and-tell' industry (albeit lucrative) is restricted to magazines like the *Globe* or the *National Enquirer* but rarely impinges on newsprint, and it does not apply in Australia, at least not to anything like the same degree; Australian journalists, indeed, are among the most vocal in their disapproval of the British tabloid press.

But then, prevailing social attitudes are different in these countries. The Americans look after their stars, they nurture them; you have to do something pretty damn terrible to be knocked off your tinselled perch in a country whose national ethic is based on the idea that you, your son or your daughter might one day attain power, wealth and stardom, too. Equally with the Australians: they may have coined the phrase 'tall poppy syndrome', but that is just a different level of adherence to the notion of egalitarianism – they will have everyone cut down to size, in a cheery, back-slapping sort of way, while the Americans will have everyone elevated . . . if only in their dreams.

The British are different. We are beset by a complicated *schaden-freude* that layers all our (very real) fascination for our 'betters' with (very real) resentment, soothed only by the knowledge of all the tiny slips, faults, ailments and minutiae of misery, be they among footballers, fashion models or dead princesses. I do not like it, you may well not like it, but to suggest that this uncomfortable facet of the national psyche is created by the tabloid press, rather than just fed by it, is fatuous. Not one journalist is more powerful than the reader who reaches out to lift us from the newsagent's counter.

The good editor, tabloid or broadsheet, understands this. It is interesting to note, in fact, how much the broadsheet editors are now being forced to absorb from their despised counterparts. Until the mid-1970s, the *Guardian* did not even review popular music; today the divorce of a popular singer will make its front page. The *Independent*, in its early days, ran the wholly principled risk of not dallying with 'royal stories'; a gamble that, in the end, proved to be an unaffordable luxury. And no matter how many grumbled snootily at the time, the fact is that Andrew Neil increased the circulation of the *Sunday Times*, at least in the short term, when in 1992 he serialized Andrew Morton's biography of the Princess of Wales – a purchase that, even ten years earlier, would have been unthinkable for such a newspaper.

Increasingly the difference between the two markets is one of presentation, not of content; it's the flesh of the tabloids, not the bones (in every sense?), that upsets those who would assume the lofty position. Yet even within the presentation I find a directness, even a strange honesty, in the nature of how the tabloids work. The broadsheets, I contend, are much more likely to say one thing and do another. For example, it is they who employ the Fat-is-a-feminist-issue Susie Orbachs of this world, they who chastise the tabloids for promoting an unhealthily slim body image on readers – again, those unintelligent readers who cannot think for themselves – and they whose own fashion pages are littered with stick-insect Lolitas, with no mention of the contradiction therein. On the same issue, all the *Sun* does is to acknowledge that most of us would like to lose a few pounds and so it employs a slimming editor to offer sensible advice. (And, by the way, on the wearisome subject of role models: you cannot be a page 3 girl if you starve yourself free of curves.)

None of us is perfect. When it comes to shame, I am hard pressed to think of anything much more shameful in the British journalism of this century than the *Guardian*'s handing over to the police of a source who trusted them – Sarah Tisdall, in 1983 – and leaving her to face trial and a subsequent prison sentence. Yet I would hate not to have my *Guardian*, just as I would hate to live without the laudable craft of tabloid journalism at its finest. And to every writer, every editor or every sub who has ever asked me why I do my little bit for it, I say this: go and try it for a couple of years. Then, if you must, go back to the sweet, safe, soft option they call *The Times* or the *Independent*. At worst, you will be the wiser for it. At best, a rather better journalist.

Dealing with Mr Murdoch

ANTHONY HOWARD

In one of his more candid moments Rupert Murdoch once conceded that what his ownership of newspapers brought him was 'a little smidgen of power' – adding (engagingly or not), 'that's the fun of it, isn't it?' Even in making that confession he was being over-modest. Whatever the precise dimensions of 'a little smidgen' may be, most people would say that Murdoch enjoys power on a far grander scale than that. Indeed, not so long ago an eminent panel assembled by the *Observer* rated him the second most powerful figure in the country, outranked only by the prime minister, Tony Blair (and on any international reckoning, given Murdoch's worldwide media dominion, that order should probably be reversed).

Murdoch can look back on a long tradition in which press proprietors, at least in twentieth-century Britain, seldom shrank from looking down upon politicians as people who should defer to them. Leaving aside the paranoid delusions of Viscount Northcliffe, that after all was what the whole running battle in the 1920s and the 1930s between the first Baron Beaverbrook and the first Viscount Rothermere on the one side and Stanley Baldwin and the Conservative Party on the other was all about. It is fashionable today to assert that in advancing claims to being the equals, if not the superiors, of politicians, the old breed of 'Runnymede' press barons merely made themselves look preposterous. But that was hardly how matters were seen at the time, especially in Conservative Central Office, which always remained distinctly windy about the degree of influence and power that 'rogue' newspaper proprietors could bring to bear, especially at election times.

The Tory high command had some reason for its apprehensions:

if Baldwin lost the December 1923 general election, it was at least partly because the Beaverbrook and Rothermere newspapers effectively deserted him; and if he massively won the October election in the following year it was partly thanks to the fact that this time the *Daily Express* and the *Daily Mail* – the latter even obligingly producing its 'red scare' with the almost certainly forged Zinoviev letter – stood solidly behind him.

The truth is that only the most arrogant, or perhaps the most insouciant of politicians (and Baldwin plainly belonged to the latter category) disregards the role that the press can play in influencing and shaping – though seldom, if ever, in actually forming – public attitudes.[1] It is this consciousness of newspapers exerting a rival power to their own that complicates the entire relationship between politicians and the world of journalism. A prime minister or Opposition leader has no difficulty at all in dealing with a manufacturer of soap powder or a producer of motor-car components: however successful their business may be, they are not remotely engaged in the same game. A newspaper owner – or, even worse, today an international media mogul – is a very different proposition. Whether either side cares publicly to acknowledge it or not, they are both competing for the same prize – the chance to mould and formulate public opinion.[2]

It is over this that the resentments arise. The politician finds it hard to accept the legitimacy of the newspaper proprietor – or even of the humbler editor – in any such role, if only because he or she does not have to stand for election and, therefore, holds no mandate

1. Alastair Campbell, the present Prime Minister's press secretary, once told me: 'I don't think you could say that a single newspaper wins or loses a general election. I do think, though, that under the Labour Party of Neil Kinnock the chances of ever winning were greatly diminished by the fact that, day in and day out, newspapers attacked the Labour Party – and Neil Kinnock in particular – virulently; and that was bound to have had an effect on the way that politics was perceived during those years in which people are actually making up their minds.'
2. Lord Beaverbrook was, on the whole, a shrewd judge of what he once called 'the armed frontier' that should exist between the world of the press and that of politics. But when he made a mistake, it tended to be a clanger – as when he wrote in his slim volume *Politicians and the Press* (1925): 'The journalist and the statesman are not fighting for the same prize.'

from the voters. There can, of course, be no arguing with that – though there is a sense in which the newspaper editor stands trial at the bar of public opinion every day of his or her professional life; a sustained slump in their papers' sales, and he or she will be out of office just as surely as a politician defeated at the polls. Popular approval thus matters as much to the one as to the other.

That brings into play the other complicating factor. The shrewdest politicians – conscious that they have in normal times only a quinquennial rendezvous with the voters – usually nurture an uneasy suspicion that those who own, edit or even work on newspapers may be in closer touch with public opinion than they are. When they come to lunch in a newspaper boardroom the questions they tend to ask are about the reactions of the readership to any particular campaign that the paper may happen to be running at the time, or even (in the absence of that) merely the contents of the newspaper's postbag on some topical issue. The current vogue for 'focus groups' deployed by political parties themselves may have altered the position a bit; but, in general, a newspaper still possesses far more access to public opinion in the raw (as opposed to the pollster's processed version of it) than any politician, however distinguished. And it is newspapers, of course, that continue to provide the day's agenda for the great mass of backbench MPs in the House of Commons. One memory that has stayed with me across the years is of being told in the early 1960s by the then Clerk of the House, Sir Edward Fellowes, that if he wanted to know in advance the type of questions that would be brought to the Table Office by Labour MPs on any particular day, he merely had to read the *Daily Mirror* that morning. And the fact that he made the remark with some distaste in no way altered its status in my mind as a piece of perceptive observation.

So it is not just the shared desire for influence but also a common thirst for information that binds the two worlds of politicians and the press together. That has never, of course, led to the two sides liking each other very much. The ultimate insult – and in many ways a far more crushing retort than the famous later passage about Beaverbrook and Rothermere aspiring to 'power without responsibility, the prerogative of the harlot throughout the ages'[1] – probably came from Baldwin at the same Queen's Hall meeting during the St George's Westminster by-election of March 1931. The *Daily Mail* had alleged that, as someone who had lost his own fortune, he was totally disqualified from restoring that of anyone else, let alone the fortunes of the country. Slightly unusually, the *Daily Mail*'s attack was signed with the one word 'Editor', and this is how Baldwin chose to reply to him:

I have no idea of the name of the gentleman. I would only observe that he is well qualified for the post which he holds. The first part of the statement is a lie and the second part of the statement by its implications is untrue. The paragraph itself could only have been written by a cad. I have consulted a very high legal authority and am advised that an action for libel would lie. I shall not move on the matter, and for this reason: I should get an apology and heavy damages. The first is of no value, and the second I would not touch with a barge pole.

Probably the most interesting aspect of the whole flavour of that reply is the clear *de haut en bas* attitude towards the press that it revealed. And remarkably, at least until the end in 1955 of the reign of Winston Churchill (who refused to allow lobby journalists even into Number 10), what contacts there were between Downing Street and Fleet Street tended to be very much on a prime minister/press baron level.[2]

It was the ill-fated Anthony Eden – with his appointment of a working journalist, William Clark, the diplomatic correspondent of the *Observer*, to be his press spokesman actually within Number

1. According to the third Earl Baldwin of Bewdley, all eleven words of this phrase were borrowed by his father from his cousin, Rudyard Kipling, who had previously used them in a private argument.
2. For Churchill this proved to be a wise investment. When he had his stroke in June 1953 three newspaper proprietors – Viscount Bracken (of the *Financial Times*), Viscount Camrose (of the *Daily Telegraph*) and Lord Beaverbrook (of the *Daily Express*) – were summoned to Chartwell and gave their sanction to a thoroughly misleading medical bulletin. Not a word about the prime minister's true paralysed condition ever got out.

10 – who changed all that. Although, no doubt, a democratic experiment entered into with the highest (or lowest) of motives – Eden always desperately wanted to be loved – it proved a total failure. Within nine months the Downing Street press office was reduced to putting out an unprecedented statement denying that the prime minister was about to resign, nine months after that Clark left his job in protest against the British and French attack on Suez, and just three months later (in January 1957) the prime minister himself was forced out of office.

The fiasco of the Suez intervention, and the subsequent fall of Eden, marked a defining moment in the relations between Westminster and Fleet Street. It was apparent even to those newspapers – and they were easily the majority – who had supported Eden's policy of trying to grab back the Suez Canal by force from President Nasser that the government had lied about collusion with Israel, that it had buckled at the knees in face of American pressure on the pound, and that, through the folly and 'crookedness' (the *Observer*'s own editorial phrase) of the military action taken, Britain had ceased almost overnight to be a world power. In the aftermath of the humiliation, the hour of reckoning had come – and part of that reckoning involved a wholesale readjustment in the relationship between the assured world of government authority and the hitherto largely deferential one of ordinary journalists.

Eden's successor – or, perhaps more accurately, his displacer – Harold Macmillan admittedly did his best to stop this incipient peasants' revolt in its tracks. Although a crofter's grandson and a publisher by trade, he chose from the moment he arrived in Number 10 to adopt a grand, feudal manner. Having appointed a brisk and efficient former civil servant named Harold Evans as his spokesman, he himself tended to keep his distance from grubby working lobby journalists. He took care, though, to cultivate proprietors – and, to a lesser degree, sympathetic editors – and, partly thanks to the intendedly ironic invention of a characterization of him called 'Supermac' by the left-wing cartoonist Vicky, rode almost effortlessly to victory in the 1959 general election. No sooner, however, was that contest over than his troubles began.

It was not just what his ultimate Labour rival, Harold Wilson, cannily called his 'grouse moor image' that began to jar with an increasingly irreverent public. His government, too, soon began to run into difficulties. Spy and security scandals followed one another in quick succession and even newspapers such as the *News of the World* (later claiming to be 'as British as roast beef and Yorkshire pudding') saw no obstacle in banging an outraged, patriotic anti-Communist drum. These alleged security lapses culminated in the Vassall affair of 1962 involving an Admiralty official employed in a minister's private office who had been caught spying for the Russians. Various newspapers, especially traditional loyalist right-wing ones, carried a series of sensational stories implicating various members of the government and hinting at a homosexual ring in high places. Outraged, Macmillan summoned up all the clanking machinery of a Judicial Tribunal, presided over by that all-purpose Cerberus of the establishment, Viscount Radcliffe. No evidence was ever adduced for any of the more lurid innuendoes; but two journalists – one on the *Daily Sketch* and the other on the *Daily Mail* – were sent to prison for refusing to reveal their sources (probably non-existent). This effectively broke the truce that had largely operated – at least when the electoral chips were down – between Conservative governments at Westminster and Tory newspapers in Fleet Street.[1]

Things were promptly made worse for Macmillan, who had only just emerged from a war-to-the-death with Beaverbrook newspapers over Britain's first (and thwarted) application to join the Common Market, by the breaking in the spring and summer of 1963 of what became known as 'the Profumo affair'. This was to prove another seminal episode in determining a more equal relationship between journalists and government, if only because the newspapers could claim that their suspicions had been vindicated while the prime minister was shown, at best, to have been negligent. At issue was the conduct of the then Secretary of State

1. One eloquent sign of this was the announcement of the resignation of John Junor from the editorship of the *Sunday Express* on the ground that he could not in any forthcoming election support a prime minister who had clapped two journalists into jail. Fortunately for Junor, Macmillan himself resigned while he was still serving out his notice. Sir John Junor went on to edit the *Sunday Express* for another twenty-two years.

for War, John Profumo, who was alleged to have had a liaison with a model named Christine Keeler – who, inconveniently, was at the same time sleeping with the Soviet naval attaché (and KGB agent), one Captain Eugene Ivanov.

Despite all the huffing and puffing by the Labour leader, Harold Wilson, there was, in fact, absolutely nothing to the security angle. But Profumo had sealed his fate by declaring in a personal statement to the Commons way back on 22 March that 'there was no impropriety whatsoever in my acquaintance with Miss Keeler'. When the truth came out – as it did by a voluntary confession on his part in June 1963 – he, naturally, had to resign. But in many quarters there persisted a feeling that – if only by reason of his failure to investigate thoroughly enough – the prime minister should go, too. For some weeks – with the newspapers holding very much the whip-hand over the government – the mood at Westminster remained febrile, with the more historically-minded politicians recalling the atmosphere of calumny provoked by the notorious Titus Oates in the seventeenth century. In the end, Macmillan felt compelled again to call for an eminent judge, this time Lord Denning, to investigate, as he put it in the Commons, 'rumours which affect the honour and integrity of public life' and to produce a report. It was another victory of a sort for the press – and it inevitably looked even more so when, by the time the Denning Report was debated by the Commons, the man who had instigated it addressed the House no longer from the Treasury bench but from the front bench below the gangway, having a month earlier announced his resignation as prime minister and First Lord of the Treasury in face of an impending prostate operation.

The newspapers had not, in fact, brought Harold Macmillan down – but they had sufficiently weakened his position to the point where many in his own party had already started to wonder whether he had not become an electoral liability. This was a view shared by Harold Wilson, who was desolate when Macmillan finally resigned and found consolation only in the Tories' choice of a third successive Old Etonian (and a fourteenth Earl to boot) to succeed him.

The still predominantly right-wing world of Fleet Street may not have joined Wilson in his sense of relief at the Earl of Home's appointment. For the next twelve months it was to find Sir Alec Douglas-Home (as he became, having renounced his earldom) a somewhat baffling prime minister.[1] Most Westminster journalists had expected R. A. Butler, who as Leader of the House for nearly five years had enjoyed very close and cordial relations with them, to step into Macmillan's shoes; when he was ruthlessly blocked from doing so, they – in common with the rest of the professional middle class – somehow felt let down. In any case, there was now a new and exciting boy on the block – the eminently newsworthy Harold Wilson, who promptly inaugurated an entirely fresh era at Westminster by insisting on treating all but the most reactionary of lobby journalists as colleagues and partners in his great enterprise of building 'the new Britain'.

It has to be said that the spell Wilson immediately cast over the working press at Westminster – not just in his twenty months as Leader of the Opposition but also in his first two years as prime minister – amounts in retrospect to one of the more shaming episodes in the history of British journalism. There was nothing, of course, wrong with his trying – by means of the use of Christian names, signed Christmas cards and all the other marks of personal favour – to tickle and seduce the normally hard-bitten corps of political correspondents who patrol the corridors of the Commons; but there *was* something demeaning in the way they nearly all rolled over and allowed him to do so.

Ultimately, it did him little, if any, good. After the 1966 election – in which Wilson converted his original majority of five into one of ninety-seven – they came to realize that he was not a miracle-worker at all,[2] and a fearful revenge was exacted. Collectively the

---

1. Most of them found him a baffling Leader of the Opposition, too – a post he gave up on the direct instructions of the *Sunday Times* in July 1965. He made way for Edward Heath, who throughout his ten-year leadership of the Conservative Party appeared to have only the vaguest idea of how the press worked.
2. For William Rees-Mogg, a former lobby correspondent of the *Financial Times* but by then deputy editor of the *Sunday Times*, the moment of truth came when he asked Wilson as prime minister why he kept on so many weak members of his Cabinet. He never forgot the reply: 'You've got to remember that the weakest members of my Cabinet are the ones who are most loyal to me.'

lobby correspondents turned on him with quite exceptional venom, only to be explained by their resentment at having been 'conned' in the first place.

Yet, in his first couple of years in Number 10, Wilson undeniably enjoyed the kind of honeymoon with the press that was later vouchsafed only to Tony Blair. (It is often forgotten that initially Margaret Thatcher did not have a smooth ride with the newspapers at all: she only became the toast of the whole of Fleet Street after her victory in the Falklands War of 1982, the defeat of the miners in 1985 and, perhaps above all, her legal facilitation for Rupert Murdoch's smashing of the print unions in 1986.) Certainly Wilson succeeded in leaving behind some tips for his successors, especially noted, in terms of Fleet Street honours, by Margaret Thatcher. No prime minister was ever more assiduous than Wilson in courting not just the hacks at Westminster but their editors and proprietors as well. Five peerages to those associated with the upper echelons of Mirror Group newspapers[1] will presumably remain an all-time record – but Wilson also showed flair and imagination more ecumenically elsewhere: both Michael Berry, translated to being Lord Hartwell (the then owner of the *Daily Telegraph*), and Patrick Gibson (at the time chairman of the *Financial Times*) were his creations as life peers.

In addition, he wined and dined almost promiscuously in newspaper and TV boardrooms, rarely showing any visible sign of discomfort over what the political views of his hosts might be – although, according to his original press aide, John (now Lord) Harris, he was, at least in the early days, never above muttering out of the side of his mouth as he went in: 'Now we go and meet the enemy.'

Alas, it was that surreptitious side-of-the-mouth suspicious attitude that his successors – at least until the coming of Tony Blair – tended to inherit. Tony Benn may not have left many lasting legacies

---

1. The lucky recipients were John Beavan (Lord Ardwick), Alma Birk, Ted Castle, Hugh Cudlipp and Sydney Jacobson. Terence Lancaster, at the time the *Mirror*'s political editor, declined the offer of a peerage in Wilson's Resignation Honours List of 1976.

to the Labour Party but one he has successfully passed on lies in his inveterate suspicion of 'the meejah'. Such a wary outlook might have been warranted as long as individual working journalists – or, for that matter, television or radio interviewers – regarded themselves as no more than vassals of their employers; but even by 1959 – when the Kemsley empire, the last newspaper organization in which that feudal attitude largely survived, was taken over by the far more commercially-minded Roy Thomson – it had effectively vanished. The peasants' revolt had succeeded, and Labour (unlike Clinton's or even Kennedy's Democrats in America) never even noticed.

One thing that it ought to have observed was the fate of the old Fleet Street ancestral ownership houses. One by one, between the end of the 1950s and the mid-1980s, they went down like ninepins: the Carr family with the *News of the World*, the Astors first with *The Times* and then with the *Observer*, the Aitkens with the *Daily Express* and its sister papers, and finally even the Berrys with the seemingly impregnable kingdom of the two *Telegraphs*. Add to that the takeover – or rather the plunder – of the *Mirror* by Robert Maxwell and it should have been perfectly clear that the whole geology of Fleet Street had changed (with only the Rothermere traditional family empire at the *Daily Mail* maintaining its position).

Of course, in Labour's eyes it was not necessarily a change for the better. International entrepreneurs, like Rupert Murdoch (who expanded his domain from the *News of the World* and the *Sun* in 1969 to *The Times* and the *Sunday Times* in 1981) or the Canadian Conrad Black (who lifted the two *Telegraph* papers from under the unsuspecting eyes of its previous owner Lord Hartwell in 1986), were hardly guaranteed to be any more friendly to what was still in the 1980s ruefully known as 'the people's party' than any of their more traditionalist predecessors.

It remained, however, probably a mistake for Labour, following its third successive electoral defeat in 1987, to settle down to doing its very best to alienate the new race of 'media moguls'. Although none of it in the end got into the 1992 Labour manifesto, there was a lot of dark talk about bans on cross-ownership between newspapers and television, threats of the imposition of much stricter limits on the extent of celestial or terrestrial TV interests any one concern should be allowed to own and, perhaps most offensive of all to the American Rupert Murdoch and the Canadian Conrad Black, a direct warning from the Shadow Home Secretary, Roy Hattersley, that a Labour government would legislate to prevent British newspapers from being owned by anyone but British subjects.

The trouble, of course, with extreme proposals of that kind is that in time they tend to produce their own reactions. In Tony Blair's game plan, the invention of 'new Labour' was from the start intended to involve the development of a whole new relationship even with those papers that had traditionally been unfriendly and hostile to the Labour Party. In Blair's eyes – and perhaps even more in those of his press secretary Alastair Campbell (who joined him almost from the moment of his election as Labour's leader in 1994) – that meant, first and foremost, courting the tabloids. The one they had particularly in their sights was the Murdoch *Sun*, and when that best-selling of all British dailies came out for Blair on the very first day of the 1997 election campaign it was a peculiarly sweet moment for all those who had set their hands to the new Labour enterprise.

Yet, as Baldwin discovered all those years ago, in the wicked world of rampaging press lords it is rare indeed for something to be offered for nothing. For a prime minister dealing with the new breed of international tycoons, the only difference today is that the stakes tend to be higher. Where Beaverbrook in 1921 started out by demanding nothing more than the ending of the wartime embargo on the import of Canadian cattle, Murdoch from the beginning has had far higher ambitions and global designs – reaching all the way to dictating policy on the Euro and asserting his right to colonize China via satellite. In the run-up to the 1997 election, it may well have appeared that any forfeit he chose to exact was worth delivering to him. But the halfway stage of the first Labour government to come to office in eighteen years may perhaps be the moment to reassess the policy of always paying the Danegeld on demand.

It is claimed that at the moments of his greatest stress – many of them provoked by the warrior press barons of the 1920s and 1930s – Baldwin's wife Lucy used to try to encourage him by muttering under her breath, 'Tiger Baldwin'. Maybe it is time – if she wants her husband to take his place in history as a man who was never afraid of making his own decisions – that Cherie Booth started murmuring something of the same sort to Tony Blair, with especial reference to Rupert Murdoch.

Reporting from the Front Line

EMMA DALY

We went looking for the fighting at a time when the war was conducted out of town, in a breathtaking rural landscape, and we found it. Face down in the damp grass, caught between my pounding heart and the whirr of a shell flying overhead, a clear case of effect and cause. I remember thinking, why are we doing this?

But all I must do is look back on my journalistic life at Canary Wharf, feigning interest in the dreary recollections of some minor celebrity, flicking through acres of vacuous lifestyle features, some of which I actually had to write, and I know now. You don't have to visit a war zone to find compelling stories and to learn about the human spirit, but it helps.

Bracing for the explosion, my mind is clear – the point is here and now, what next, how to proceed, which way to go. Rolling over in a lull to consult the others, Ron, David and Jehona – no idle chat, a quick assessment and a decision made: time to leave this muddy track leading nowhere.

The few soldiers who had passed by (in retreat, we later realized) did not want to chat and, frankly, there is no value in watching shells crash into an abandoned village. A few minutes and a few miles later, safe again, adrenaline still pumping, chest still tight with fear even though we had not been so close: the shells we could hear burning the air above us with a strange rhythmic rush were landing at least 300 yards away. This battle was of no particular account – just a small step along one army's road to domination and destruction of the area. I don't think it made a line in the copy – but for me the morning offered another fragment of knowledge and experience to add to the imagined landscape of this particular war.

Reporting from the front lines of the late twentieth century does not often mean we don a uniform, accept an honorary rank (officer class, naturally) and move with the advancing army. Even in the Gulf War of 1991, with its multiple press pools, much of the actual news came from journalists travelling alone. The nasty truth of modern warfare is that civilians are routinely targeted – so correspondents trying to document the fight hang out on street corners, in dusty villages and sophisticated cities, in cellars and schools and hospitals, more often than in trenches and bunkers.

For my generation of war correspondents – not that I have ever heard any of them say, 'Me? Oh, I'm a war correspondent,' they normally leave it at 'journalist', though my friend David likes the prefix 'shithole' – the defining conflict was Bosnia. It was our Vietnam, though we are still waiting for a decent film. Thousands of journalists must have passed through Sarajevo, not to mention Mostar, Vitez, Prijedor, Gornji Vakuf, Srebrenica and dozens more obscure villages made infamous by villainy on a hideous scale. Hundreds of them stayed for weeks, months or years, living without water or electricity or fresh food; without heating in icy winter or fridges in high summer, reading by candlelight, writing on computers powered by truck batteries, calling on bulky satellite phones that cost at least $25 per minute.

'You are all freaks, you're sick,' railed Sabina, a Sarajevan working as a war correspondent because she had no choice. It is true that many of our childhoods are the makings of multiple Hollywood weepies – random death and destruction teaching the visceral early lesson that shit happens anywhere, that you can die as swiftly and suddenly in a traffic accident as in an ambush.

Sarajevo offered an escape from one kind of reality – and anyway, we lived far more easily there than the locals. We could afford petrol at £10 a litre and Marlboro reds at £1 a pack (tax-free, cheaper than Britain), we owned flak jackets and, most important, we could leave town at almost any time. With so much misery around, our lives did not seem so bad. But still we ran the gauntlet of snipers and shells, and in those grim four years several journalists were killed and many more wounded.

So why did so many choose to stay, to return time and again, to put themselves in harm's way for the sake of a story? Why do we do it? By 'we' I mean my colleagues, my friends, in a way my second family, the small, dissolute, dedicated band of reporters, photographers and camera crews who choose to document the worst that man can do, who put themselves, their lives, their relationships, at risk of death or serious injury. I know it is not for the cash. We are not badly paid – especially those freelance TV crews on a handsome day rate. But I have lost count of the people who ask, 'Do you get danger money?' The answer is absolutely not, or not if you work for the British press. I cannot think of anyone who is motivated by the pay. It might be for the glory – but I doubt it. In Britain, media fame is generally restricted to pundits, opinion-formers, columnists and news-readers, and rarely extended to those who pursue the stories, the facts, the news. 'War reporters' – by definition we make careers of the suffering, the misery of others, but so do many journalists, dealing as we do in the currency of misfortune, be it in Beirut or Birmingham.

Perhaps our work sounds more glamorous, more dramatic, sexier. Perhaps. Sometimes at parties people would ask, 'What is it like to live in Sarajevo?', and sometimes they really wanted to know. How it looked and sounded and smelt, how we lived a medieval life without mod cons, surviving on tinned food and Balkan tobacco, how we witnessed unbearable horrors. But not often, which is why we would gather in London or New York or wherever for dinners that bored outsiders rigid – so that we could argue, gossip, trade war stories and discuss the latest political response to a crisis that did not, could not, engage others to the same extent. Some correspondents are drawn to the excitement, the intensity of experience, good and bad, unmatched in peacetime. Because covering a conflict is never dull – it is horrifying, exhausting, terrifying, soul-destroying, awe-inspiring, uplifting and even, at times, uproariously funny. Sarajevans lived by the concept that you had to laugh or you would only cry. Survival can be addictive, the high that kicks in as you realize you are safe again, that the mortars were sending up smoke and fragments of burning metal on the road behind, on the verge, up ahead, but that every one of them has somehow missed your speeding car. You grow accustomed to distant gunfire, a lullaby soothing you for another night. Sometimes you thrill to the thunder of artillery, adding an edge to sex, arousing in the way of a violent storm raging against the windows back home.

War brings out the best and worst – as some sink to the lowest depths of depravity and cruelty, so others rise to display a generosity of spirit, a courage that is overwhelming, and that, for me at least, outweighs the evil. The horror is physical and emotional – in the human wreckage of war you notice strange and disgusting, repelling things. Brains often get left behind when the bodies, the limbs are picked up, and the blood is hosed off the street. Dogs and cats, even fluffy, cuddly ones, will happily feed off the dead. The memory of smell, especially that sickening combination of death and disinfectant, will haunt you in any hospital or morgue, but unless it is really bad you can learn how to breathe without really taking it in. I can usually examine bodies and describe them, even if they are mutilated and torn, faces frozen in terror or surprise or anxiety, because my job does not require me to look too closely. I trade in words. But my friends who are cameramen or photographers – and many of the most perceptive and intelligent chroniclers of conflict work in film – are haunted by these physical images, since they must focus, literally, on the bloodied detritus that was once a person.

For me, the anguish comes when people speak, when they tell their stories, when they describe their loss, their despair. When they ask, as if I could possibly know, 'What shall we do now?' When they weep silently or wail aloud, when there is so much pain and so much distress that I can hardly bear to watch and I think, How must it be to live this? Or when someone else, a jolly, hospitable, charming someone else, explains it all: 'These people, these others, are not really suffering, they are faking, telling lies, it's all a plot and hey, they would kill us if we did not kill them, believe me . . . I am afraid and that is why I do what I do . . . Not that I have done anything bad, you understand, it is all the fault of the others.'

Perhaps we work for the intellectual challenge, the mental

discipline that is constantly tested by circumstance. First, can I do the job in hand well, without unforced errors, can I convey adequately the reality I see, the stories I hear, with some kind of context? Can I show the readers back home why life goes on in this desolate place, how people keep up bourgeois standards against all the odds because that is one form of resistance? And, more important, can I function under extreme duress? Can I hold on, keep going, stay calm? I know that if a gunman rips open the car door screaming in a foreign language and brandishing a rifle, I can respond with soothing words and gestures, that I will not panic. I know, because it has happened more than once.

It is impossible to predict how someone will behave under fire, though there is some satisfaction in knowing that you can do your job, that you can keep going – at any rate, that you have yet to encounter the situation that defeats you in the moment. The payback comes later, at home, with nightmares or flashbacks or depression or aggression, excessive emotion, or any of the multiple symptoms of post-traumatic stress disorder. (It is no wonder so many of us drink heavily or not at all, do drugs, ruin relationships. Nor is it a coincidence that so many of the Bosnia crew decided after the horrors of the war to settle down, to marry, to have children, to try to build the 'normal' life that is an early casualty of war reporting – though most showed up again for the next chapter in Kosovo.)

At any rate, staying calm is a strange sort of talent – certainly it is a characteristic you seek in others you plan to work with, and most of us are pretty careful about choosing our travelling companions to dangerous places. You don't have to like them, though it helps, but you must trust them to watch your back, to share their instincts, to shout out loud when they hear the fire coming in.

That is one of the (many) obstacles facing a newcomer. It is expensive to watch a war – you need cameras and/or computers, access to satellite phones and flak jackets, insurance and someone to pay for the $50,000 medical evacuation plane (just in case), black-market food and fuel, translators or language lessons. Then you need to persuade someone to show you the ropes, tell you the safe routes in and out, the tricks of survival. After that, you apply all that background reading and try to work out what the story actually is and how to report it, without getting yourself and anyone else killed – since first-timers are very often the subjects of anecdotes about dead journalists.

Which is why 'war reporters' are self-perpetuating. I never planned to cover conflicts (I did not even mean to become a journalist) but my first job came at an English-language newspaper in Central America in 1987 and war – in Nicaragua, El Salvador and Guatemala – was the biggest story around. I ended up, two years later, in Panama City during the US invasion – and by then I had become, without realizing it, a war correspondent, a member of the tribe.

Because of that experience, I was sent to the Balkans at the start of 1994 – and I spent my first night in Sarajevo sleeping on the floor of a friend, a photographer I had worked with in Central America. On her say so, I was welcomed by the Bosnia crowd. Editors like that, they like to know that if they drop you somewhere nasty, you will find a friend. It gives you a head start, and it means that you, in turn, must do the right thing when someone new arrives in town.

Journalism can be a dirty game, in which competition drives people to shameful deeds. But in times of trouble, most of my colleagues will do all they can to assist – share material with their rivals, help the competition to call in, lend equipment, supplies, whatever it takes. Being surrounded by death and destruction does help to put things in perspective – an 'exclusive' tag is really not the point when the story is about a mass grave.

It is not that we are great humanitarians, that we suffer for the sake of others. But I think we are motivated to continue, at least in part, by the people we meet in these not-so-distant lands. I never thought I could change the world, but I would like to show you what I have seen. I want to give a voice to so many: to the 12-year-old girl who watched her 5-year-old sister ripped apart by a shell in the playground; to the grieving parents mourning a 17-year-old daughter whose death was stolen and re-broadcast as propaganda by her killers; to the 29-year-old keening, with great gasping sobs, over the body of her mother, to all those whose lives have been destroyed in the pursuit of power. To those friends whose memories and stories I never noted down – because sometimes you just want to talk as people, to set the job aside for a few moments. To all who survive with grace and humour and dignity, offering coffee to every stranger who crosses the threshold and time to every curious journalist dropping by to ask, 'And how do you feel/What do you think/Show me your scars.'

We can do no more than record as faithfully as we can what we see and hear and smell and taste and touch. Each one of us is influenced by our history, our beliefs, our prejudices, and each of us has a responsibility to try to identify such traits and to work around them. By now I almost expect the work of reporters in the field to be dismissed as 'naïve' by diplomats, pundits and other specialists who rarely leave their comfortable Western capitals yet who have an unshakeable faith in their own knowledge, garnered mostly from official briefings. 'You simply don't see the big picture,' is the patronizing phrase often used by those who choose to see only in the abstract. Or, as a colleague once said to me, 'All you people in Sarajevo are obsessed by dead children and that is simply not the point.'

But I think that exactly is the point. I think that war is the greatest human-interest story there is. The martial metal, the acronyms in which soldiers speak, the decisions made in offices far away – their significance comes from their ability to shatter the lives of real people. Progress has dragged war off the battlefield and into the home – and I'm not talking about CNN. In the past we used soldiers as cannon fodder, but now the military machine devours civilians, before our very eyes. There was some discussion, after the Bosnian war ended in 1995, of the changing nature of war reporting – the genre was thought to have been feminized, since a cold, dispassionate ideal had mutated into the more emotive 'journalism of attachment' described by Martin Bell, journalist and MP.

What was a reporter following the journalist grail of objectivity to do if he or she found out that some stories really had only one side? Consider, for instance, the 10-year-old boy who describes in hideous detail the murder of his mother, sisters and neighbours by gunmen. Gasping for breath, he tells of how they broke in, howling like wolves, and set the house ablaze, calling forth its terrified residents and shooting them, one by one. He says that he faked death and then scrambled into a smoke-filled room to hide from the executioners, that he had to leave his small sister behind, to burn alive, since he could not carry her. In his right arm there is a bullet wound but no one survived to corroborate his account. The government routinely denies such stories, though we have heard hundreds, thousands of similar tales. Should we simply report the denial straight – the small boy's word against the minister's? Because if we do, we are questioning the boy's veracity – as are the editors who insert the word 'alleged' into the story. Is it any 'truer' to create doubt than it is to assert certainty?

How to report a story fairly and accurately is especially tough in the fevered, overwrought atmosphere of a war zone, where you too are at the receiving end, where you too are under a death threat. Here it is especially important to cross lines, to experience life on the other side – especially when you find that the fight is not equal, that army A is attacking city B simply because its leader wants more power, or wants to wipe out an entire people, or is claiming to avenge some ancient wrong long forgotten by everyone else.

In Bosnia-Herzegovina, for instance, the Western media were accused of bias, of partiality, of taking sides. But that implies that we knowingly manipulated information to make one group look better than another – which is not true. The reality was that in this particular conflict, the huge majority of war crimes were committed against the Bosnian people (Serbs, Croats and Muslim among them), just as in Rwanda the massacres of spring 1994 were conducted by Hutus against their political enemies (mostly Tutsis, but including some Hutus and foreigners).

There are times when the reporter has a responsibility to apportion some kind of blame – not to an entire people but to individuals, if possible, and to a leadership whose aim, whose *raison d'être*, is to wage war, as was the case with President Slobodan Milosevic. It is not enough simply to say, bad things happen in war. But the good reporters – and I worked with many – spent time pondering this topic, arguing back and forth about good and bad and blame, questioning their own assumptions and beliefs, trying to strike a balance, trying to come as close as possible to the truth. Bringing emotion, passion and commitment to a story does not make a journalist partisan, unstable, unreliable. After the fall of Srebrenica, in Bosnia, sensible reporters dismissed survivors' testimony of mass executions as exaggerated – we simply could not believe in state-sanctioned murder on such a scale, so close to home. But a few months later we walked across the killing grounds they had described in such detail, dislodging bones and strips of the pink cloth used to blindfold the victims. How could we not respond with rage and pity? How could we not demand justice for the victims, punishment for those who ordered the atrocities, and an honest accounting from those who saw it happen but were too frightened to admit it?

Four years later, I stood and watched as men, women, children, dozens, hundreds, thousands, a numberless multitude, struggled to make their agonized way across the border from Yugoslavia into Albania – forced out of their homes at gunpoint, taunted and threatened, stripped of their possessions, their documents, their humanity by an army, a government, that claimed its place among the civilized nations of Europe. It does not matter that I was numb with grief, that I wept for these people, that there came a point where I could hardly bear to listen again to another story of a family destroyed. The only purpose was to record these scenes so that no one, not those who would rather ignore this nastiness, not even those in whose name the crimes were committed, would have an excuse to say: 'I did not know.'

Why I Hold Journalists in Low Regard

ALAN CLARK

I am always wary of corporate – as opposed to collective – nouns. 'The Palace', 'No. 10', 'Central Office', and so on.

What is 'The Press'? Sometimes 'it' preens itself on a courtesy title . . . *The Fourth Estate*. But, once personalized, 'The Press' can be seen as no more, surely, than a bunch of journalists. Fellows with, in the main, squalid and unfulfilling private lives, insecure in their careers, and suffering a considerable degree of dependence on alcohol and narcotics.

These are not characteristics inseparably associated with discernment or a fastidious taste. And they are observable, it would seem, at practically every rank within the 'profession'. Reporters, the lowest form of pond life, are bullied, and their self-esteem reduced, by news editors. Editors are anxious about relations with their proprietors.

Periodically editors may go through periods of congenial self-delusion, related to the amount of power that others believe them to dispose. All of them (with only one honourable exception known to me) must aspire to reincarnate Beaverbrook's verdict on Northcliffe in 1917:

His influence, particularly when he was assaulting the public reputations of ministers, was something which had constantly to be reckoned with. Politicians, therefore, feared and hated him. (But) . . . He would use his papers to urge that they should be replaced and *to prepare public opinion* [my italics] *for the reception of a new and determined Administration.* (*Men and Power*, p. 62.)

The late Sir David English, for example, strongly believed himself to be a 'broker' of power and influence. And this was reinforced by politicians who sought his favour and employees who were alarmed at the prospect of his disapproval. In fact, though, his impregnability was a myth. If Lord Rothermere had got sick of him, English would have been belly-up in twenty-four hours.

More self-consciously insecure was Mr Max Hastings, who will end – one must assume – his career editing an evening tabloid in the Rothermere group. Hastings displayed many of the appurtenances of a Conservative gentleman-politician, including a yo-ho-ho conversational style and a propensity to shoot (easy) birds on the weekend. But this did Hastings little good; and he compounded the error by espousing pinkish causes and increasing the price of the paper. Both of these men, in common with most of their editorial confrères, 'flirted' from time to time with other proprietors, notably Mr Conrad Black. But they avoided Mr Rupert Murdoch, whose brutal realism and capacity to equate personal quality and strategic objective made him awkward company.

Notwithstanding the self-regarding vortices of those 'Award' ceremonies in which the different newspapers co-operate to give medals to one another's staff, the real criterion of survival, both personal and institutional, and subject to so intense and continuing a scrutiny as to qualify, in medical parlance, for status as an obsessional disorder, are the circulation figures. These are in the forefront of the minds of all those staff who attend each day's editorial conference, at which the paper's attitude (sometimes dignified by the word 'policy') towards events and 'personalities' is determined.

Much of this meeting is occupied, in its initial stages, by scrutiny of what 'the competition' is doing. To have been scooped – by an eye-catching headline that may cause random bookstall visitors to prefer the look of, and to purchase, a rival – is thought to be deeply humiliating, and may lead instantly to recrimination. Sometimes it will provoke counter-scoop, or even 'spoiling' (an attempt to anticipate what is coming next, and to both trail and degrade it). At the back of everyone's mind will be William Randolph Hearst's primary injunction: *Girls make news*, itself no more than a commercially grounded restatement of the first law of criminal investigation in France – *Cherchez la femme*. With the guise of 'human interest,' sex, by its combination of power simultaneously to arouse voyeuristic curiosity and puritanical indignation, is the mainspring.

Thus a primary element in any scoop is to acquire (and prevent the competition from acquiring) the 'story' of the principal characters involved in any episode that has caught the attention of the public – aka *hit the headlines*. Where the essence of the case is criminal behaviour, even murder, but where it has an overtly sexual content – as in the case of the Saudi nurses, or Fred and Rose West (the use of Christian names is part of the technique for showing them as 'real' people) – then the titillation-factor escalates, and the participants have hot potential.

If a newspaper has bought an 'Exclusive' relating to a particular person, then it feels, with perhaps some justification, proprietary. And certainly this claim is implicitly confirmed by the manner in which rival organs will do their best to rubbish whatever, or whoever, is claimed as their own property by a competitor. This is the 'Blackie-the-Donkey' syndrome where one tabloid, having worked its readers into a state of high indignation at the cruel fate awaiting an amiable female donkey ('Blackie') at some Spanish village festival, managed to present them with a triumph. Blackie had been saved, and was coming to a peaceful farm in the Home Counties where she would live out her remaining days in comfort. 'Ah but . . .' the rivals declared, Blackie was crippled and disease-ridden. Her proposed importation was a disgrace. Who knows what strange viruses and other troubles might not attend on this 'stunt'?

Similarly, when a particular celebrity has been the object of fulsome attention, then a particular paper – often the entire press – may feel that it has 'made' them, and can thereafter treat them as it chooses (regardless of whether or not the celebrities have so conducted themselves as to be charged in the criminal courts). Actors, singers, politicians, whizz-kids have only a tenuous life-expectancy within this convention. Anyone who has sought, and received, publicity enters that long and vaulted corridor in the temple whose priesthood, waiting by the altar, are ready at their own choosing to practise and enjoy the ritual of human sacrifice. It is the traditional pattern of the circus. In ancient times the Roman emperors would distract and placate the mob by first displaying the chosen hero then contriving his humiliation, and wounding, before the jeers of a spectating crowd. A phenomenon perpetuated still in these days, where modern circuses manage to arouse simultaneous fear and admiration as 'wild' animals are displayed – later to suffer torment and subjugation.

First, the setting up. And here a bogus sense of righteousness legitimizes every device of entrapment: 'wiring up' (the *Sunday Times*); burglary (the *Sunday Mirror*); forgery (the *Guardian*); and always an approach – sometimes wheedling, sometimes intimidatory, often in disguise – towards the subject's family, including, and particularly, their children. I recall one prominent and (genuinely) respectable MP being first embarrassed, then shamed, after being invited to listen to, and comment on, tapes of his daughter soliciting on the telephone. Finally, the destruction. At the end the hunt has transmogrified into a blood sport whose objective is to inflict misery on the victim and titillate the audience with *schadenfreude*. Not infrequently it may come to climax with that ultimate notch on the portable WP – the 'kill', when the demented victims cheat the pursuers by taking their own life.

Lady Caithness, Lady Green, Mr Tommy Graham MP, these are examples of human beings, who have been goaded beyond endurance by endless harassment on the telephone or on the doorstep concerning their own sexuality or that of their spouse. When I predicted the demise of Princess Diana, a Mr Alan Cochrane (whom I had never mentioned or even, as far as I can recall, met, although apparently he intermittently occupies various junior editorial positions) wrote a piece of some length to assert that I had 'finally taken leave of my senses'.

This is a charge sometimes levelled against me by those unwilling to engage in rational debate. So plainly the word 'finally' is not only inappropriate but it is also illiterate. Syntax is seldom a dominant consideration in this milieu. Let me add, though, that it is impossible to overestimate the level of crude vindictiveness that reporters are encouraged to apply. Little regard need be paid to their protestations that, like concentration camp guards, they were 'only acting under orders'. The sadistic delight of the paparazzi (or, as the vernacular has it, 'monkeys') who take continual pleasure in the intimidating effect of their weight of numbers, of the sound of cameras clacking on motordrive, and of the blinding of the victim by high-intensity flashbulbs: all these, from individuals who will never converse or even communicate a greeting other than an obscenity designed to provoke, find counterparts in the crudities and contrived falsehoods of their deskbound colleagues.

Look, for an example taken at random but most recently, at the *Mail on Sunday*. This paper had bought, one must assume for a substantial sum, the trashy (and plainly contrived) 'diaries' of a backbench Tory who lost his seat after only one Parliament. Plainly there was a commercial requirement to spice them up a bit. And so when a reference was made to the author's predecessor as MP for the City of Chester, himself a sad and lonely alcoholic who (fortunately for the Associated Press lawyers) died one year ago but had in his time been returned by the electorate with far higher majorities than his successor, it was delegated to a sub-editor. This individual, within the confines of a heavily framed 'box', told readers that the 'Old Etonian' (much deployed indicator-code for *privilege*, so the reader is put on notice to be prepared to spit) was 'rumoured to be a pervert who preyed on small boys'. This extraordinarily hurtful allegation was without any foundation whatsoever. Nor is it possible to make much sense of it even within a context of the ever-present requirement to increase the paper's circulation. It can be understood only as an example of sadistic falsehood, whose overt homophobia embellishes the 'story' with an added prurience.

Certainly it is often possible to predict, from even the most sidelong glance at the intended 'subject', how their achievement, or misfortune, will be handled. Here, in this great cauldron of alphabet soup, to be 'snooty' (like Selina Scott), or fastidious (like Graham Le Saux), or even (like Sir Alec Douglas-Home) courteous, means that you deserve to be 'taken down a peg'. Any insult, however crude, any accusation, however fanciful (a denial is always good for a headline), is permitted.

Even, and most indicatively, it was often possible to detect in some parts of the press an editorial preference (during the period when the two women could be said to have been competing for public affection) for the Duchess of York, who could have been depicted as vulgar, bloated and predatory, over the beautiful, public-spirited and vulnerable Princess Diana.

'Dumbing down' is an expression minted for the *Sun*, the *Mirror*, and to a slightly (very slightly) lesser extent the *Mail* titles. I recall one of the many occasions on which I have been invited to appear on television in order to review the newspapers. I was in the company of a distinguished visiting American, and we were looking at the *Mirror*. 'In my country,' he said, 'the people at whom this paper is aimed can't read.'

In fact this brutish culture, part base prejudice, part leering innuendo, which colours and informs the style in which these papers compete one with another is a transposition of the technique of the playground bully: where the 'sensitive' child is held up to ridicule by the mob and their confidence shattered, their innate sense of modesty, truth and value deliberately extinguished.

What can we do about this? As individuals – *particularly* I should say as individuals – nothing. Absolutely nothing.

Sue? Impossibly expensive, outcome unpredictable.

Complain to the Press Complaints Commission? Complete waste of time – you might as well refer a fraudulent pension scheme to FIMBRA.

Always remember that once you have drafted a press release, or spoken – even on the telephone – to a reporter, you place yourself at their mercy. And for all time.

Just as there is no such thing as gratitude in politics, so there is no such thing as mercy in the media. Individuals suffering bereavement, distress, or the consequences of some especially gruesome criminal episode, are significant only as circulation fodder. They are weak, and thus to be despised and exploited. All that will temper the cruelty of the press is a demonstrable level of exposure-fatigue in their audience. Only this can force a change of direction and cause the editorial conference to search round for another target.

So much for the treatment by the press of individual human beings and their predicaments. But what on the macro scene, be it global or domestic, of an editor's proudest claim (most recently asserted by Mr David Yelland, the newly appointed boss of the *Sun*) – to *set the agenda*? Here analogous, though not necessarily identical, considerations apply.

Editors are subject to Focus Group Syndrome. This often, and misleadingly, will raise the 'profile' of an issue to a level well beyond that of genuine public interest. A *campaign* is launched, treading that narrow strip of territory between boring blue the majority of the readership, and earning the plaudits of a category (first identified by the beleaguered Ted Heath) known as 'right-thinking people'. Temptingly, if recognition is imposed on the audience, then later – and in the condign sense of the word – it may be bestowed on the editor and those prominent in his entourage.

Lead-free petrol, dangerous dogs, hand-guns. On many different subjects Parliament has been pressured into responding, and the press has been able to claim a victory. Never mind that the additive-laden vapours of lead-free fuel, inhaled at the pump, are carcinogenic to a far higher degree than the old stuff. Or that the enjoyment, and abuse, by the police of their additional powers has inflicted misery on many families and individuals who keep pets, without (in any measurable degree) reducing the always minuscule number of victims bitten by dogs. Or that hand-guns remain easily and cheaply available among the criminal fraternity; the number of persons killed or wounded by hand-guns has increased, and the confiscation, punitive in its severity, inflicted on gun clubs, marksmen and Olympic teams has caused great hardship and disillusion. If the rationale behind a campaign is held up to the light, still more if it be contradicted, those who express doubt will be held up to obloquy.

This is also true when a paper, for its own mix of reasons, intrudes upon the wider stage of international politics and diplomacy. In the 1930s a civil war raged for several years across Spain. It was marked by indiscriminate brutality, and characterized a proxy confrontation between democracy and totalitarianism of both right and left. In no time *demonization*, the indispensable tool of the propagandist, was brought into play: – 'Reds rape, burn alive nuns' was a headline that several times found its way on to the front page. 'Fascists slaughter hundreds' could also occasionally be found, though not – surprisingly – in many newspapers after Guernica.

As I write, another European civil war disfigures the Balkans. But the reportage has its own propaganda ethic. 'Investigative' journalism is scarcely permitted, blocked by a tacitly agreed, and self-imposed, censorship. To question NATO's targeting disciplines, the institutional lack of scruple that characterizes the United States Air Force, the linkage between the Albanian and Calabrian Mafia and their joint exploitation of immigration and drug-traffic rackets, is to run a risk – as even the mild and conscientious John Simpson of the BBC was to discover – of being stigmatized as 'a tool of Milosovic'.

Newspapers entertain. For quite a lot of the time they can also inform. As for censorship, its ritualized denunciation is part of the litany recited by career-conscious journalists. But it should never be forgotten that those who seek to 'set the agenda' are themselves assiduous in excluding anything that might seem contradictory, or even discordant, within their own preferred frame, an unwelcome rule that applies whether the topic is a 'personality' or an 'issue'.

What Columnists Are Good For

STEPHEN GLOVER

Once I thought I only had two columns in me. Perhaps I still have. I've forgotten one of them but I can recall the other, which was about the evils of tourism. My not very original line was that tourists destroy the very thing they seek to love. In an ideal world there would be no tourists, only ourselves, wandering knowledgeably among deserted ruins, a thin though erudite book nestling in one pocket, and perhaps a lump of delicious local cheese, known only to the *cognoscenti*, resting in the other.

I can't remember how many times I wrote that column. Three times over a period of five years? Four? I wasn't a columnist in those days, being occupied in perhaps more useful forms of journalism, but from time to time an editor or someone would notice that the resident pundit was away, and ask me to fill in. Then I would fall into a kind of panic. What to write about? One of my two stock columns would be dusted off – the one about the subject I have forgotten about, or the other about the evils of modern tourism.

Looking back, it seems odd that I should have assumed that column-writing required an encyclopedic understanding. A few years earlier, at the comparatively tender age of twenty-six, and in an altogether different world, I had found myself writing editorials for the *Daily Telegraph* on all manner of things about which I often knew absolutely nothing.

The paper's editor, Bill Deedes, had thoughtfully fixed the leader conference at quarter to four to allow us time for a leisurely lunch before arriving at work. The conference, which normally lasted about three-quarters of an hour, was discursive and rather witty, like a high table dinner (I then imagined) after the port had passed around a couple of times. If you didn't have to write an editorial, which was quite often as there were three leaders every day and perhaps as many as eight or nine leader-writers would bother to turn up, you went off to have a coffee with a colleague. But if you were asked to produce, you had only a couple of hours to acquaint yourself with the latest developments in Central America, or to work out why the government was right (or, as it might be, wrong) to raise interest rates.

Leader-writing is an ideal training ground for a political columnist. Bernard Levin, William Rees-Mogg, Henry Fairlie, Charles Moore, Hugo Young, Peregrine Worsthorne and many other famous columnists have gained the courage to pontificate under their own names by first pontificating under a paper's. (All men, I fear, probably because until recently politics, even more than journalism, has been a male business.) But at the time I am speaking of – when I had those two column ideas – I had put leaders behind me, and I half believed that a columnist must know a great deal about a subject before setting pen to paper.

This is what many people think. *How do you do it?* That is the first question columnists are asked by non-column-writing humanity, usually suspiciously, as though there might be an element of trickery involved. How is it possible for one person to write with even a modicum of authority about so wide a range of subjects? One answer, devised by a new generation of columnists, is to write exclusively about themselves. But that is likely to be a short-term solution, since in the end the reader will usually grow tired of an intimate account of their lives and deaths, however interesting they may be. The really successful columnists, who keep at it ten, twenty, thirty or forty years, write about the external world, though they may allow the reader an occasional glimpse into their own lives. They have to write about many subjects and there will always be someone who knows more about each of them than they do. Leslie Stephen, founder of the National Dictionary of Biography and father of Virginia Woolf, sneered that 'by journalism is to be understood, I suppose, writing for pay about matters of which you are ignorant'.[1] That, put in the most derogatory terms, is the art of column-writing. Of course, columnists should have a considerable general knowledge and obviously, unless they are writing pieces about themselves or bits of whimsy, they need to follow the news and read the papers assiduously. They must have a good number of contacts, though not be on such intimate terms that they find themselves writing to please these contacts rather than the readers. But however many books one has read, however impressive one's mastery of the news and the scope of one's contacts, it is inevitable that columnists will find themselves straying into subjects in which they are far from expert.

I Ie, or she, will then experience the curled lip of the specialist, the superior tut-tut of the person more in the know. There is an answer. Could you do better? Could you in your ivory tower or Whitehall ministry or university department, tilling and hoeing as you do your tiny parcel of land, knowing the names of every plant and counting every blade of grass, bring a single, organizing and moral intelligence to the wide variety of human experience? Ah, did I hear you say you wouldn't bother to try? And that no one should? Well, you're wrong there. We all live in our tiny boxes, knowing a lot about a little, and the columnist moves between us, making connections we may not have understood as individuals, attempting to explain a more complete picture to those who have seen only part of it.

Columnists of the sort I am describing are old-fashioned essayists writing for the modern world, the last of the generalists. One of my heroes is William Rees-Mogg of *The Times*. It is true that as a forecaster he leaves something to be desired, and generally speaking if he says something won't happen it will, and if he says it will, it won't. (This led Francis Wheen to call him 'Mystic Mogg', after 'Mystic Meg', a one-time adjunct of the National Lottery.) But he remains a hero of mine because he casts out his net with such abandon. He can write about John Locke, the Church of England and the state of the Conservative Party with equal plausibility. The academic philosopher, the Bishop and the Tory grandee will

1. Leslie Stephen, ed., *The Letters of John Richard Green* (London, 1901), p. 66.

complain that he doesn't know his onions, which may be very slightly true, but at least he is prepared to step outside his bailiwick. He may charge around a bit, and trip himself up and bang into things, but the point is that he has dared to venture out.

Columnists don't have to be experts. If they were, they wouldn't be columnists. They may have their little areas of expertise to which they can return, a sort of port in a storm, but most of the time they are on the wide-open seas. And it is a moderately difficult occupation, I think, though not necessarily more so than welding or cattle rustling. Almost anyone can knock out five or ten columns if they really try, though I thought I only had two, but to turn out 100, 500 or 1,000 is another matter. You need stamina and patience and large dollops of chutzpah. Week after week, day after day, you're exposing your intellect for all to see. A columnist is only as good as his last piece, or perhaps, if his reputation is very considerable, his last few pieces.

There is a vital distinction between a leader, which by definition is not signed, and a column, which is. A newspaper editorial, even if written by an ignorant young leader-writer, carries the authority of the newspaper. A leader in the *Sun* may be intellectually flawed (perish the thought) but that is not really the point. What matters is that the *Sun* has said what it has said. That is the paper's view, and it must be taken note of. Even a silly leader is imbued with some significance unless it is so bone-headed as to invite derision, and it draws strength in proportion to the size of the paper's readership. The *Sun* is read by 10 million people a day, and so its leaders are considered rather important. By contrast, so-and-so will not be excused for writing nonsense in his *Sun* column merely because he is addressing 10 million souls. A columnist is on his own – or her own – and will be judged on the merits of his or her piece.

It is a bit like performing on the stage, I think. You step out into the lights. But it is an unruly, distracted audience whose attention you must grab – much more the Globe *circa* 1600 than the National Theatre *circa* 2000. You have to retain the interest of your readers, who will have many other things to do, for 1,100 or 1,200 words with prose that is your own, not put into your mouth by some obliging playwright. Admittedly people can't throw rotten cabbages at you if they get fed up, though it is disconcerting to hear nothing but silence when your column disappears into the void, and I think I'd rather have a live audience. After a few days the letters arrive and a few of them are certainly stinking. I once received an ominous-looking parcel, which I did not open as I had strong suspicions as to its contents.

The very worse thing a columnist can do is to show boredom. You may not want to write about the government's latest difficulties or the problems of one-parent families, and sometimes, because news doesn't flow evenly, you may be short of a good subject. Whatever your feelings, you must demonstrate 100 per cent commitment. There is nothing more fatal than to betray *ennui*, since why should the reader bother if you will not? At the beginning of *Goodbye to Berlin* the young Christopher Isherwood imagines his life defined by the number of beers he will drink, an image evoking endless, futile repetition. The columnist who looks ahead, and measures out his own columnar life in such a way, is doomed. Of all necessary attributes I have mentioned stamina is the most important – but a stamina informed with an unflagging curiosity, and touched by passion. For me the best columnists are those who care. Give me an engaged columnist with whom I disagree, give me the *Guardian*'s passionate but sometimes wrong-headed Polly Toynbee, rather than a flaccid writer whose every word is unobjectionable. You can't maintain the stamina without belief. Columnists must believe in something other than themselves. They must have a view of the world, and readers will exchange this, and accept it by way of compensation, for failings in knowledge, even for mistakes. It may be a wry or even flippant world view, or it may be altogether more portentous, but either way it has to hang together and make a kind of sense. This is the voice that every columnist needs.

So far as I can make out, half the youth of Britain intends to take up column-writing, and it would be as well for them to know what they are letting themselves in for. I recently met a young girl of about fifteen of no very obvious academic attainment, who seems not even to skim the newspapers. None the less, she told me that she might like to be a columnist, her breezy tone implying that the choice was largely hers. Before long the editor of the *Times* or the *Daily Mail* or the *Guardian* would be on the line imploring her to bend her considerable talents to the art of column-writing. And she might very well accept.

There are certainly more opportunities for column-writing than there used to be. Our young friend will join a growing army. To a large extent signed columns in the British Press are a post-war phenomenon. Thirty or so years ago the good columnists on broadsheet newspapers could still almost be numbered on two hands: Bernard Levin, Katherine Whitehorn, Peregrine Worsthorne . . . The *Daily Telegraph* in those days actually had no regular weekly or daily columnists at all, apart from the satirical Peter Simple, because its proprietor, Lord Hartwell, regarded them as self-indulgent. Far better to have a news story than a chap banging on about his personal opinions. As recently as 1986, the page facing the leader page in the *Telegraph* carried news. Now it is bursting with columnists.

Their multiplication on this and every other national title partly reflects the much fatter newspapers following the demise of the restrictive Fleet Street printing unions: editors have got to fill them with something, and a columnist is a dependable performer, certainly not cheap, but without the expensive overheads a foreign correspondent or an investigative reporter may carry. But I think there is more to it than that. Editors believe that readers want columnists to help navigate them through the conundrums, personal and political, of the modern world, and ideally to entertain them in the process. The good ones do that; the bad ones are a waste of time.

Our young friend would be well paid for as long as she held the job, though, as I say, if she writes only about her love life she may have a short life as a columnist. Papers like the *Independent* or the *Guardian* offer between £400 and £600 per column to their lesser stars, and a good deal more to their big names. The rates are higher on *The Times* and the *Telegraph* and higher still on the tabloids, where a few star columnists command £200,000 a year or more for a couple of columns a week. Not bad work if you can get it, but you have to keep it up. Recently Matthew Parris of *The Times* was rumoured to have turned down an offer of £300,000 a year to work for the *Independent*. Suzanne Moore was paid a signing-on fee before joining the *Mail on Sunday*, and is said to receive some £140,000 a year for writing one column a week, admittedly composed of several items, that cannot take her more than a few hours to compose. I suppose she might reply, like the painter Whistler when asked how he could justify asking 200 guineas for a picture that had taken him two days' work: 'I ask it for the knowledge of a lifetime.'

Columnists such as these will find themselves courted by editors. Few of them actually sell many newspapers single-handedly (Lynda Lee-Potter of the *Daily Mail* is believed by her employers to be a rare exception). The proof of this is that when famous columnists leave newspapers, or are dismissed, there is never any discernible effect on the circulation figures. There wasn't when Richard Littlejohn quite recently left the *Daily Mail* for the *Sun*, or when Peregrine Worsthorne was (disgracefully) sacked in 1997 by the *Sunday Telegraph* after thirty-six years as its star columnist. John Junor is said to have taken tens of thousands of readers with him when he moved his column from the *Sunday Express* to the *Mail on Sunday*, but the circulation figures do not bear this out. So why do editors tend to make so much fuss of columnists? Partly because they believe that they are an ingredient in a mix, one element among many that make a successful newspaper, and if it is removed the recipe will be subtly changed. And partly because they like having them on their papers as a kind of intellectual praetorian guard. Columnists can bring snippets of information back from the political front – not always published if they are too scandalous or confidential – and they can lend lustre to an editor at a dinner party or official function. The words an editor most likes to hear on these occasions are, 'I must say that your so-and-so hit the nail on the head this morning. He certainly knows what's going on.' An adverse criticism, if it comes from someone important, is also valued, because it shows that a columnist is read. Resentment is a sure proof of influence.

But who remembers these stars who bestrode their worlds? Who remembers J. L. Garvin, who dominated the *Observer* for thirty years? Every week, Harold Macmillan later recalled, 'We read the *Observer*, not really for anything in it, but to see what Garvin had written . . . Everybody wanted to know what Garvin's views were.'[1] Few modern journalists could even tell you who Garvin was, or would know that during his editorship between the wars the *Observer* was a Conservative newspaper. Which journalist today is aware of Hugh Massingham, also of the *Observer*, or for that matter his father, Henry? In the 1950s Hugh was one of the most famous columnists of his day. Who thinks of Henry Fairlie, whose star blazed across the firmament during the 1950s and 1960s before he left for America? Fairlie was unusual in being practically forgotten in his own lifetime – and he was only sixty-six when he died. He drank too much. I met him once around the mid-1980s in the offices of the *New Republic* magazine in Washington, where towards his end this impoverished, tramp-like figure sometimes slept the night.

What of the great Sam White, who for many years wrote a column for Lord Beaverbrook's *Evening Standard* from Paris, usually ensconced in the Crillon bar, where he once picked up the telephone and commanded the operator: 'Get me his Lordship at sea.'[2] I once saw White at a *Spectator* party, some time in the early 1980s. He was an old man making his way laboriously through a throng of people, attended by a retinue of admiring journalists, some of whom were carrying chairs in case he wanted to sit down, while others parted the way. A great statesman could not have been more honoured. Who thinks of him? And who spares a thought for the tireless Peter Jenkins, who was writing only the day before yesterday? Two or three times a week throughout most of the 1970s and 1980s, Peter wrote a column, first for the *Guardian*, then briefly for the *Sunday Times* and finally for the *Independent*. He died,

1. Speech by Harold Macmillan, 7 December 1977. Garvin's articles were unsigned, but it was known that he invariably wrote them and, as Harold Macmillan's remark implies, they seem to have been regarded as a personal column as much as an editorial. After he was dismissed as editor of the *Observer* in 1942, he wrote signed columns for the *Sunday Express* and *Daily Telegraph*. He died in 1947.
2. Ben Bradlee, *A Good Life: Newspapering and Other Adventures* (Simon & Schuster, New York, 1995).

virtually in harness, as recently as 1992, and his memorial service in St Margaret's, Westminster, was attended by former and existing cabinet ministers, ambassadors and droves of MPs. A lesson was read by Michael Heseltine, then practically the most important politician in the land. Which person under thirty even knows who he was? Who over thirty can recall a single column that he wrote?

And what of Bernard Levin, in his day a more famous columnist even than Peter, and happily still with us? Everyone knew who Bernard Levin was, and had an opinion about him, good or bad. Whereas Peter Jenkins was of the school of columnists which seeks, often sympathetically, to unravel the political process, Mr Levin's view of almost all politicians was a plague on all their houses. I remember a bishop preaching a sermon and cracking a joke about him – calling him the deputy prime minister in deference to his enormous power. How the congregation tittered, even if all of them did not read his column in *The Times*, a paper which was then lucky to sell 300,000 copies a day. Who now recalls what he wrote? Even in my own mind, his columns, hundreds of which I have read as though he were my master, seem to have coalesced around the simple themes that communism is bad, politicians are untrustworthy and judges are often foolish. After twenty-seven years of service, *The Times* 'let go' Mr Levin in 1997.

Where are their columns now? Their gibes and flashes of merriment? Columns die, and the reputations of columnists usually die with them, if not before. Not especially brilliant novelists are sometimes still read and revered thirty or forty years after their deaths, but dead columnists who outshone them in fame and influence and perspicacity and even their mastery of English prose are only half remembered by a few odd people like me. It's not just that columnists appear in the easily disposable form of newsprint whereas novelists are immortalized between hard or soft covers and can remain proudly in your sitting room to gather dust. Even when columnists collect their works in book form, or have them anthologized by someone else, they seem to have little to say to us across the years. A friend of mine quite recently brought out a huge tome containing the articles of once-famous columnists since the end of the last century, a considerable work of scholarship. It was practically unreadable. Some of the lighter columnists who tended to write about timeless themes – men such as H. L. Mencken or James Thurber – could still bring a smile to one's lips. But the more serious political columnists, who plunged into the controversies of their day, were mostly unbelievably dreary. Political columns are written for the moment, and the very qualities of specificity which make them irresistible at the time render them almost irrelevant to posterity, of little interest to anyone but the historian.

So our fifteen-year-old friend will be forgotten in the end. We all will be. But how much better to be Bernard Levin than some novelist plodding through the minutiae of Hampstead lives! Her brilliant columns that may move men to tears and laughter and flashes of understanding will end up in a pile of forgotten and never-to-be-read-again newspapers in an attic, or sit unvisited in some database until they are finally wiped away. Not for her the comforts of immortality, the treasured place on the top bookshelf in the upstairs room. Her voice will not carry across the years, but she will have spoken to her time.

About the Contributors

LYNN BARBER was born in 1944 and joined *Penthouse* magazine immediately after Oxford and had an early, exciting career as a writer of sex books. She only began to specialize in celebrity interviews when she joined the *Sunday Express* magazine in 1983. Since then she has written for the *Independent on Sunday*, the *Telegraph* magazine and *Vanity Fair*; she currently writes for the *Observer*. She has won four British Press Awards and a 'What the Papers Say' award. Two collections of her interviews have been published by Viking/Penguin – *Mostly Men* (1991), and *Demon Barber* (1998). She is married, with two daughters, and lives in London.

ANDREW BROWN was brought up in Egypt, Yugoslavia, Sweden, Germany and Surrey. He first earned an honest living at the age of twenty-one in a rural Swedish factory, where he nailed together wooden pallets for Volvo marine diesel engines until rescued by paternity leave. He then started writing heartfelt articles on the awfulness of Swedish drink laws and other flaws of that nature, which led to the prestigious, though virtually unpaid, posts of Scandinavian correspondent and, later, chief reporter of the *Spectator*. His only subsequent paid employment has been as religious affairs correspondent, parliamentary sketch-writer and other odder things at the *Independent*, from 1986 to 1997. He is the author of a book about the London police, *Watching the Detectives* (1988), and of *The Darwin Laws* (1999). He won the first annual Templeton Prize in 1995 as the best religious correspondent in Europe.

ALAN CLARK is Conservative Member of Parliament for Kensington and Chelsea. From 1974 until 1992 he was MP for Plymouth (Sutton). He was Minister of Trade from 1986 to 1989, and Minister of State at the Ministry of Defence from 1989 to 1992. He is the author of *The Donkeys: A History of the BEF in 1915; The Fall of Crete; Barbarossa: the Russo-German Conflict, 1941–45;* and *Aces High: the War in the Air Over the Western Front 1914–18.* His *Diaries*, an account of the Thatcher years, was published in 1993. He has written for many newspapers, and has been a columnist for the *News of the World* and the *Mail on Sunday.*

EMMA DALY fell in love with journalism during an accidental encounter in Central America in 1987 and realized she was unfit to hold any other office. Within weeks she was reporting on the effects of civil wars in the region, visiting Nicaragua, El Salvador and Honduras. She covered the US invasion of Panama for Reuters news agency, then moved to London and joined the foreign desk of the *Independent.* She moved to Sarajevo in February 1994 as Balkans correspondent for the *Independent*, and spent two years covering all three sides of the war in Bosnia-Herzegovina, and the culmination of the war in Croatia. Since the summer of 1997 she has been based in Madrid, working as a housewife and as a correspondent. She covers Spain for the *Observer* but continues to visit war zones, making trips to the Gulf, Kosovo and northern Albania for the *Independent* and the *Express.* She has contributed to *Crimes of War*, a handbook on the Geneva Conventions as they are applied (or not) in modern conflicts, published in 1999.

STEPHEN FAY is the son of Gerard Fay, the last London editor of the *Guardian.* His first proper job was on the *Glasgow Herald*, where he wrote leaders and became industrial correspondent. Covering the trade unions was one of his many jobs for the *Sunday Times.* He was correspondent in New York, Europe, and Washington DC, worked for 'Insight' and wrote features, often about the arts, and edited 'Atticus'. His first editor's job was on

Business Magazine in the late eighties. Fay found his true vocation as deputy editor of the *Independent on Sunday*, a job he did twice. Being fired first time round did not deter him from becoming Rosie Boycott's deputy. He edited the paper briefly after her flight to the *Express*. What he likes doing best now is writing about cricket.

NIALL FERGUSON is Fellow and Tutor in Modern History at Jesus College, Oxford. He has just published *The Pity of War* and *The World's Banker: The History of the House of Rothschild* (both 1998). He has also written numerous articles on nineteenth- and twentieth-century financial history, including an influential critique of Keynes's *Economic Consequences of the Peace*. A prolific commentator on contemporary politics, he writes and reviews regularly for the national press, notably the *Daily Telegraph*, for which he used to write a weekly column. He lives with his wife and two children in Oxfordshire.

JAMES FERGUSSON has been obituaries editor of the *Independent* since it was launched in 1986. He is also an antiquarian bookseller.

PAUL FOOT has written for a wide variety of newspapers and magazines, most notably *Private Eye*, *Daily Mirror*, *Guardian* and *Socialist Worker*, and has won Journalist of the Year award twice. He has also published many books including *Murder at the Farm: Who Killed Carl Bridgewater?* (1986), *Who Framed Colin Wallace?* (1989) and *Words as Weapons* (1990).

STEPHEN GLOVER was one of the three founders of the *Independent* and the founding editor of the *Independent on Sunday*. He has written in a wide variety of roles for the *Daily Telegraph* and the *Evening Standard*, and now writes a weekly column for the *Daily Mail* and the *Spectator*. He is married with two children and lives in Oxford. The paperback of his previous book, *Paper Dream*, was published by Penguin.

ZOË HELLER was born in 1965. She started out in journalism writing book reviews. Her first staff job was at the *Independent on Sunday*, where she worked as a feature writer from 1989 to 1993. After leaving the *Independent on Sunday*, she moved to New York and took up freelance work. From 1994 to 1997 she wrote a 'girl' column for the *Sunday Times*. Her writing has appeared in a variety of publications including the *New Yorker*, *Vanity Fair* and the *London Review of Books*. Her first novel, *Everything You Know*, was published in June 1999.

ANTHONY HOWARD retired as obituaries editor of *The Times* earlier this year. Before that he was editor of both the *New Statesman* and the *Listener* and, from 1981 to 1988, deputy editor of the *Observer*. He has also worked in radio and television. He claims to have 'stumbled' into journalism, having originally intended to be a barrister (he was called to the Bar while on active service at Suez in 1956). He is the author of two political biographies – of Rab Butler and Dick Crossman – and is currently working with Michael Heseltine on the latter's memoirs.

RICHARD INGRAMS was born in 1939 and educated at Shrewsbury (along with Paul Foot and Willie Rushton) and University College, Oxford. He was editor of *Private Eye* for over twenty years and has written a regular column in the *Observer* since 1989. In 1992 he helped found *The Oldie* and has been its editor ever since. He has appeared regularly on radio and TV, notably on Granada's *What the Papers Say* and Radio 4's *News Quiz*. He has written a number of books, most recently a biography of Malcolm Muggeridge.

ANN LESLIE is special correspondent for the *Daily Mail*. She has written and presented programmes for the BBC and Granada/Sky TV, and is a frequent contributor to British and American networks. Since the 1960s, her assignments in seventy-two countries have included conflicts in El Salvador, Ethiopia, Bosnia, Albania and Central Africa; developments in China since the time of the Cultural Revolution; many superpower 'summits' and US presidential elections; and events in the Soviet Union, Central America, Eastern Europe, the Falklands, South Africa and the Middle East. She has been an award-winner eleven times in the British Press Awards, as well as Feature Writer of the Year in the Granada/BBC 'What the Papers Say' awards for her work in the Philippines, the Soviet Union and Iraq. In 1997 she received the Media Society's Lifetime Achievement award. Married with one daughter, she lives in North London.

PETER MCKAY began working for newspapers in the north-east of Scotland in 1960. He was the Scottish *Daily Express*'s 'unusual mortalities' correspondent in news-starved Aberdeen, a post which required careful study of death notices. He was brought to London and the *Sunday Express* in 1964 by Sir John Junor and has since written columns for a wide range of papers – the *Daily Express*, *Daily Star*, *Daily Mirror*, *Evening Standard*, *News of the World*, *Sunday Times* and *Daily Mail*. From 1968 to 1986 he contributed to *Private Eye* and wrote an unauthorized history of the magazine, *Inside Private Eye*.

CHRISTOPHER MUNNION, born in Essex, was the *Daily Telegraph*'s correspondent in Africa for more than twenty-five years, covering many of the wars, coups and upheavals on that continent in the post-colonial period. He is now a freelance journalist and author, and lives in Johannesburg.

AMANDA PLATELL was born in 1957. She started her journalistic career as a cadet trainee on the Perth *Daily News* and was soon promoted to run the Sydney bureau for the same paper. On leaving, she became sub-editor of the Sydney *Sun* before moving in 1985 to live in the UK, where she joined the launch team for *Today*. She moved next to the London *Daily News* as sub-editor and then deputy arts editor. She returned to *Today* as features production editor before being promoted to become deputy editor. Amanda Platell then moved to become group managing editor, and later marketing director, of the *Mirror*. Subsequent appointments as managing director at the *Independent* and executive editor at the

Sunday Express were followed, in March 1999, by her present position as Head of News and Media of the Conservative Party.

HENRY PORTER is a freelance writer. He contributes to the *Guardian, Daily Telegraph, Observer, Sunday Telegraph, Daily Mail* and *London Evening Standard*. He is also the London editor of *Vanity Fair* magazine and the author of *Lies, Damned Lies*, a study of the fiction that masquerades as fact in national newspapers. In 1999 he published his first novel, *Remembrance Day*, a thriller set in London. He estimates that he has worked for some thirty different editors and has himself edited two magazines, the *Illustrated London News* and the *Sunday Correspondent* magazine.

FIAMMETTA ROCCO writes for the *Economist, Granta* and the *Telegraph Magazine*. She was recently named Feature Writer of the Year in the UK Press Awards.

CAROL SARLER has worked her way around the communications world, taking in spells as an advertising copywriter (J. Walter Thompson), a radio reporter (BBC *World at One*), a magazine editor (*Honey*, for IPC), a television producer (independent for Channel 4), but has repeatedly returned to print. Early days included subbing (she was the first woman on the stone at the *Sunday Times*). She has written for every British national broadsheet except the pink one. For the past six years she has added to her portfolio a weekly column in the *Sunday People*. Her essay in this collection is based on one published in the *British Journalism Review* in 1998.

LYNNE TRUSS edited weekly book review sections for the first twelve years of her career (latterly as literary editor of the *Listener*) and became a full-time writer in 1990, with the *Independent on Sunday*. In 1991, *The Times* made her its television critic; in 1996, the year she was made Columnist of the Year for her magazine work, the same newspaper sent her to football, after which her journalistic profile went a bit weird. She has written three comic novels, several radio plays and scripts (including a limpet monologue for Dame Judi Dench), and a small book about the nineteenth-century portrait. She lives in Brighton.

ALAN WATKINS joined the editorial staff of the *Sunday Express* in 1959. Since 1963 he has written a political column in the *Express* (as 'Crossbencher'), *Spectator*, *New Statesman*, *Sunday Mirror*, *Observer* and, most recently, the *Independent on Sunday*. Since 1986 he has been rugby columnist of the *Independent*. He is the author of *The Liberal Dilemma*, *Brief Lives*, *A Slight Case of Libel*, *A Conservative Coup*, *The Road to Number 10* and, jointly, *The Making of the Prime Minister 1970*.

FRANCIS WHEEN started in Fleet Street as an office boy more than twenty-five years ago. A regular broadcaster and the author of several books, he has also written for many newspapers including the *Independent*, the *Independent on Sunday*, the *Daily Mirror*, the *Observer* and the *Guardian*. In 1997 he was named Columnist of the Year in the 'What the Papers Say' awards. His latest book is a biography of Karl Marx.

MICHAEL WHITE was born in 1945 and has been political editor of the *Guardian* since 1990. He was previously Washington correspondent during the 'Teflon presidency' of Ronald Reagan. Married with three children, he was raised in Cornwall and is a graduate of London University. A reporter on the *Reading Evening Post* and the London *Evening Standard*, he joined the *Guardian* as a feature writer/sub-editor in 1971. Between 1977 and 1984 he was the *Guardian*'s parliamentary sketch writer. In November 1991 he engaged in a press gallery altercation with Alastair Campbell, then political editor of the *Daily Mirror*, over the death of Robert Maxwell, which he mistakenly assumed would be welcomed by his employees. The fact that he struck Mr Campbell back is rarely mentioned in the press cuttings. That too is a tribute to good spin.

A. N. WILSON was born in Staffordshire, where his family had manufactured pottery for generations. After seven years of teaching, he became literary editor of the *Spectator*. Some years later, he became literary editor of the *Evening Standard*, a post which he occupied for another seven years. He is also a regular weekly columnist for the *Standard*. He writes for other newspapers, including the *Independent on Sunday* and the *Daily Telegraph*. His first book, *The Sweets of Pimlico*, was published in 1976. Since then he has published seventeen novels and a number of biographical studies. His latest book, *God's Funeral*, published in June 1999, is an account of the loss of religious faith during the nineteenth century in Europe and America.

SIR PEREGRINE WORSTHORNE has written in a number of roles for various newspapers, and was editor of the *Sunday Telegraph* from 1986 to 1989, where he also wrote a political column for thirty-six years. In addition, he has published several books including *Peregrinations: Selected Pieces* (1980), *By the Right* (1987) and *Tricks of Memory* (1993), his autobiography.

PETRONELLA WYATT was educated at St Paul's Girls' School in Hammersmith and University College, London, where she read History. After leaving university she worked on the *Daily Telegraph*'s 'Peterborough' column before becoming a leader writer for that newspaper. She edited the 'Mandrake' column in the *Sunday Telegraph* and wrote a weekly column under her own name. Since 1997 she has been deputy editor of the *Spectator*, to which she also contributes 'Singular Life', and political interviewer for the *Daily Telegraph*. Her first book, *Father, dear, Father*, a comic account of an eccentric English upbringing, will be published by Hutchinson next year. She lives in London.

Index